Polygamy

Polygamy

A Cross-cultural Analysis

Miriam Koktvedgaard Zeitzen

BERG

Oxford • New York

First published in 2008 by
Berg
Editorial offices:
First Floor, Angel Court, 81 St Clements Street, Oxford OX4 1AW, UK
175 Fifth Avenue, New York, NY 10010, USA

Berg is the imprint of Oxford International Publishers Ltd.

Library of Congress Cataloging-in-Publication Data
Zeitzen, Miriam Koktvedgaard.
  Polygamy : a cross-cultural analysis / Miriam Koktvedgaard Zeitzen.
    p. cm.
  Includes bibliographical references and index.
  ISBN-13: 978-1-84520-220-0 (cloth)
  ISBN-10: 1-84520-220-1 (cloth)
  ISBN-13: 978-1-84520-221-7 (pbk.)
  ISBN-10: 1-84520-221-X (pbk.)
  1. Polygamy—Cross-cultural studies. 2. Polygamy—History. I. Title.
  GN480.35.Z45 2008
  306.84'23—dc22
                                                        2008004852

British Library Cataloguing-in-Publication Data
A catalogue record for this book is available from the British Library.

ISBN 978 1 84520 220 0 (Cloth)
       978 1 84520 221 7 (Paper)

Typeset by JS Typesetting Ltd, Porthcawl, Mid Glamorgan
Printed in the United Kingdom by Biddles Ltd, King's Lynn

www.bergpublishers.com

Contents

Part I
Defining Polygamy

–1–

Forms of Polygamy

Introduction

Aims

This book is an ethnography of polygamy with a cross-cultural scope. Polygamy is the practice whereby a person is married to more than one spouse at the same time, as opposed to monogamy, where a person has only one spouse at a time. In principle, there are three forms of polygamy: polygyny, in which one man is married to several wives; polyandry, where one woman is married to several husbands; and group marriage, in which several husbands are married to several wives, i.e. some combination of polygyny and polyandry. This broad definition is based on the etymology of the word polygamy, which contains *polys* (= many) and *gamos* (= marriage). Polygamy literally means 'often married' in Late Greek.

During the Winter Olympics at Salt Lake City, UT, in 2002, Mormon polygamy grabbed the headlines because an advertising campaign for a new beer named Polygamy Porter had offended members of the Mormon faith. In the state of Utah, in Southwest USA, 70 per cent of the population are Mormon, and officially monogamous. But the Wasatch Beers Company played on deep-seated American stereotypes linking Mormons with polygamy to promote its new product. The beer label featured a man with several women along with the inscription 'Why have just one'. The advertising slogan urged buyers to bring some home 'for the wives'. Mormons were not amused, but the brewery countered that since the Mormon Church is officially against polygamy, it had not anticipated that the campaign would offend. It had been more concerned about the risk of targeting minors, since 'so many polygamists marry under-age girls', a barbed reference to arrests of Mormons accused of marrying and having sexual relations with very young girls.[1] The furore over the beer illustrates the peculiar circumstances surrounding contemporary Mormon polygamy: officially banned by the Mormon Church, but still practised by small groups of Mormon fundamentalists, and thus still associated with Mormonism by the American public. The fact that Mormons reacted angrily to the commercial reinforced non-Mormon beliefs that Mormons still endorse polygamy even though it is illegal, whereas mainstream Mormons felt targeted once more by a resentful American public who will not acknowledge that Mormons have rejected the practice over 100 years ago.

The beer incident underscores that polygamy is not an exotic non-Western custom, practised by people who have not yet entered the modern world. Polygamy is worldwide, cross-cultural in its scope, it is found on all continents and among adherents of all world religions. Its practitioners range from modern feminists to traditional patriarchs, illustrating the great versatility of polygamy as a kinship system. An overview of the many peoples practising polygamy, in contemporary as in past societies, illustrate that a majority of the world's cultures and religions have condoned some form of polygamy. For many of the societies described here, polygamy used to be an integral part of their kinship systems, but modern times have brought a streamlining of marriage patterns to all societies around the world. The spread of Christianity and European-based legal codes through colonialism, and the imposition of state laws on aboriginal peoples living within the borders of modern nation-states, have spelt the end of polygamy for many people. The Arctic Inuit (Eskimo), for example, practised polygamy in the recent past, as described in older ethnographic literature; if still practised, it may be in clandestine or irregular ways. This is the case for numerous populations that used to practise polygamy, but have now become integrated in the global community where monogamy dominates.

There are few books dealing exclusively with polygamy, and they are mostly concerned with polyandry in the Himalayas or Mormon polygyny in the USA. The more numerous articles tend to focus on Africa, the world region with the highest prevalence of polygamy. Polygamous practices in Africa are perhaps better described and analysed than anywhere else in the world. Africa is where much of the early anthropological scholarship was developed, and a practice as alien as polygamy was inherently interesting to Western observers. The resilient polygamy–Africa equation thus came into being. Those untroubled by anthropological wisdom may have some vague image of a polygamist as an old African chief surrounded by numerous wives servicing his every need. Those with some anthropological exposure might have read such classic ethnographies as Rebecca Reyher's wonderful *Zulu Woman* (1948) or Mary Smith's *Baba of Karo* (1953), confirming their views that polygamy was and is an African institution. As this book will hopefully show, polygamy is so much more than an exotic African custom. Africa remains synonymous with polygamy, nonetheless, a treasure trove of ethnographic information, which will be used prodigiously throughout this book.

It should be noted that many of the book's descriptions of polygamous practices are based on old ethnographies, requiring the usual 'suspended ethnographic reality'. For example, the Mende people of Sierra Leone lived through a brutal civil war in the 1990s, which undoubtedly influenced their polygamous patterns. Those patterns are here described as they were in the pre-1990s, however, because most of the available Mende research was carried out prior to this period (e.g. Crosby 1937; Little 1951; Bledsoe 1990).

A further point is that the study of polygamy in Africa has often been biased by Western perceptions of African society and matrimonial arrangements (Clignet and Sween 1981: 467). 'Most Whitemen see polygamy as an attribute of primitiveness, and they think that the African cannot really attain civilization unless he has discontinued polygamy and adopted monogamy' (Maillu 1988: 1). Western research agendas informed by such (subconscious?) views may as a result linger between contradictory concerns of nostalgia for traditional African culture versus critique of polygamy as oppressive to women or detrimental to development. Such conflictual views of polygamy appear to have been internalized by Africans themselves. Many Africans (and other peoples practising polygamy) now consider polygamy less socially, morally and culturally legitimate than monogamy, in line with Western views. This tends to make polygamous practices ethnographically 'invisible', making studies of polygamy increasingly difficult in many societies. Men will present their official wife to the world (and the researcher) and 'hide' their other wife. It comes back to the anthropological truism that what is legal, and is advocated as the ideal or the right way with respect to marriage, does not necessarily represent the reality people practise.

A study of polygamy in contemporary societies must not only grapple with the practical problem of identifying such 'irregular' and perhaps 'invisible' unions. It must also grapple with a theoretical problem that has existed since the earliest attempts at anthropological analysis of polygamy, namely its definition. In China, as well as among diaspora Chinese worldwide, it is customary for rich men to have more than one wife. With the advent of marriage laws abolishing polygamy in most countries where it used to be practised (including China), the practice did not disappear, but simply took another form. According to state laws a Chinese man can only be married to one wife, but he may then 'marry' a second wife by performing a ceremony according to customary laws. But is the couple in fact married if the state legal system says they are not? If the marriage is not socially accepted, then the second 'wife' is only a concubine, and it is not polygamy. If it is socially accepted as a marriage because the man has a committed, long-term relationship with, and maintains, the second 'wife', as well as acknowledges paternity of the children born, then it may be called *de facto* polygamy (see below). The definition of polygamy in other words hinges on the definition of marriage, and there is no consensus in anthropology about what exactly marriage is.

This definitional challenge is further complicated by the vast variety of polygamous systems cross-culturally, many of which are borderline cases and hence difficult to categorize. Australian Aborigines in the Northwest Territory, for example, practised a diffuse form of polygamy, in which polygamous males would 'lend' wives to younger men or ignore their wives' adultery. In doing so, senior men could create political ties with 'brothers' who might otherwise become their enemies in their competition for wives. Similarly among the Arctic Inuit, polygamous males would 'lend' wives to other men. It is difficult, however, to define a system as polygamous in which wife-sharing is common, because the line between 'marriage' and a woman's extension of sexual services to men other than her official husband is blurred.

The book will therefore deal not only with the three main forms of polygamy – polygyny, polyandry and group marriage – but with the endless variations on the polygamous theme that exist in matrimonial systems across the world as well. Theoretical considerations form a natural part of the ethnographic analysis, ranging from an examination of the foundations of modern anthropological theory regarding polygamy to addressing contemporary concerns facing modern polygamists such as Westernization, HIV/AIDS and women's emancipation. Polygamy is faced by numerous economic, sociocultural and political challenges wherever it is practised today. At issue is polygamy's survival as an institution in a world where monogamy is dominant. Thus, one effect of globalization, and its concomitant sociocultural streamlining of the world's societies, has been the emergence or reinforcement of internal opposition to polygamy even in societies where it has formed part of the cultural repertoire for generations. In traditionally polygamous non-Western societies, where such 'modern' factors as economic progress and women's emancipation have challenged polygamous practices, these practices have not disappeared, however. Rather, they have adapted to the new circumstances, perpetuating old ways in new forms. In monogamous Western societies, contemporary individualistic culture and lifestyle choices are used a basis for promoting polygamous practices by some segments of the populations. The various polygamous forms that exist today encourage research outside traditional polygamous homelands to include new grounds, not least by following the slipstream of the modern world's migrating peoples. Polygamy has become part of the social and political discourse in contemporary societies.

The aim of the book is thus to give readers a general understanding of polygamy, its forms, foundations and functions, as well as providing insights into polygamous patterns and practices in contemporary societies. This cross-cultural examination of polygamy ultimately aims to illustrate that a majority of the world's cultures have some form of polygamous practice and to demystify it as an exotic non-Western practice into one found also in Western societies.

Outline

The book contains nine chapters divided into three parts. Part I, containing chapters 1–3, is an examination of the forms and foundations of polygamy. It seeks to define polygamy and polygamous society, as well as examines polygamy in anthropological theory. First, it seeks to establish the parameters that would allow researchers to differentiate between various forms of polygynous and polyandrous systems. An important variation in polygamous practices concerns formal or legal polygamy versus informal or illegal polygamy. Today, many countries have banned polygamy, but because it remains culturally entrenched, people continue to practise it informally. Another fundamental distinction concerns polygamy based on religious doctrine versus polygamy based on cultural practice. Particular attention is therefore paid to polygamy's place in the major religions, as well as the cultural foundations of polygamy. American Mormons are a contemporary example of people practising polygyny despite its illegality. Christian polygamy is probably the most alien form of polygamy to Western observers: a majority of Westerners will share some religious and cultural understanding with the polygamists, but are conditioned to think of monogamous marriage as the only acceptable form. In the USA, the surrounding Christian populations reject polygamy, both as a marriage form and a religious right. This is quite different from other Christian populations who have polygamists in their midst. In West Africa, for example, polygyny is a traditional cultural custom that is independent of the religion practised by the polygynist, inasmuch as Christians, Muslims, followers of native religions and others practise it. Polygyny in West Africa is thus an accepted part of local culture and kinship systems, though not necessarily accepted by Church or State. In the USA, in contrast, polygyny is a religiously based custom practised by a very small subset of a religious minority, the Mormons, which enjoys no support from the majority population.

Second, Part I outlines the main anthropological theories concerning the foundations of polygamous practice. Early theorists worked on kinship systems in order to trace the development of human culture. Polygamy formed an integral part of their theories that humanity had in its early stages of cultural evolution gone through various developmental phases, and ideas about 'primitive man' and his polygamous tendencies influenced the formulation of early anthropological theories of man, kinship and culture. Modern anthropological explanations fall, with some overlap and variation, into two main groups, focusing on production and reproduction versus power, politics and prestige. On some level, they cannot be differentiated, because any particular polygamous system will probably contain elements of all those aspects of polygamy. Production and reproduction are intimately linked in many polygamous systems, just as polygyny may confer prestige precisely because it confers political power. The explanations are not meant to be mutually exclusive, but rather to highlight those aspects of polygamous systems which anthropologists have found important in understanding polygamy.

Part II, containing chapters 4–6, deals with polygamy cross-culturally and provides selected ethnographic examples of polygamy: Muslim polygyny in Malaysia, Christian polygyny in the USA and Hindu polyandry in India. For each ethnographic example provided, patterns of polygamous marriage, family life, sex life and social life are examined. Examining each population through the same set of parameters will help the reader compare and contrast the great variety of polygamous arrangements that exist worldwide.

Part III, containing chapters 7–9, deals with polygamy in contemporary societies. It expands on the theoretical and ethnographic overview of polygamy given in parts I and II by moving the analysis to polygamy's place in contemporary societies. Polygamy as it relates to gender and modernity is examined, involving such elements as female emancipation, economic development and cultural globalization. Finally, the future of polygamy is discussed, with particular emphasis on the contemporary cultural and legal challenges facing polygamists.

Polygamy is, by its very nature, a gender issue. It is important to address the gender dimensions of polygamy because of its inherent gender asymmetry; the fact that one man can be married to several women but one woman can only be married to one man, or vice versa, paves the way for potential conflict between the sexes. In polygamous societies that have seen the emancipation of women through education and economic opportunities, polygamy's creation of inequality and power differentials has become a key aspect of contemporary gender relations. The 'threat of polygamy', the possibility that their present or future husband might take another wife, is influencing women's perception and management of relationships, marriage and family life. In a polygamous society, it may on some level be wrong to call any marriage monogamous because all marriages are potentially polygamous, and both men and women organize their relationships on this assumption. This in turn has a profound effect on gender relations both inside and outside marriage. Particular attention is therefore paid to power relations between husbands and wives as well as gender-based status differentials in polygamy. A key theme within a gender-based examination of polygamy is the notion that polygyny subjugates women, and the associated idea that economic development and women's emancipation will undermine and eventually eradicate polygyny.

Like gender, modernity is a crucial determinant of contemporary polygamous systems, their future form and function. There is a widespread notion, in Western as well as non-Western minds, that modernity will make the 'traditional' practice of polygamy disappear. It appears to go against modern ideas of nuclear families as espoused in most state development and population policies. Particularly in urban areas, people feel that being monogamous projects a more modern image. Urban areas also cannot provide the same socio-economic foundations for polygamy as rural areas. As women become more emancipated, better educated and increasingly independent socially and economically from their families and husbands, polygamy is seen by many as a form of 'development reversal', a wrong direction to take with respect to gender relations. In urban areas, however, a reinvention and adaptation of traditional ways to modern conditions has given new life to polygamy, which appears to be increasing rather than disappearing. In urban Ghana, for example, sugar daddies (*de facto* polygynous husbands) and gold-diggers (their *de facto* polygynous wives) redefine polygamy, both as a theoretical concept and as a practical lived institution. For many urban Ghanaians, to be polygamous is to be modern.

Forms of Polygamy

Polygyny

Polygyny is a form of plural marriage in which a man is permitted more than one wife. Where co-wives are customarily sisters this is called *sororal polygyny*. The other main form is *non-sororal polygyny*, where co-wives are not related. Polygynous marriage is generally correlated with those economic and political systems where the most important resources are human resources. Polygyny allows a man to have more children, providing him with a broader productive base, as he controls the labour of his wives and children to a large extent. It also provides him with more affines,[2] permitting him to manipulate factional and/or kin group ties to his advantage. In some societies, polygyny may be the exclusive privilege of leaders or chiefs; an Amazonian Indian leader's multiple wives are both a sign of his power and an important element in building up and maintaining his power base, for example. Polygyny is often associated with age asymmetry in the marriage relationship, such that older men marry young girls, and younger men are obligated to remain celibate for extended periods, or alternatively marry widows of older men. Polygyny may in such cases be interpreted as part of the age-gender stratification, where older men control human resources and thus control the productive and reproductive resources in a society. Where resources such as land or other forms of private property predominate, like in Western societies, monogamous nuclear family forms tend to be the rule (Seymour-Smith 1986: 228). Polygyny does exist in Western capitalist societies, but then always as a result of religious doctrine. A contemporary example is American Mormons who practise Plural Marriage, a form of polygyny associated with the nineteenth-century Mormon Church and its present-day splinter groups (see Chapter 5).

An unusual variety of polygyny is practised among the Lovedu of Southern Africa. Within the Lovedu system of 'woman marriage', a woman can become a female polygamous 'husband'. High status females such as queens and other power-holders could sometimes use their wives and cattle as polygamous currency in the same way as male kings and chiefs. The Lovedu Rain Queen, for example, regularly received wives as tribute from all districts of her realm, and she had numerous wives. Some wives would later be reallocated to important men (Krige and Krige 1943: 165). It was politically significant who the fathers of a rain queen's wives' children were, especially as a Lovedu queen could be succeeded by a woman; it could be her own daughter or that of one of her wives (Kuper 1982: 59). These all-female Lovedu unions are polygamous, because the wives are all married to their female husband, but whether they are polygynous depends on whether gender is crucial in defining the common spouse. In principle, they might as well be called polyandrous, because the main spouse is a woman. However, as the Rain Queen is ascribed what is normally a male power status, it may be more correctly seen as polygyny, as she is pursuing a normally male power strategy by marrying several women. Anthropologists have therefore argued that female husbands are culturally conceptualized as men for the purposes of the marriage. Their overall gender status remains ambiguous, however, as some female husbands may themselves be married as wives to male husbands (Oboler 1980). Without a thorough examination of local gender constructs, it is not possible to establish whether a female husband is a 'man'. Returning to the Rain Queen, her position underscores that in Lovedu society, to rule is as much a feminine as a masculine role; similarly, marriage to a woman may be undertaken by either gender, and as such a female husband is not necessarily taking on a male role (Buijs 2002: 123).

The *levirate* is a marriage form in which the heir of a deceased male inherits his assets and liabilities including his wife or wives. It specifies that when a man dies leaving behind a wife, the widow should marry a kinsman of her husband, typically his brother. The levirate thus provides social and economic security to widows and their children. It also represents a way for the husband's family to maintain their rights over the wife's sexuality and her future children, as well as keeping the dead man's children and his wealth within his family. The levirate also maintains the bond established by the original marriage between the two families (Haviland 1983: 240). In practice, the inherited wives may be beyond their childbearing years, rendering the marriage symbolic. For example, upon the death of his father, a senior son may inherit his father's wives, the mothers of his siblings, in order to make his position as elder more evident (Whyte 1980: 138; Wolfe 1959: 182). If the woman is in her childbearing years, she is expected to have children for her new husband.

Levirate is differentiated from *widow inheritance*, which varies according to whether the social father of the child will be the present husband and biological father or the deceased husband. In the 'true' levirate, as practised among the Nuer of Sudan, for example, or in ancient times by Jewish populations, the social father of the child is the deceased husband of the mother. In systems of widow inheritance, the social father is the present husband of the mother (Radcliffe-Brown 1950: 64). Both systems ensure the continuation of the lineage and the protection of resources within the household, and both systems may be practised within the same society. Levirate or widow inheritance are found in most of traditional Africa, where they take many forms, but they all ultimately constitute a way of ensuring that most women and children get an economically and socially secure home. The age differentials between husbands and wives on which high levels of polygyny are based (see below) typically result in many widows, as older men tend to die before their often much younger wives. These widows are inherited by men who are almost invariably already married. Extensive practice of the levirate hence typically contributed to high levels of polygyny in a society, or was in fact the foundation of polygyny in some societies (Goody 1976: 64). Today, levirate and widow inheritance are declining or completely disappearing in many societies for various reasons, and polygyny levels in those societies are falling as a consequence (see Chapter 8).

The *sororate* specifies that a widower should marry a sister of his deceased wife. The sororate is akin to the levirate, and fulfils the same function of maintaining relations between two families even after a spouse's death. They may be practised in the same societies. In essence, a family provides another spouse to take the place of the member who died, and both families usually encourage this remarriage because it continues the bond between them. Local kinship systems ensure that enough brothers and sisters are available by providing 'classificatory siblings' when there are no biological siblings available (Haviland 1983: 240). Among the Tonga of Zambia, for example, sororatic marriage is only allowed with classificatory sisters (Colson 1958). The sororate may also function without death being involved: if a wife is barren among the South African Zulu, her family may provide a sister to bear children in her name. The children are socially the children of the barren woman, just as children are socially the children of the dead husband in the levirate (Radcliffe-Brown 1950: 64).

Polyandry

Polyandry is a form of plural marriage where a woman has more than one husband. Polyandrous marriage is relatively rare and is concentrated in the Himalayan areas of South Asia. It is sporadically found in Africa, Oceania, America and the Arctic. There are two main forms of polyandry: *fraternal* or *adelphic polyandry*, in which a group of brothers share a wife, and *non-fraternal polyandry*, in which a woman's husbands are not related. The commonest form is fraternal polyandry where joint husbands are brothers (real or classificatory). For example, Nyinba brothers (ethnic Tibetans now living in Nepal) live together in large households, sharing a common estate and domestic responsibilities, as well as a common wife with which each maintains a sexual relationship. Generally, each child of the marriage is acknowledged by, and develops a special relationship with, one of the possible fathers, even where biological paternity cannot be determined (Levine 1988).

The Nayar of India practised a form of non-fraternal polyandry in which several men were simultaneously the 'husbands' of one wife. Usually only the first husband underwent a ritual marriage with the woman before she entered puberty. He was then given a special position as a 'ritual' father of all the woman's subsequent children, who like their mother had to observe the customs connected with his death. Any of the men with whom a Nayar woman engaged in sexual relations and had children could be called upon to acknowledge (potential) paternity, however; this was usually done by giving a gift to the woman and paying midwives' expenses. The central Nayar domestic unit consisted of a mother, her daughters and their children; husbands and wife did not set up house together. Descent was reckoned exclusively through women, and children derived their group affiliations and claimed their inheritance through their mothers (Lienhardt 1964: 93–4).

The Nayar case illustrates that the dividing line between true polyandry and a woman's extension of sexual services to men other than her legal husband is not always clear. Generally the label polyandry is used for those systems in which paternity is assigned to more than one man, which is most clearly the case in adelphic polyandry. But as the definition of polyandry depends on the definition of marriage itself, the Nayar case makes it difficult to formulate an all-inclusive definition of marriage. This impasse creates a typological continuum of polyandrous societies, from those where people practise 'pure' polyandry in which one woman is officially married to several husbands, to doubtful cases involving no marriages that can no longer be called polyandry but may share certain familial patterns. In between those two extremes one may find societies where polyandrous practices do not necessarily involve formal marriage but rather one woman having sexual relations with more than one man in a regular and lasting fashion, societies which allow passing connections between one woman and more than one man, as well as societies where people live in *conjoint* marriages, containing both polygynous and polyandrous arrangements. The definitional challenges relating to the Nayars will be revisited in Chapter 7.

In *serial marriage*, a man or woman either marries or lives with a series of partners in succession. Researchers coined the term to describe the marriage patterns of West Indians and lower-class urban Blacks in Western societies. Here, women often lived in female-headed households in which a series of men fathered children, who remained with their mother. The grandmother was typically the head of the household; she cared for all children while her daughters worked to support the whole group. An adult man's loyalties might thus be to his own mother, his kin and friends, rather than to his present wife or partner (Haviland 1983: 240; Stack 1975). Serial marriage may not be polygamy in an anthropological sense, because the multiple matings tend to sequential rather than simultaneous, and may not involve formal marriage. If a man (or woman) maintains several simultaneous relationships with women (or men), one of which was in the form of formal marriage, it could be said to approximate *de facto* polygamy. In contemporary America, some African American activists have indeed been calling for the legalization of polygamy to accommodate the lifestyle and circumstances of urban Blacks (see Chapter 9).

Group Marriage

Group marriage is a polygamous marriage form in which several men and women have sexual access to one another and consider themselves married to all other members of the group. Group marriage is sometimes termed circle marriage or *polygynandry*, from a combination of the words polygyny and polyandry. Group marriage may exist in a number of forms, but typically consists of more than one man and more than one woman who together form a single family unit, with all members of the marriage sharing parental responsibility for any children arising from marriage. Group marriage must be contrasted with polyfamilies, which is similar to group marriage but where some members may not considered themselves married to all other members. Group marriage appears to be have been rare in traditional societies: the Kaingang people of Brazil practised group marriage most frequently, but even among them, only 8 per cent of the unions were group marriages (Murdock 1949: 24).

In the West, a long-lived example of group marriage was the Oneida Community founded by the Congregationalist minister John Humphreys Noyes in 1848. Noyes believed that he and his followers had undergone sanctification, making it impossible for them to sin; for the sanctified, marriage and private property were abolished as expressions of jealousy and exclusiveness. The Oneida commune practised sexual communalism and shared parental responsibilities, and in effect functioned as a large group marriage until around 1880. Communal groups of the late twentieth century, among people seeking alternatives to traditional Western marriage forms, have also tried out group marriage. The Keriste Commune, for example, practised group marriage in San Francisco from 1971 to 1991 (Haviland 1983: 240). It is difficult to estimate the actual number of people practising group marriage in modern societies, as this form of marriage is not officially recognized anywhere; it is probably a very limited practice today because of the inherent strains among its members.

Assessing the prevalence of group marriage is mostly a definitional problem. Researchers tend to lean on Lewis Henry Morgan's nineteenth-century definition of group marriage, which must contains all ten basic kinship relations: wife, co-wife, husband, co-husband, mother, father, daughter, son, brother, sister (see Chapter 2). In addition, all children born to the group marriage must be acknowledged by all men and by all women. The problem arises because several unions may contain most of these characteristics, but may fail on one account, which then disqualifies them as group marriage. As will be discussed in Chapter 6, polyandry suffers from a similar definitional straitjacket, which makes some proclaim polyandry or group marriage to be very rare, while others consider them more widely practised, albeit with modifications. Following a wider definition, the marriage practices followed by some Pahari peoples in the Central Himalayas of India (see Chapter 6) may be called group marriage. The dominant Pahari marriage form is fraternal polyandry, in which a woman marries the eldest of a group of brothers, all of whom are then the woman's husbands. Pahari marriage is fluid, however, and within the same village one might find monogamy, polygyny and polyandry, and within the same family all three forms might exist at some stage or even simultaneously. Researchers working among Pahari people have coined the term polygynandry to accommodate the fluid nature of local marital arrangements. Many of the family forms grouped under polygynandry approximate group marriage, as they contain all ten basic kinship relations of Morgan's group marriage. However, whereas all men acknowledge all children in a Pahari marriage, all women do not acknowledge them. The paternity of children is shared by all 'fathers', while the biological mother of each child is known and socially recognized within the family, even if this child refers to all its father's wives as 'mother' (Berreman 1975). This last point disqualifies Pahari marriage as group marriage for some.

Poly relationship (from polygamy, polyamory, etc.) refers to forms of interpersonal relations in which some or all participants have multiple marital, sexual and/or romantic partners. Such relationships are also termed non-monogamous. One variant is polyamory, which refers to romantic or sexual relationships involving multiple partners, regardless of whether they involve marriage. Any polygamous relationship is polyamorous, and some polyamorous relationships involve multiple spouses. Polygamy is usually used to refer to multiple marriages, while polyamory implies relationships defined by negotiation between its members rather than marriage. Polyamory can be contrasted with polyfidelity, where participants have multiple partners but restrict sexual activity to within a certain group. Open relationships involve one or both members of a couple who are sexually active with other partners, sometimes in the form of an *open marriage*. The terms referring to marriage forms involving several spouses or partners (polygyny, polyandry, polyamory, group marriage, etc.) are by nature flexible and difficult to define, not least because practitioners themselves might disagree as to what their relationships entail and where their boundaries are. The term 'poly relationship' is generally used only where all participants acknowledge the relationship as non-monogamous, and not applied where one person has multiple partners due to infidelity.

Defining Polygamy

Polygamy as Matrimony

In G.P. Murdock's *Ethnographic Atlas* (1967), an overwhelming 85 per cent of recorded societies were polygamous. It is a percentage which reflects ideals not realities, however, for most of the societies in Murdock's survey are listed as polygamous because they allow for and prefer polygamy, but in fact the majority of marriages in those societies are monogamous. The resources necessary to be able to marry more than one spouse make polygamy unaffordable to most people. It is usually only rich or powerful men in polygamous societies who can marry several wives, just like rich men in monogamous societies marry one wife and may have one or more mistresses; poor men are monogamists all over the world. Humans are nowhere strictly monogamic, but while polygamous societies practise permissive polygyny and actual monogamy, monogamous societies only allow monogamy. It has been argued that, from an evolutionary perspective, the optimal strategy for humans is monogamy when necessary, and polygamy when possible. Polygamy is mostly advantageous to human males, whereas females may opt for monogamy; 'infidelity' would then assure reproduction in case of infertile partners. Polygamy, securing genetic variation, may have been the preferred mating pattern for early humans, just like the majority of primate species are polygamous. Some smaller species of monkeys and all of the smaller apes, such as gibbons, do mate monogamously for life, but none of these primates are closely related to human beings. Monogamy probably developed as an adaptation to economic, ecological or other circumstances, which made polygamy impractical for some or most members of human societies. This tendency to social monogamy is subject to strong reinforcement by cultural factors, particularly religion. This has made monogamy the predominant mating system (in terms of practitioners) in most human societies today (Haviland 1983: 239; Obi 1970; Schuiling 2003; Stone 2006: 32–4).

Polygamy as a concept is used in various ways within the different branches of the social and natural sciences. In sociobiology, polygamy is used in a broad sense to mean any form of multiple mating, whereas zoologists use it in a narrower sense to include pair bonds that might be temporary or sequential. In the social sciences, polygamy is furthermore often used in a *de facto* sense, applying regardless of whether the relations between the 'spouses' are socially or legally recognized. Thus, while polygamy is legally forbidden in the Western Christian world, it has long been argued that it exists there in various pseudo or *de facto* forms (Gallichan 1914: 283). People typically point to *serial marriage* or serial polygamy, which is marriage followed by divorce, remarriage followed by divorce and so on any number of times. Other forms include a man married to one woman, or indeed unmarried, while maintaining one or several mistresses. This view of *de facto* polygamy is based on a very broad definition of the formality of marriage in ascribing polygamy. Anthropologists generally consider formal marriage the foundation of polygamy, leading to the three main forms of polygamy described above. The definition of formal marriage is very contentious among anthropologists and other social scientists, however, leaving room for multiple forms of unions to be included under the umbrella term polygamy.

This definitional challenge is illustrated by the myriad forms of marital relationships that traditionally existed among the Kota people in South India. They encapsulate the problem inherent in classifying polygamous practices: in many polygamous societies, marriage forms are fluid both structurally and temporally, and several forms may coexist within the same family. The Kota are usually classified as polyandrous, but on some level they practise all the marriage forms described in the book, including polygyny, polyandry and group marriage. They are not polyandrous in the classic sense, as a woman only has one husband, and would have to divorce or become a widow before she could marry another husband. However, her husband's brothers have free sexual access to her, and when her husband is ill, incapacitated or otherwise unable to fulfil his husbandly duties, his brothers take his place. This makes the husband's brothers his wife's *de facto* husbands, and the arrangement is then *de facto* polyandry. A Kota household typically consists of several brothers and their wives and children. As a man may marry more than one wife, polygyny as well as polyandry can be practised within the same household. A woman lives in house of her legal husband and he is recognized as the social father of her children, even if the biological father is known to be the husband's brother. A husband has preferential access to his wife, but in his absence his brothers have a right and obligation to take his place. A brother's rights to a man's wife apply not only to uterine brothers, but also to classificatory brothers, as well as male parallel cousins and male lineage members. Though sibling sets tend to be small among the Kota, there may nonetheless be ten to twenty men related to a man, who then have access to his wife. This principle of the 'equivalence of brothers' is carried over to sets of sisters, such that a man has sexual access to all his wife's sisters. If a newly married couple is incompatible, for example, a husband can exchange his wife for one of her sisters. This 'equivalence of sisters' is more difficult to put into practice, however, because female siblings are often married and living in other villages, and are hence unavailable for marriage or intimate relations for brothers-in-law (Mandelbaum 1938).

How one defines polygamy is hence very much related to how one defines marriage, kinship and the family. Research into polygamy, typically based on demographic surveys, has often been influenced by Western family norms that do not leave much room for non-Western family forms. A person being investigated is either married, divorced, widowed or single, leaving little space for alternative, multiple or polygamous unions, especially if they occurred in a previous period of the respondents' lives. The notion of the universal nuclear family as the basic building block of family life has been a constraining norm, because the nuclear family – father, mother, children – is intimately associated with monogamy. The problems involved in defining polygamy have hence often circled around whether a nuclear family can exist when there are plural husbands or wives. G.P. Murdock (1949: 2) suggested that nuclear families do exist in such situations, in that a man or a woman simply belongs to more than one nuclear family at the same time, linked by a common spouse. Others argue that polygamous marriage creates a domestic situation very different from that created by monogamous marriage. Polygamous sexual arrangements and reproduction, for example, are quite different from those characteristic of monogamous marriage. In polygamous households, a father relates to several half-siblings through a hierarchy of wives, rather than focusing on a small group of full siblings in monogamous families. Distinctive patterns of infant care also arise when a mother sleeps alone with her children while the father sleeps with a different wife each night. In economic terms, a polygamous household often consists of an extended co-resident family production team rather than separate husband–wife teams. In Africa, for example, a man may typically marry a second wife to relieve his first wife's work burden in nursing, grooming, cleaning, fetching water, cooking, etc. and thus increase domestic output. This can only be effective within a non-nuclear family setting. It might therefore be inappropriate to equate a nuclear family in a monogamous domestic context with a husband–wife–child unit embedded in a polygamous domestic context (Harris 1983).

In this book, polygamy is considered based on unions in which several people are married (in one way or another) to one common spouse, usually, but not always, of the opposite gender. They may or may not share domestic responsibilities and residence. It follows that *de facto* polygamy is not considered polygamy, because the defining characteristic of polygamy is that a marriage has sealed the relationship between the spouses. *De facto* polygamy is a useful label to describe a social phenomenon based on the principles of polygamy, but without the transference of rights and obligations involved in formal marriage (cf. Mair 1971; Solway 1990). A Western man who is married but maintains a mistress is not *de facto* polygamous, rather he is monogamous but cheats on his wife. In order to become polygamous, he would have to marry his mistress, in which case he would become a bigamist within Western law, not a polygamist! *Bigamy* refers to someone who has entered into any number of 'secondary' marriages in addition to one legally recognized marriage. Many countries have specific statutes outlawing bigamy, such that a man with three wives, for example, would be charged with two counts of bigamy, for two 'secondary' marriages after the first legally recognized one. Before the twentieth century, Western rulers and the elite were sometimes 'married to the left hand', if their informal unions were recognized as *de facto* (rather than legal) marriages. Today, this is no longer acceptable for legal, social or moral reasons in the West. *De facto* polygamy is nonetheless an important part of contemporary polygamous practices cross-culturally, and as such will be included in the discussion.

De facto Polygamy

De facto polygamy is not a separate form of polygamy, but rather a variant that applies to all three main categories of polygamy discussed above. Its characteristic feature is that it does not involve formal marriage between some of the partners, distinguishing it from 'real' legally recognized, or *de jure*, polygamy, which involves formal marriage for all partners. The term acknowledges, however, that the domestic and personal arrangements resulting from *de facto* polygamy are similar to 'real' polygamous ones. *De facto* polygamy has been primarily applied to the new forms of polygyny practised in urban Africa. It is also found in other parts of the world, but the discussion will focus on Africa, where the phenomenon is growing to the extent that it is replacing traditional forms of polygyny in many areas.

Polygyny in Africa has deep and ancient roots, providing security and immortality to its practitioners. Elders traditionally relied on their numerous offspring, made possible through polygyny, to provide material security as well as spiritual security by securing the family line among their ancestors; ancestors will live on as along as they have descendants. The modern world's demand for individual self-reliance therefore threatens the very basis of polygyny. So it is in Africa that polygyny shows its strongest weaknesses, but also its resilience in the face of rapid and revolutionizing change. Globalization and Westernization, industrialization and urbanization, and all other forces of modernization have been changing Africa for over a century, and with it, polygynous practices. Many have predicted, and indeed wished for, their demise. However, as Ware notes, '[p]olygyny is not a dying tradition in (West) Africa, it is a flourishing institution' (1983: 16). African polygyny is not only flourishing, but constantly changing as well, adapting to ever changing circumstances and new interpersonal relations.

Today, polygynous practices are being transformed along with the circumstances in which (would-be) polygynists find themselves in modern Africa. They are confronted with such problems as conflicts between customary and post-colonial policies, urbanization, female education, the spread of sexually transmitted diseases, decreasing availability of land, women's control over productive resources, and penetration of the cash economy. Such problems act as agents of change which rearrange and slowly disintegrate the traditional kinship patterns and social structures, which formed the basis for polygynous marriages (Gwako 1998: 331). As modernity marches all over Africa, the matrimonial patterns, like so many other aspects of social life, begin to approach Western forms. In theory, the majority of African peoples are polygynous, but it has always been permissive polygyny and actual monogamy, because the majority of men cannot afford to be polygynous. In Africa's economic environment today, polygyny has become even more unaffordable. Those bent on being polygynous are increasingly practising *serial polygyny* instead, by marrying and divorcing several spouses in succession; some claim this form of polygamy is practised in the West as well, as previously mentioned. Serial polygyny emerges when there are enough women available to marry, but they are too expensive to maintain. Women may similarly be forced to engage in multiple transient marriages with men as a means of supporting themselves and their children, and perhaps a widowed or divorced parent as well. Their husbands then have to support a large number of dependants, including children who are not theirs. This not only threatens marital relations between the spouses, but also undermines the institution of marriage as husbands tend to leave such unions quickly (Guennec-Coppens 1987: 239–40).

In contemporary urban environments, with economic recession and competition for jobs, combined with high costs of living, schooling and health care, men cannot afford to maintain large polygynous households. They may engage in serial polygyny, or more typically, they marry one wife and are officially monogamous, but maintain concubines. This is again an approach to Western ways. These various forms of 'outside marriages' involve conjugal relations but rarely lead to formal legal marriages. A woman who has a child by a man may nonetheless consider herself married to him, as she probably would have been in traditional rural Africa. She is his 'outside wife', a wife in all but name. This form of 'outside marriage' has become so common in urban Africa that some governments are now debating the legalization of polygyny, not least because women's rights are better protected within formal marriage. It may also be an acknowledgement of the fact that unions based on polygynous principles, whether formal or informal, are still sought after, not only by men but also by women. Urban educated elite women may choose to become part of polygynous unions, for example, because they may find greater personal autonomy in polygyny than as partners in monogamous marriages where their husbands may have 'outside wives'. Some elite women choose to head their own households, while engaging in serial unions or in polyandrous arrangements with several men. Through their actions, and their demands that men accept and adapt to their decisions, elite women act as a 'reference group' for other women, and may thus transform the behaviours and beliefs surrounding marriage and the family in Africa. Many women in Africa, especially in rural areas, remain primarily producers of men's food and children, but they may help change matrimonial patterns by refusing to participate in polygynous marriages, for example (Parkin and Nyamwaya 1987). Freedom for women, however, gives even greater freedom for men to pursue those marital strategies that are most suited to their needs, while not necessarily respecting the needs of women. While many modern urban African men are no longer officially polygynous, they do practise *de facto* polygyny by maintaining several women, regardless of the legal status of their marriages.

It should be noted that while polygamy in Africa almost invariably equals polygyny, there are some populations with polyandrous arrangements (Levine and Sangree 1980a). In Northern Nigeria, for example, several populations traditionally practised 'secondary marriages', in which a wife married and lived with another husband without divorcing her primary husband. Her 'secondary marriage' was legitimized by her new spouse's marriage payments to her father or guardian. The wife would on occasion return to, and temporarily cohabit with, her primary husband, thus oscillating between her spouses. Such secondary marriages differ from polyandry in that the wife only cohabits with one husband at any time, though she remains married to several husbands simultaneously, whereas in polyandry the wife cohabits with, and is married to, several husbands simultaneously. Secondary marriages may thus more correctly be labelled a form of *de facto* polyandry, though the fact that the woman is legally married to several men simultaneously would allow the practice to be labelled polyandry per se. Please see Chapter 2 for a further discussion of this typological challenge. Today, such practices have almost entirely disappeared, as a result of a law institutionalizing divorce and forbidding the remarriage of women without prior performance of *Idda*, the three-month period of sexual abstinence required by Islamic law before a divorce becomes final (M.G. Smith 1953, 1980). In modern Africa, polyandrous arrangements are increasingly found in the form of *de facto* polyandry in urban areas. In many African cities, motherhood is becoming more important than marriage in defining a woman's status and giving her access to a man's resources, and this has created a category of women practising 'polyandrous motherhood'. While a woman may not have several simultaneous husbands, she may have several simultaneous recognized fathers to her children, thus effectively managing several men at once. Because these men typically have different lineage affiliations, their children have access to different kinship networks, thereby optimizing the woman's and her children's access to resources (Guyer 1994).

The distinction between *de jure* and *de facto* polygyny raises one of the central questions in the book, namely how can one define polygamy based on the fluid definition of marriage? Numerous kinds of unions are recognized in most African societies, many of which are not ritualized or formalized. They include unions sanctioned by legal or statutory ceremonies, various religious or customary procedures, or consensual agreements. The many types of socially acceptable marriages in African cultures result in many types of domestic categories, rather than the binary system in the West where one is either married or unmarried. During the past century, various reform movements have attempted to regulate the perplexing African 'marriage market' by approving some forms of unions and banning others. Colonial administrators and Christian missionaries especially considered it imperative to distinguish clearly between 'married' and 'unmarried' people. However, rather than clarifying what marriage entails by limiting options or removing ambiguity, reform attempts have usually made it more ambiguous. They have also inadvertently given people new grounds for creating new types of unions by adding more criteria to the definition of marriage. The numerous changes in systems of authority have also regularly led to disputes, as Africans may marry under various systems of legislation containing elements of customary, colonial and post-colonial law. Legally it can become a problem when people are unable to clearly establish whether, or according to what 'law', they are married. Especially in inheritance cases, there are numerous conflicts about whether a marriage really occurred, thus entitling the person to inherit from a deceased spouse.

African 'marriages' are fluid and flexible, and as partners continuously restructure their relationships, different people perceive unions differently at different times. Researchers have therefore argued for a processual approach to marriage in Africa, in which marriage is not considered a single event in time, but rather 'a process built up out of visits, transfers of wealth and symbolic tokens, the births of children etc.' Fulfilling particular responsibilities to spouses, children and affines helps define marriages and make them reality, rather than the other way around. African marriage is thus not a linear process but a fluid, ever-changing process, as people constantly move around among different kinds of unions, each involving different conjugal and affinal relationships and each having different social values (Bledsoe and Pison 1994: 4–10; Mann 1994: 175). A fluid definition of marriage necessarily entails a fluid definition of polygamy.

–2–

Foundations of Polygamy

Polygamous Marriage

Definitions

The definitional challenge involved in analysing polygamy as matrimony is particularly great with regards to polyandry. Polyandry can be most simply defined as a form of marriage in which one woman has more than one husband at a time. So far, it mirrors the definition of polygyny, in which one man has more than one wife at a time. The definitional similarity ends here, however, because unlike polygyny where a man is formally married to all his wives, this is not the case in polyandry, where a woman may only be married to one husband, who then represents the group of men to whom she is socially but not legally married. So the first definitional challenge is what precisely marriage entails in polyandrous unions.

In fraternal polyandrous societies, the common wife will typically be married only to the eldest brother of a group of brothers. She will also have legitimate sexual and other relations with her husbands' brothers, who socially but not necessarily legally form part of the marriage. Technically then, the woman is not married to most of the men with whom she has intimate relations and with whom she may have children. This depends entirely on the definition of marriage used, however. As Leach (1955) has pointed out, it is virtually impossible to formulate a definition of marriage that is universally applicable, because marriage entails different expectations, obligations and behaviours in different societies. The definition of marriage must by nature be open, for even if one could formulate a list of elements normally associated with marriage, one can always find cases that do not fit. That is the usual conundrum in anthropology. The definitional challenge is increased with regards to polyandry precisely because its very definition rests on the definition of marriage. In polyandrous societies, a husband's brothers (or co-husbands if not related) typically have sexual access to his wife, but these brothers may not have married her through the performance of the same ritual which marked the wife's marriage to the eldest brother. The question then becomes whether their socially approved but not necessarily formalized sexual relationship with the wife constitutes a marriage, that is, are they her husbands? If their union is not considered a marriage, many, if not most polyandrous societies would no longer count as polyandrous (cf. Mair 1971: 143).

The uncertainty about what constitutes marriage, and whether it should be the defining criteria of polyandry, has created a range of explanatory models. At one end of the range are the very loose definitions of polyandry that defines it as one woman mating with more than one man (cf. Westermarck 1891). This would include all those regular sexual relations, which are practised with or without marriage, such as cicisbeism, free love and conjoint marriage (see below). At the other end of the range are the very restrictive definitions based on formal legitimate marriage. They contend that, as the primary purpose of marriage is to make a woman's children legitimate, it would be sufficient for a woman to marry one man only. This would render true polyandry very rare, and many of the practices traditionally considered polyandrous would instead involve women in monogamous marriages engaging in *polykoity*, or multiple matings, without involving marriage (Fischer 1952). The term *cicisbeism* has been introduced to deal with this problematic aspect peculiar to polyandry; it refers to the practice of one woman having sexual relations with more than one man, in a regular and lasting fashion outside marriage (Meek 1925: 197). Cicisbeism, a female version of concubinage, allows women to have legitimate sexual unions with men with whom they have not gone through what their particular society normally would consider a marriage ceremony. The introduction of this concept meant that most cases of polyandry could in fact be cicisbeism instead, because they typically involve a man's brothers having free sexual access to his wife without being married to her, as polyandry would 'require'. People in such societies would be practising monogamy with fraternal cicisbeism rather than polyandry. The principle of fraternal cicisbeism is indeed often seen in populations where polyandry is disappearing. For example, among the Lepchas of India, the majority have now become monogamous, but younger brothers are still permitted to have sexual relations with an elder brother's wife (Raha 1987: 18–19).

Polyandry is probably a rare phenomenon in the ethnographic record if one follows a strict definition, which uses the criterion of marriage as crucial; on the other hand it becomes impossible to define and discuss polyandry if there are no boundaries to adhere to. A central problem is whether socially approved sexual relations qualify as 'marriage' for the purposes of identifying polyandrous practices. Various people have attempted to put qualifiers on what sorts of sexual relationships were practised in polyandrous societies. Some suggest that temporal aspects are crucial, such that the permanency of a union is a better criterion than its state of formal legitimacy for differentiating polyandry from cicisbeism. Stephens (1988) defines non-adelphic polyandry as a lasting and simultaneous sexual union between a woman and two or more unrelated men, such that the children born to the woman are considered legitimate offspring. This temporal condition involves both the duration of the unions as well as the fact that they are simultaneous. A woman's involvement in several consecutive monogamous unions would not qualify as polyandry, nor would cuckoldry be involved as the shared and simultaneous sexual access to one woman is implicitly agreed among the partners. Such a broad definition of marriage means that the Nayars of Southern India (see Chapter 7), where a woman is not necessarily married to any of the men with whom she has sexual relations but with whom she has 'legitimate' children, would be considered polyandrous.

Polyandrous Parenthood

Many researchers indeed focus on the importance of conferring legitimacy on children as a distinguishing feature of polyandry. It is based on the view that conferring legitimacy and affinity are universal features of marriage. In the case of polyandry, the criterion of legitimacy allows it to be distinguished from cicisbeism or other forms of plural relations of women (Levine and Sangree 1980b: 388). Hence, having a socially approved sexual relationship with a woman would not constitute marriage, because marriage is considered determined by social parenthood, i.e. that a man may be recognized as a father to the woman's children. This would imply that a polyandrous union in which children have only one legal father, and a woman only has one legal husband, would not be polygamous. If marriage is a social arrangement by which a child is given a legitimate position in society, the legitimacy of a woman's children is secured by her first marriage, and it is therefore not necessary for the woman to go through formal marriage rites with her other partners. The tolerated sexual access of a woman's other 'husbands' constitutes *polykoity*, or plural mating, since they are not married to her, even though they may officially form and function as a social and economic unit. Critics have pointed to several problems with this argument. First, people marry not just to confer legitimacy on potential children, but because of social convention, economic advantages or personal feelings. Second, in many polyandrous societies the biological father of a child may be unknown, and legitimacy is ensured by the fact that the mother gave birth to the child. Among the Nayar, for example, a child is automatically granted full birth-status rights in his society if he was conceived in accordance with approved norms of sexual relations (i.e. within appropriate castes) for his mother (Gough 1959; Leach 1955; Nandi 1987).

Unknown fathers are particularly a feature of matrilineal[1] polyandrous societies, where a mother's eldest spouse will typically be her children's social father, while her other co-spouses are referred to as uncles. Social fatherhood may also be ascribed to a collective group rather than an individual, as for example among the polyandrous Irava in colonial Ceylon (present-day Sri Lanka). In Ceylon, British-based Sinhalese law did not recognize the existence of polyandrous marriage despite its widespread practice. All 'husbands' of a wife were considered fathers of her children, resulting in children who were not officially legitimate offspring of both their parents, as non-married co-husbands could not be on their birth certificates, but who were nevertheless legitimate heirs of both their parents. This was based on customary rules of inheritance and property rights according to customary rules of descent, where fatherhood reflected a husband's sexual rights. This implies that if legitimacy can be defined in terms of property rights rather than officially recognized descent, then Sinhalese customary unions should be regarded as marriages. Legally it was not marriage, but for the people involved it was: what the system could not confer in terms of legal recognition, it conferred in terms of customary inheritance. This contradiction stemmed from the conflict between English law and customary law: based on English law, Irava marital arrangements would involve polykoity creating legitimate children for the official husband, but based on customary law, those arrangements would be considered polyandrous because they involved marriage (Leach 1955).

There are, in other words, alternative ways to ensure the legitimacy of children than marrying their mother. Because it is not always possible to determine which man is biologically responsible for the birth of a particular child in polyandrous societies, one of the mother's 'husbands' typically becomes the social father of the child. Social paternity can be ascribed either through the performance of certain rituals or through social conventions; if one of the 'husbands' is actually married to the woman he will be the social father of children born to that woman. A classic example of a ritual conferring fatherhood on a man is the bow and arrow ceremony performed by the Toda of the Nilgiri Hills in India. The Toda practise fraternal polyandry, and biological paternity is not considered important, because it is the extension of the clan's life force which is crucial: the actual man responsible for a pregnancy is less important than the fact that a child is conceived. Fatherhood must, however, be socially established. This is done through the performance of the bow and arrow ceremony, which involves several rituals culminating in the presentation of a bow and arrow, signalling that a man has achieved social fatherhood. Performance of the ceremony is not required when a child is born to a man and woman of different Toda groups, for one clan's life force is of no importance to another clan (Goswami 1987; Peter 1963: 508–10; Raha 1987).

Typologies

The peculiar problems involved in distinguishing polyandry from other forms of socially approved relationships are not just definitional, but by extension typological as well. There appears to be endless variation in how 'polyandrous' households are set up. In an attempt to lessen definitional and typological confusion, especially in those systems that may be described as polygynous polyandry (Levine 1980: 286), Majumdar (1962) coined the term *polygynandry*. It refers to any marital union involving several husbands and wives; the term is a combination of the words polygyny and polyandry. For example, fraternal polyandry with multiple wives is the common and preferred domestic arrangement in the Jaunsar Bawar region of India, described in Chapter 6. It may in principle be called fraternal group marriage, because a new wife usually marries the eldest brother but becomes a shared wife to all brothers. The new term allows researchers to deal with the fact that, in societies where polyandry is practised, the form and composition of domestic groups typically vary to the extent that forms of monogamy, polygyny, polyandry as well as group marriage may all be practised within communities and individual families, sometimes simultaneously. The various forms of marriage practised are not mutually exclusive, being all based on the same principles and beliefs; they are rather responses to the particular internal and external circumstances facing a family. Over time, the composition of a domestic group usually undergoes many developmental changes as a result of marriages, births, divorces and deaths. A family might start out with a polyandrous set-up, developing over time into a fraternal group marriage with an equal number of husbands and wives, go through a polygynous phase, only to end in monogamy. The term polygynandrous thus underscores that a polyandrous marriage system is rarely static but rather a fluid combination of forms, which change as family composition changes. As such it follows a *domestic cycle*, or cyclical development, which all domestic groups whatever their marriage patterns go through (Berreman 1975).

Peter (1963) argues that polygynandry should rather be called *conjoint marriage*, for although it can on some level be considered a combination of polyandrous and polygynous practices within individual families, it bears little relation to polygyny per se. Conjoint marriage emerges out of a polyandrous union when one co-husband wants to take another wife for whatever reason. All husbands, however, share the new wife and as such conjoint marriage is a development of polyandry without actual polygyny; polygyny is reserved for the few men who can afford more than one wife on their own. Polygynandry does indeed differ crucially from polygyny in involving brothers sharing common wives, whereas polygyny typically involves one man with exclusive access to several wives. Sexual exclusivity is important because it offers him individual reproductive and productive power as well as social prestige, whereas polygynandry may diminish power and prestige for the individual man through the process of sharing.

Such typological problems are well illustrated by the polyandrous arrangements of the Native American Shoshone and Northern Paiute of Nevada. Northern Paiute marriage was not marked by ceremony or exchange of gifts, rather a marriage was thought of as established when a man and a woman had sexual relations. When one man and several women or several men and one woman were known to be living together and having sexual relations, they were similarly regarded by public opinion as being married without requiring further formalities. Polyandry was not common, but it was socially recognized as a legitimate union. There were no particular economic incentives to polyandry, nor was it apparently a response to one husband being away from home for prolonged periods, a reason often given for polyandry. Among the Northern Paiute, polyandry may rather have been linked to the frequency of polygynous marriages, including the levirate, where one man marrying up to four women may have led to a shortage of females (Park 1937). It parallels the situation described among the similarly small-scale Inuit societies, where high-ranking males practise polygyny, forcing low-ranking males to practise polyandry (see Chapter 3). In societies practising the levirate, it could possibly act as a catalyst for polyandry, as a man could, in anticipation of sexual access to his brother's wife after his death, be encouraged to 'try her out' while the brother was still alive. This might have been the foundation for polyandry among the Northern Paiute. Polyandrous relations, at least *de facto* ones, may thus have accompanied the levirate in more societies than acknowledged. Among the Shoshone, who practised fraternal polyandry, as well as sororate and levirate, a man might bring his younger brother to live with himself and his wife. The wife would perform domestic duties for both men, but only engage in sexual relations with the younger brother when her husband was away. The arrangement was temporary, as the younger brother was expected to marry a wife of his own at some point, and any children resulting from the cohabitation called him uncle (Steward 1936).

Should the Shoshone and Northern Paiute be classified as polyandrous? And can their societies be called polyandrous if polygyny is also practised, and may in fact be the culturally preferred form of polygamy? They seem to fail along several definitional parameters, including permanency of union or formality of marriage to at least one man. But if the Northern Paiute consider a woman to be married to two men once she starts having sexual relations with them, then one probably does violence to their way of relating to each other if one refuses to call the system polyandrous just because some form of formal marriage between the woman and at least one man is lacking. A definition of marriage is perhaps best based on what people in the particular society in question consider marriage to be. Marriage may not necessarily involve the performance of a ceremony, which might include negotiating the specifics of the union and various rituals including the exchange of wows and/ or gifts, in order to render the union legitimate. In many societies, marriage is a lengthy process, not marked by any single event, but rather emerges gradually as an established union, recognized by the community and the couple (Solway 1990: 45). The Tshidi of South Africa, for example, arrange their unions along a continuum marked by their duration and jural state; in an everyday context, however, there are few distinctions between people legally married through transfer of bridewealth[2] and other rites, and those simply living together as a couple. Married status is continually negotiated, and 'the formal elements of the marriage process are not reducible to a jural device for the legitimization of marriage' (Comaroff 1980: 170). Among the Nuer, payment of bridewealth through family-owned cattle constitutes a marital relation between two lineages, and when a Nuer man dies, 'there is no question of the widow being married to one of his brothers, for the brothers already count as her husbands. The dead man's lineage has a right to inherit his wife because she is their wife, the wife of their cattle' (Evans-Pritchard 1951: 45). The widow hence does not need to go through a new marriage ceremony in order to count as her husband's brother's legitimate wife through the levirate.

Returning to polyandry, Leach (1955: 182) noted half a century ago that it might be pedantic to discuss whether (adelphic) polyandry does or does not involve marriage, and whether its defining feature is conferring legitimacy on children, for what is marriage, and what is legitimate offspring? In the end, it is up to the individual researcher which parameters he or she feels must be included in a definition of polyandry. Those following very strict definitions of marriage and polyandry will find very few societies practising it; those subscribing to broad definitions will find more, thus transplanting the definitional and typological problems into the ethnographic record.

Foundations of Polygamy[3]

Polygamous Society

The attempts at defining various forms of polygamy (and hence by implication marriage) lead to the next important question, namely how does one define a society as polygamous? This is a troubling question to which there is no immediate answer, because of the great range of polygamous practices found cross-culturally. This means that, depending on how broadly one defines polygamy, it could on some level exist everywhere and virtually all societies could be labelled polygamous. Boundaries need to be set through various parameters that can establish what aspects of a society make it polygamous. Among some groups polygamy is virtually unknown, practised by a few fringe elements that break the law in doing so; among other groups it is common, a cultural and religious norm that people aspire to. Thus, at one end of the continuum, there are people like the Mandinka of Gambia among whom: 'polygyny is a widespread cultural practice legitimized by the Islamic religion, the Gambian State, and by Mandinka customary practice' (Wittrup 1990: 117). In other words, it is legitimate religiously, culturally and legally. At the other end of the continuum, there are groups like the fundamentalist Mormons of the USA, who practise polygyny in spite of the fact that the surrounding society finds it religiously, culturally and legally illegitimate. Those Mormons practising polygyny believe it to be legitimate according to their own sacred beliefs, hence absolving them of their duty to respect civil laws banning polygamy in the USA. Classifying societies as either monogamous or polygamous based on whether they permit polygamy or not is therefore tempting, but this strategy works best for Western monogamous societies which unambiguously prohibit polygamy, legally as well as culturally. In polygamous societies, legal and sociocultural prohibitions against polygamy do not always coincide, making the approach ambiguous and potentially arbitrary. Populations in the Cote d'Ivoire (Ivory Coast), for example, have some of the highest levels of polygyny in Africa, though the State legally abolished polygyny in 1964 (Bledsoe and Pison 1994: 11).

The problem involved in defining a society as polygamous is crystallized in the following quote: 'polygamy was in Ganda, as possibly everywhere else [in Africa], the ideal: men generally aspired to it, peasants seldom managed to have more than two or three wives, and the majority, as probably everywhere else, were fortunate to have one' (Betzig 1986: 76). Should one label Ganda society polygamous if polygamy remains the privilege of a minority, but a majority aspires to be polygamous? What weighs more heavily in the definitional equation, the fact that it is permitted or that it is practised? Many if not most African societies condone polygamy, but typically only a small part of the population of those societies actually practise it. A typical example are the Southwest African Suku, whose marriages are about 80 per cent monogamous, whereas important chiefs could have ten or more women, and the king up to forty wives (Betzig 1986: 73). It is therefore important to look at people's attitudes in describing a society as polygamous: most people would probably intuitively label a society like the Ganda polygamous because most male members strive for polygyny, regardless of the actual numeric levels of polygamy in Ganda (cf. Murdock 1949: 28). In contrast, polygamy in Malaysia is legal only for Muslims, among whom only some strive for it and even fewer achieve it. Ganda society may be called polygamous because it represents the ideal marriage form, whereas Malay society would not generally be considered polygamous, because it does not represent the ideal in the same all-encompassing way. That it is legally sanctioned does not make it socially or culturally sanctioned. It is a matter of definition and labelling, and one must be clear on whether an ideal or a fact is described. That is, what are the norms and numbers relating to polygamy of the particular society in question?

Some kind of parameters for describing a society as polygamous are needed, in other words. As described above, polygamy as a social institution can be divided into such main types as polygyny and polyandry. Moving on to the foundations of polygamy, however, a much more complex set of differentiations is needed, such as religiously versus culturally based polygamy and official versus unofficial polygamy. Various researchers have tried to come up with generalized models that reduce the complex sets of variables into simple schemes to address this explanatory problem. One model looks at the different frequencies of polygyny in different societies, thereby attempting to set numeric standards for when a society is polygamous. This avoids the difficulties of defining an institution based on ideal judgments. The model, developed by White (1988), and incorporating Murdock (1949), lists societies along a polygamy continuum involving six levels:

Level 1: general polyandry;
Level 2: exclusive monogamy/monogamy prescribed/no polygyny permitted or encouraged;
Level 3: monogamy preferred but with limited polygyny/polygyny permitted but incidence below 20 per cent for married males/occasional or limited polygyny;

Level 4: polygyny preferred but of low incidence;
Level 5: polygyny and polyandry may coexist;
Level 6: polygyny common or general/incidence 20 per cent or above.

In order to operationalize this model, one might first look at the rates of men and women who marry polygamously within a society. Factors affecting the demography of polygamy directly, through the relative population of adult males and adult females who are married, are relative age at marriage, relative ease of divorce or remarriage, and rates of bachelorhood and spinsterhood. Factors affecting the demography of polygamy indirectly are the adult sex ratio versus natal sex ratio, the relative male/female mortality, relative rates of labour migration and the relative movement of men and women in or out of a community at puberty or marriage. Second, one could try to distinguish which categories of men and women are married polygamously. One of the most important factors to examine is the frequency of multiple wives for elites as opposed to commoners as well as the prerogatives of rulers, because in most polygamous societies elites have disproportionately high polygamy rates compared with commoners. A high frequency of polygamy, for example, tends to indicate the presence of social differentiation based on age, or *gerontocracy*, since older (and hence typically richer and more powerful) men have access to a greater number of wives (see Chapter 3). As with all schemes trying to describe societies numerically, the model encourages unilinear interpretations, which makes it difficult to understand an institution as rich in diversity as polygamy. But simultaneously, it is precisely its rich diversity that makes it necessary to break the institution down into component parts if one is to understand it.

Polygamous Parameters

Probably the most fundamental parameter one can use to distinguish various forms of polygamy is polygamy based on religious doctrine versus polygamy based on cultural practice. Polygamy is found among people practising all major religions of the world, Islam, Christianity, Judaism, Hinduism, Buddhism, as well as local native religions. Polygamy is also found on all continents, Africa, Asia, America, Europe and Oceania, where various populations may practise polygamy because it forms part of their cultural repertoire. The legitimate basis for polygamy in a particular society is like a swinging pendulum, however, sometimes found in religious codes, sometimes in cultural codes, such that this legitimacy may change foundations over time. Religious and cultural codes may work against each other or reinforce each other, and within any particular group of people practising polygamy, there will always be some people justifying their belief in polygamy based on precisely those codes that are rejected by their opponents. In Malaysia, for example, the basis for practising polygamy is Islam and thus religious. Culturally, however, polygamy is less accepted, but women's activists are not using cultural norms as a way to speak out against polygyny, because its legitimacy stems from its religious basis. Women hence use Islam to argue against, whereas men use Islam to argue for, polygamy. In other words, the legitimacy of polygamy always tends to be contested, with some leaning on cultural codes and some on religious codes to defend their own ways, often using the same codes to argue opposite views.

Just as there are religious codes, there will be cultural codes constraining or encouraging polygamy in a particular society. In societies that permit polygamy, there are typically a great variety of culturally accepted marriage strategies that may lead to polygamy. In many societies, extraordinary individuals such as leaders, shamans, hunters, nobles or wealthy men have a socially prescribed right to take a second wife. Some societies allow polygamy only through cultural rules such as widow inheritance, levirate, sororate or wife capture, for example in war. Other typical culturally and socially acceptable reasons for taking a second wife include barrenness of the first wife, post-partum sex taboos,[4] the need for economic assistance from co-wives, fluctuations in the sex ratio, male mortality and male migration. It is also important to examine people's culturally based attitudes towards polygamy, as mentioned, particularly that of parents towards their daughters' potential polygamous marriages. In any given society, there is always a great many and often conflicting norms, expectations and behaviours at work in polygamous unions, making it difficult to generalize as to what polygamy is and means on a local scale.

The same situation applies with respect to formal versus informal polygamy in a particular society. In countries that legally allow polygamy, only people who qualify for this type of marriage may in principle formally engage in it; the rest may then engage in informal, or not legally sanctioned, polygamy. In traditionally polygamous societies where many or all members of the population are now prohibited from marrying polygamously, there will often be a fringe element, or perhaps a large sub-group of people, engaging in informal polygamy. The resulting secret 'outside wives' live a double life, officially single but unofficially married. This notion of 'outside wives' (or more rarely 'outside husbands') that defy the laws of the land is common in many colonial and post-colonial settings where the advent of Christianity or adoption of Western-based laws may spell the abolition of polygamy in that country (see Chapter 8). That people who used to practise polygamy *de jure* can no longer marry a second wife does not prevent them from doing it *de facto*. The difference is rather one of men's strategies to obtain more than one wife.

An important set of parameters to examine when trying to define a society as polygamous are the particular rights and statuses applicable with respect to polygamy, legal, cultural and religious. Understanding the legal system in a particular society, and how it regulates polygamy, is absolutely vital, because it provides the foundation for examining an institution that is defined through legal marriage. Important aspects to examine are the requirements which exist for a man who wishes to take secondary wives, (religious and) legal codes as sources of restrictions on the number of wives a man can take, the legal status accorded to secondary wife, etc. The most important aspect of the legal system that one must examine is the marriage system itself. First, this means looking at the degree of formality of marriage. In a society where marriage is formal, concubines are recognized as a separate category from second wives; where marriage is informal, concubines may be considered second wives. The marital status of concubines thus needs to be investigated. Ranking and differentiation among co-wives is another important aspect that has both social and legal implications, as does the status of children by different types of marriage. For example, in societies with formal marriage, children of concubines typically do not inherit their father, even if he has acknowledged paternity.

Polygamous Arrangements

Polygamous societies are differentiated by their legal, cultural or religious foundations, as well as by how polygamous families arrange themselves. Societies can be differentiated according to such parameters as whether there is separate or common residence of co-wives, and whether there is separate or common residence of the husband with his wives, and with which wife. For example, there tends to be a strong correlation between non-sororal polygyny and co-wives occupying separate houses. Residential arrangements can signal the form of polygamy practised in a particular society, though it may be difficult to assess such arrangements. In societies where most houses are communal, for example, polygamous families may share a house because everybody in that society does, not particularly because they are polygamous. At one residential extreme are the large African polygamous compounds where the household includes a husband and all his wives, their children, and sometimes daughters-in-law and grandchildren as well. Communal living here signifies one common social and economic unit that is mutually interdependent. At the other extreme are urban Malay polygamous unions, where the husband usually lives only with his first wife, whereas he may not cohabit at all with his other wives, who live in separate houses. In fact, Malay co-wives are often unaware of each other's existence. Such polygamous families have component parts that are socially and economically completely independent of each other; their lack of collective identity and interaction may indeed disqualify them as families in a narrow sense. In between the two extremes one may find various residential arrangements, some of which are described in the ethnographic chapters in Part II.

Polygamous societies are also differentiated by how multiple wives are recruited, as well as how they relate to each other. Examining the recruitment process as an explanatory parameter involves examining, first, the extent of widow inheritance or levirate as a source of secondary wives; second, whether the first wife encourages the husband to take a second wife; third, whether the first wife's permission is required for the husband to take a second wife; fourth, whether the first wife helps to recruit her own kin or non-kin as co-wives; and finally, whether there is marriage of girls and women captured in war within the society. Relations between co-wives will differ not only on the basis of how they were recruited, but will also differ markedly depending upon which type of polygamy is practised, and its residential and other domestic arrangements.

Relations between co-wives are first and foremost affected by their internal kin-relations. In most polygynous societies there is general non-sororal polygyny. In some societies sororal polygyny is permitted or preferred, and some societies have exclusively sororal polygyny. In other words, polygamous societies differ markedly with regards to allowing kin, especially sisters, to become co-wives. Sororal polygamy is practised in some societies because it is believed to foster greater cohesiveness among co-wives sharing values and norms, whereas it is specifically forbidden in other polygamous societies. For example, ancient Jewish law permitted polygamy, but generally forbade marriage with sisters, for it was believed that jealousy and antagonism was stronger among kin than among strangers.[5] In contrast, other ethnic groups believe that sisters raised in the same household have had the opportunity to work out personal adjustment with one another and can move into the household of a common husband with a minimum of friction. In Indonesia, for example, aristocratic co-wives are often kinswomen, a state of affairs that is believed to foster friendly relations between them. The women appear to object less to polygamy if their co-wives are related to them, and from the same caste and village. The shared background of sisters is thus believed to create conflicts between co-wives in one cultural context, but to alleviate them in another (Clignet 1970: 54; Clignet and Sween 1981: 453; Krulfeld 1986: 203).

The social relations between co-wives are naturally also affected by whether there is solidarity or conflict between them. Broadly speaking, cooperation and competition among co-wives vary markedly even within local regions, making generalizations about them regarding 'types of polygamy' difficult. In Cameroon, for example,

> Co-wife competition is a main problem for women in the district. Instead of helping each other with domestic tasks – as the local normative discourse prescribes – co-wives frequently fight for the money and the sexual favours of their husband. The unequal division of money causes sharp arguments and competition between the co-wives, since these women do the agricultural work and almost totally depend on their husbands for money. (Notermans 2002: 345–6)

Jealousy and competition among co-wives is typically focused on economic resources, especially when they are (perceived to be) insufficient. Economics appears to be a greater source of conflict in modern polygynous families than sexual jealousy, reflecting local concerns of co-wives rather than the usual Western focus on problematic sexuality (Kilbride and Kilbride 1990: 216). Sexual and emotional jealousy may of course emerge when the husband favours a particular wife, typically the most recent and youngest wife, and neglects the emotional and sexual needs of his other wives (Meekers and Franklin 1995: 321). Co-wife jealousy tends to be lessened by such factors as adequate financial maintenance of all wives, shared domestic responsibilities such as cooking and childrearing, and, most importantly perhaps, the enforcement of strict rules for the husband's sleeping schedule. Generally, whatever the object of envy between co-wives, there is an unspoken agreement within most polygamous systems that a husband must share himself and his resources equally between all wives. If this agreement is broken, it typically triggers jealousy (Madhavan 2002).

Religious and Cultural Foundations

Polygamy in World Religions

Judaism.   Historically, polygamy was practised in Ancient Hebrew society, typically in the form of bigamy or through the levirate. The levirate is indeed named after Levi, son of Jacob in the Old Testament. The levirate was practised when a deceased man had no son to succeed him, as male heirs were necessary to continue a man's lineage. His widow should marry his brother in the hopes of begetting a son, though she was still considered the wife of the dead man. The dead brother rather than the living biological father therefore became the acknowledged or social father of a child born after its mother entered the levirate (Radcliffe-Brown 1950: 64). Some European Jews practised plural marriage well into the Middle Ages. Changes in cultural and religious practices have made polygamy illegitimate, and Jewish populations no longer officially practise it. Secular law in most Western countries with large Jewish populations does not recognize polygamous marriage, though few such countries have any laws against living a polygamous lifestyle.

Christianity.   Polygamy has never been culturally or religiously legitimate for Christians. In most Western countries with predominantly Christian populations secular law does not recognize polygamous marriage. Few such countries have any laws directly banning living a polygamous lifestyle, however. Polygamy was indeed practised by some Christians at various times throughout the centuries; there were small polygamous Christian groups in late medieval times, for example. In the Middle Ages, as in other ages, powerful men married monogamously, but mated polygynously. Both laymen and clergy tended to have sexual access to as many women as they could afford (Betzig 1995). One of the most prominent proponents of Christian polygamy was Martin Luther who joined other theologians of his time in accepting, albeit reluctantly, the desire of the social and political elites to practise polygyny, in order to retain their support and ensure the success of the reformation

(Altman and Ginat 1996: 42; Cairncross 1974). Martin Luther could lean on good Catholic precedents in these matters. The Catholic Church did not accept polygamy, but neither did it consistently prevent it, even sanctioning a few special cases over the centuries. The fact that there are no specific prohibitions against polygamy in the New Testament allowed various religious leaders to advocate it on moral and religious grounds, such as the need to replenish the male population after wars. In eighteenth-century France, arguments in favour of marrying several women were put forward based on population concerns and the 'rights of man'. The proposed legalizing of 'simultaneous' polygamy caused controversy, however, and the idea was abandoned; the notion that one male would enjoy an advantage at the expense of others was associated with despotism and as such was antithetical to the principle of equality (Blum 1998).

Today, the Christian Church clearly condemns polygamy, not least as a result of the last 200 years of colonial history, where the intercultural confrontation between colonizer and colonized often took the form of religious confrontation. Faced with polygamous, animistic peoples, European administrators and missionaries made polygamy one of the main issues with which to force their way of life upon their new subjects. By banning its practice as religiously illegitimate, it was assumed that the subjects would convert to Christianity. To most Western Christians, polygamy is wrong and totally unacceptable from all points of view – legal, religious, moral and social. That the people who have practised polygamy for generations may find that it can be combined with being a practising Christian has been, and still is, a problem for the Christian Church, especially in Africa (see below for a discussion of Christian polygyny in Cameroon). But African 'traditionalists' are not the only Christians practising polygamy today. The most famous (or infamous) example is the Mormons, a Christian group that arose in nineteenth-century USA. So-called Mormon fundamentalists continue to practise polygamy today, more than 100 years after the mainstream Mormon Church discontinued the practice. Several of the US states criminalize polygamous lifestyles, unlike most other Western countries; these laws originated as anti-polygamy legislation designed to allow Utah to ascend to statehood within the USA. The laws used to be rarely enforced, but some recent high-profile convictions have brought up the issue of polygamy again. For a full discussion of Mormon polygamy, see chapters 5 and 9.

Hinduism. There are small pockets of Hindus who, based on centuries-old cultural norms, continue to practise polygamy. They are the polyandrous peoples of India, Tibet and Nepal, described in Chapter 6. But in the Hindu motherland of India, polygamy is legally and religiously prohibited. However, for those Hindus bent on being polygamous, culture comes to their rescue, for 'a man who fails to produce sons by his first wife may by custom marry again. Even the Hindu Code Bill, which prohibits polygamy among Hindus, has not been effective in this respect, so forceful is the imperative for male heirs' (Sharma 1980: 199). Among Hindus, then, polygamy is not formally permitted, but this does not prevent it from being practised informally, through local custom. In Malaysia, where about 10 per cent of the population is Indian and primarily Hindu, the debate about whether non-Muslim Malaysians should be allowed to engage in polygamy periodically surfaces in the media. The 1982 Marriage and Divorce Act of Malaysia banned the practice for non-Muslims. Proponents in the Hindu communities typically claim that Hindu women acknowledge a man's conditional right to take another wife under certain circumstances, such as a wife's sub-fertility, since not having children is antithetical to manhood. Hindu women typically deny this claim. The proponents are typically Hindu men seeking legal recognition for their secondary marriages, probably contracted according to customary practice; these marriages may be legitimate within Hindu communities, but not within the larger Malaysian State. There is thus a dual society with respect to polygamy, where several people live in *de facto* polygamous relationships while being formally monogamous.

Buddhism.   For Buddhists, like for Hindus, there is a strong divide between the religious and legal foundations for polygamy on one side, and its cultural foundations on the other. Legally, there is no ground for polygamy in most Buddhist countries, although it has been customary for rich men to have more than one wife or concubines. Looking at Malaysia again, where about 30 per cent of the population is Chinese and primarily Buddhist, Buddhist Malaysians wishing to engage in polygamy face the same problems as their Hindu counterparts, described above. With the advent of the marriage law abolishing polygamy for non-Muslims, the practice did not disappear but simply took another form. A Chinese man can be married only to one wife legally, but can then marry a second one by performing the traditional tea ceremony through which they were married according to the customary laws of the Chinese community. Again a dual society with respect to polygamy is created, one that is formal and one that is informal, because cultural practice overrules religious and legal codes. There are Buddhist populations that are polygamous, however, where the practice is based on a cultural foundation. This has made Buddhist Tibet home to the largest and most flourishing polyandrous community in the world today. Tibetans typically practise fraternal polyandry where brothers become husbands to a common wife, but also allow polyandry of fathers and sons who sometimes combine to have one wife in common, a unique phenomenon not found anywhere else in world. Indeed every form of marriage appears to be permissible in Tibet – polyandry, polygyny, monogamy, group marriage – reflecting the cultural diversity of the area (Peter 1963).

Islam.   Polygamy has always been a permissible if not integral part of Muslim religious practice. It is often seen as a hallmark of Islam by non-Muslims, but not necessarily by Muslims themselves. Many populations within Islam neither practise nor condone polygamy, religiously or culturally. For a full discussion of these matters see Chapter 4 on Muslim polygamy. Suffice it here to say that among many Muslim populations, particularly in South East Asia, cultural and social patterns discourages polygamy, although it is religiously and legally permitted for Muslims to practise it. Just as religious and legal codes proscribe polygamy in Buddhist and Hindu countries, and cultural codes may prescribe it, so cultural codes may proscribe polygamy in Muslim countries, and religious and legal codes actually prescribe it. Returning to Malaysia, Muslim couples wishing to engage in a polygamous marriage may therefore do the reverse of their Hindu and Buddhist neighbours, namely keep their officially sanctioned second marriage secret by being married by Islamic officials, but not go through the community-based ritual of the *adat* (customary law) ceremony, thereby not alerting a potentially disapproving community or family of their plural marriage.

Native Religions. The traditional or customary polygamy practised by people who are followers of their traditional native religions, rather than one of the major world religions, such as Christianity or Islam, cannot really be described in generalized terms, because it is, by its very nature, dependent on the particular sociocultural context from which it springs. Usually, local polygamous patterns will be based on cultural practice rather than being religiously prescribed or allowed. It may however be supported by religion, making it a very strong feature of a particular society. An example is Mali in West Africa, where over 90 per cent of the population identifies itself as Muslim. Almost half of all women live in polygamous marriages, making Mali one of the countries with the highest polygamy rates in the world (Madhavan 2002). Here, the Muslim injunction that a man may have up to four wives works to strengthen traditional Malian polygamy. However, religion may also work against the customary practice, as is the case in Cameroon, described below. Here, the spread of Christianity, with its uncompromising condemnation of polygamy, is in direct conflict with local traditional polygamy. The Christian mission has been very successful in Cameroon, but has not succeeded in eradicating polygyny, which remains culturally entrenched. People must then practise it in spite of the religion, not because of, or in tandem with it.

Christian Polygyny in Cameroon

According to the definitions given earlier in this chapter, Cameroon is a polygynous society. Over 90 per cent of men prefer a polygamous marriage, but only 30–35 per cent will actually be able to achieve it. Cameroon thus lives up to both numeric and normative criteria for classifying a society as polygamous. Since a marriage in the Cameroon is typically considered a temporary arrangement and not a lifelong association, marriage is not seen as being permanently monogamous or polygamous. Unions may oscillate between polygamous and monogamous forms several times over the lifetime of the spouses. As polygamy represents the ideal marriage form, the majority of men are monogamous by circumstance and not by choice. Administrators from the colonial governments, as well as missionaries, typically focused on two reasons why polygamy was so strongly present in Cameroon: long post-partum sexual abstinence and female population excess. Both these reasons have since been refuted. Instead, the most commonly voiced reason given by people in Cameroon for the persistence of polygamy is the desire to have numerous children. Children are great productive assets in traditional Africa, where they contribute to household production by working in their father's fields or tending his cattle. In situations where it is difficult to find or pay hired labour, children can help augment cash crop production, a major source of income for rural households. The desire to have numerous children is not driven by economic considerations alone, however. It is also driven by a strong belief in the future continuation of life in general, and of the ancestors in particular, which a child represents (Reyburn 1959). A recent study in Cameroon showed that currently monogamous men's desire for more children drives their desire for additional wives, rather than the other way around (Speizer 1995).

With the advent of European contact with Africa came the Christian mission. It started to take on a much larger and more formalized role in the nineteenth century when the emerging Western colonial powers were able to protect and provide logistical (and moral) support to missionaries in all corners of Africa. From the end of the nineteenth century onwards, Christian churches condemned polygyny as incompatible with Christianity. Polygyny was thought to victimize women. To be 'true Christians' and respectful spouses, Africans hence had to reject polygyny and marry monogamously. Simultaneously, most colonial governments attempted to formalize African law and custom within their native territories. Colonial administrators and African traditional leaders alike were particularly concerned about the gender relations prevalent in African society. The colonial administrators, who were influenced by missionary thinking, viewed customary practices such as polygamy and bridewealth payments as retrogressive and oppressive to women. They emphasized the relative superiority of European gender ideology and its treatment of women. African traditional leaders attempted (in vain) to counter accusations of cultural inferiority and subjugation of women by asserting the appropriateness and value of such practices as bridewealth and polygamy (Erlank 2003).

In a study discussing the conflict between Christianity and polygamy in Cameroon, Reyburn remarked that, 'Polygamy is an institution which appears to many modern Africans as something natural to Africa. As some say: "Polygamy is beautiful; it is a symbol of that which is truly African"' (1959: 2). Polygamy is, in other words, deeply entrenched in the culture of Cameroon and is not based on any particular religious foundation. This gives the practice a flexibility to adapt to the modern world and to the many religions now on offer to save African souls. In much if not most of Africa, polygyny represents a traditional cultural custom which is independent of the religion practised by the polygynist, inasmuch as both Christians,

Muslims, followers of native and other religions can and do practise it. Polygyny is thus an accepted part of local kinship systems in Cameroon, and surrounding non-polygamous populations mostly do not condemn the polygamists in their midst, whether Christian or not.

Christian churches may indeed unwittingly reinforce polygamous patterns. In a study of polygamous women in Cameroon, Notermans (2002) describes how they have created their own interpretations of Christianity in which polygyny becomes an aspect of 'true' Christianity (there are clear parallels to Mormon fundamentalists here, see Chapter 5). First wives especially see the Christian message of 'love thy neighbour' as particularly useful for resolving the interpersonal conflicts emerging in polygamous households. They regularly read the Bible to learn how to avoid and to handle conflicts, to settle down and to repair inner peace. They have developed a way of integrating Christianity into their polygynous marriage, which allows them to prove themselves to be true Christians by being a successful polygamous wife. So while Christian churches officially condemn polygyny and see monogamy as a prerequisite for being a true Christian, these women state it the other way around: being a Christian for them is a prerequisite for being a good polygynous wife. They do not consider being Christian and being polygamous as inherently conflictual, because they focus on the content and not the form of the Christian message. This makes being married monogamously or polygamously less important than being a good Christian.

Some contemporary local churches have recognized the convictions of polygamous women seeking to become good Christians, and allow polygamous members to practise and worship in their churches. Other churches, and in particular the Catholic Church, completely reject polygamy and refuse to admit any members who are polygamous. The missions and churches in Cameroon have at various times attempted to legislate the admittance of polygamous women into their churches. Typically, the husband was seen as being guilty of polygamy while the wives were considered innocent. Since a church could accept only one wife, the first wife was always admitted, unless the husband took his favourite wife, no matter what her 'number', into the church with him and repudiated his other wives (Reyburn 1959). As a result many churches attract mainly women, especially first wives, who see their position strengthened by the churches' uncompromising insistence that there is only one true wife for each husband. Many polygynous women, however, also consider the churches' emphasis on Christian monogamy as the ideal marriage to be hypocritical, constituting a veiled form of polygamy even less desirable than formal polygamy. This is because monogamy is considered to encourage a husband to have informal concubines which the first wife cannot control and from whom she derives no benefits. 'It is better that a husband marries all his wives formally and takes them home than that he loves them outdoors' as one of Notermans' (2002: 346) informants expressed it. In other words, women find it preferable that their husband has several wives rather than several concubines. One might of course argue that this defence of polygyny is based on the false premise that Cameroonian men are innately polygynous, since women might just as conceivably argue that men should marry monogamously and remain faithful to their wives. But on a local, lived level, it probably appears more realistic for women to assume that their husbands will have other women, and thus prefer to have a regulated relationship with these women. The spread of Christianity has therefore not been able to eradicate polygyny, quite the contrary. Polygamy, gender roles and Christianity in Cameroon will be discussed further in Chapter 7.

Polygyny thus has cultural, normative and numeric strength in Cameroon: the vast majority of people consider it the ideal domestic arrangement and levels exceed the suggested 20 per cent indicating a polygynous society. Moving beyond the form into the content of polygyny in Cameroon, it becomes less straightforward, however. Local practices often blur the line between true polygyny and the economic exploitation of second wives that are wives in name only. First, the codification of adultery as an offence against colonial law had the effect of removing traditional controls on adultery. Instead, infringements had to be settled with fines, and monetary compensation paid to the offended party. These fines soon became a profitable venture, as husbands would induce several of their wives to engage in affairs, allowing them to secure a monetary reward when 'discovering' and exposing the perpetrators. The resulting institutionalized speculation in adultery thus greatly encouraged extramarital sexual relations rather than preventing them. Another form of economic calculation has reshaped the traditional practice of '*wandja*', in which two closely befriended men trade wives for sexual purposes. The giving of a wife creates a new relationship of '*so*' (friend) between the two men and their wives, which involves trading gifts. The *so* relationship is no longer primarily concerned with wife exchange, but rather with material gain through a form of institutionalized gaining of gifts (Reyburn 1959: 11–12). In other words, the sharing of wives for material gain, either unofficially through encouraging extramarital affairs with strangers, or officially through wife-sharing with close friends, challenges the definition of polygyny as being a marriage between one man and several wives, since the women extend sexual services to men other than their official husbands. The Cameroon case thus presents the same problem as the Nayar of India, where women extended sexual services to several men. Such arrangements must lead one to question whether they in fact constitute polygamy or rather represent economic arrangements between a woman married to one man but having several suitors. Both the examples serve to show that definitions of polygamy are fluid, contextual and subject to local modifications.

–3–

Theories of Polygamy

Culture and Kinship

Polygamy in Early Anthropological Theory

Polygamy figured prominently in the formulation of early anthropological theories of man, kinship and culture. During the nineteenth century, theories of culture were dominated by the idea of cultural evolution: cultures were considered to move through various stages of development, ending up with the pinnacle of human development, Euro-American civilization. One of most influential schemes was that proposed by the American lawyer turned anthropologist Lewis Henry Morgan (1818–81), in his book *Ancient Society*, published in 1877. Building on a tripartite scheme developed by the eighteenth-century French philosopher Montesquieu, Morgan suggested that the evolution of culture passed through the main stages of savagery, barbarism and civilization. Each evolutionary stage was subdivided into lower, middle and upper stages, characterized by technological developments such as the use of fire, pottery or bow and arrow, as well as by advances in subsistence patterns, family and political organization. Morgan held that in the lower savagery stage, people mated promiscuously and the basic unit of society was a small nomadic 'horde', which owned its resources communally. By upper savagery, brother–sister marriage had been prohibited and descent was reckoned through women, i.e. *matrilineal* descent. With the transition to barbarism, further restrictions in spousal choices were instituted as incest prohibitions were extended to include all descendants in the female line, and clan and village became the basic units of society. By the upper phase of barbarism, descent shifted from the female to the male line, i.e. *patrilineal* descent, and polygamy was practised as men married several women at one time. Finally, the emergence of monogamous families marked the beginning of 'civilization' (Harris 1983: 321; Seymour-Smith 1986: 105, 200).

Morgan's *Ancient Society* was the most influential statement of the nineteenth-century cultural evolutionary position. Other nineteenth-century thinkers, such as John McLennan (1865) and Johann Bachofen (1861), also made important theoretical contributions to anthropology by putting forward different schemes of development of society, religion, kinship or legal institutions. Evolutionists like Morgan, Bachofen and McLennan were all concerned with the moral evolution of the human species, and a common thread running through all their works was the belief in the inevitable moral advancement of humankind. The idea of promiscuity, as used by the early evolutionists, denoted the contrast between the original, immoral condition of humanity and its ultimate stage of monogamous family life, i.e. the moral perfection of Western civilization. Through a series of stages or key developments humankind moved from licentiousness to chastity. Non-Western marriage forms such as polygyny and polyandry were hence, although imperfect, viewed as moral improvements compared to the absolute promiscuity of the original human state (Cucchiari 1981). A typical exponent of this nineteenth-century view of cultural evolution is the Duke of Argyll's 1881 treatise 'On the Moral Character of Man Considered in the Light of the Unity of Nature'. He proposes that polygamy represents a departure from man's primeval state, for 'there can have been no polygamy as yet when there was only a single pair'. The Duke finds the origins of 'a custom still more barbarous and savage, namely that of polyandry' in 'the previously acquired habit of female infanticide' (Argyll 1881: 194), setting an explanatory standard that has lasted to the present day (see Chapter 7). In the spirit of the times, the Duke looked to contemporary 'primitive' peoples in search of 'early man', seeing them as extant representatives of the earlier stages of cultural development through which the Duke's own people had also passed. Favourites among nineteenth-century thinkers were Australian Aborigines, who were considered to be living on a Stone Age level, as well as Arctic Eskimos or Inuit (see below). The racist implications of such analyses have rendered most evolutionary schemes unacceptable to modern research.

Nineteenth-century evolutionary schemes are today considered unilinear, since they argue more or less categorically for a single series of stages through which it is assumed that all human groups will progress, albeit at uneven rates. An early challenger to such schemes, based on an assumed universal psychological make-up of humankind, was diffusionist theory. It postulated that important cultural elements had been invented in only a few places and then diffused. Unilinear evolutionary schemes were also undermined by newly gathered ethnographic evidence about the diversity of sociocultural systems. Most contemporary anthropologists believe that evolutionary schemes do not adequately reflect the particular history of each sociocultural system and the unique meanings and events created by its history (Seymour-Smith 1986). This modern theoretical stance has naturally influenced the view of polygamy's role in human culture and society. Polygamy is no longer considered an inevitable stage through which all human societies must pass, but rather forms part of the idiosyncratic kinship system of a particular group. In contemporary anthropological thinking, polygamy is no longer considered merely a form of marriage, or a single unified institution, which can be generalized for all people through time. Rather, polygamy is considered to be produced by diverse strategies under a range of different conditions and comprising different systems of meaning and function. The great diversity of marriage strategies that may give rise to polygamy, and the different strategies of resource intensification that may be involved in polygamy, make it useful to examine polygamy as a 'complex' or system of interrelated variables and interactions. Simple sets of attributes such as wealth flows, wars or marriage systems are important in understanding polygamy in a particularly society, but any one of them cannot explain it, because polygamous systems as 'complexes' need to be understood in the context of a larger totality (White 1988). This is not to say that ideas combining the explanatory force of evolution with polygamy have been abandoned altogether.

Inuit Polygamy in Arctic Canada

The Inuit or Eskimos, caught in a constant struggle for survival in inhospitable conditions on the edges of the world, have fascinated scholars from anthropology's early days. Their marital arrangements are particularly fascinating, because they appear to accommodate every form of polygamy imaginable. Their myriad forms underscore the complexity of polygamy and the dangers of generalizing statements: polygamy is in flux among the Inuit, always changing to accommodate the particular circumstances under which they live. Nineteenth-century evolutionists concerned themselves with the Inuit primarily as examples of earlier, and hence lower, levels of mankind. Like Australian Aborigines, most Inuit lived in small communities in harsh environments, which at the time of Euro-American contact were on lower technological levels than Euro-American societies. The Inuit were seen as early 'primitives', replicating the conditions for early Western man. Inuit polygamy also provided an example of a polygamous system based on a cultural foundation, thus providing ethnographers with a window into cultural evolution, undisturbed by religious belief systems.

Early ethnographers suggested that, true to his original state, 'the primitive Inuit has never developed a complex ceremony by which the husband and wife are bound in wedlock', and the main concern in Inuit mating was the wife's ability and willingness to bear children (Garber 1935: 219). The Inuits' free sexual relations, particularly among their unmarried youths, were considered expressions of their primitive even innocent nature. It could therefore not be called licentious, for that would require a moral code with which the Inuit was not considered equipped. Rather, sexual freedom was seen as a biological development for propagating the race, whereas 'the lewd side of Inuit life developed as a result of their contacts with the white man' (Garber 1935: 217). Because of their sexual freedom, Inuit girls were considered easy victims of unscrupulous white men. This contact was not without rewards, however, for the girls 'have quickly recognized the marked improvement in the mental and physical characteristics of their offspring when they cross their own blood with that of the white man' (Garber 1935: 221). The Inuit loss of innocence through the white man's corrupting influence was thus balanced out by the resulting offspring moving up the evolutionary ladder, away from their Inuit ancestors towards the pinnacle of physical and mental achievement, the white Euro-American man. White men, in other words, helped the Inuit reach the next evolutionary stage through an infusion of both technology and genes.

Early forms of kinship were considered reflected in Inuit kinship patterns: monogamy was prevalent because the simple economic and social conditions of early man or Inuits made polygamy untenable. However, among the Inuit (and early man?) exceptional men such as chiefs or very skilled hunters could have more than one wife, when their affluence or power required them to have a second wife to maintain their prestige and larger households. Western Inuit refer to polygamous marriage in legends and folktales, describing men who could afford two wives as great men. The usual, almost exclusive pattern in Inuit polygyny was to have two wives only. Men who had three wives were hence revered, not just because they had three wives but because they must possess extraordinary power and wisdom (Birket-Smith 1948; Garber 1935: 222). Polygyny typically became relevant if a wife was barren, or only bore female children, giving the husband the right to take a second wife for childbearing purposes. This second marriage often took place not only with the first wife's acceptance, but with her encouragement as well. Polygyny was not uncommon among the Inuit, but they were generally monogamous because of the difficulties involved in maintaining more than one wife and her children. The increased resources, responsibilities and labour required of men with more than one wife tend to limit the prevalence of polygamy among hunters. In some areas, the scarcity of women in proportion to men also made polygynous practices difficult, as did frequent divorce, which was easily obtained (Betzig 1986; Kumlien 1880). Furthermore, polygynous men had to deal with the jealousy and ill feeling from other men who could not find wives for themselves. 'The Inuit polygamist, therefore, must be a man of great energy and skill in hunting, bold and unscrupulous, always ready to assert himself and uphold his position by appeal to force' (Jenness 1922: 161).

Three aspects of Inuit kinship in particular – wife trading, infanticide and polyandry – aroused the interest of early ethnographers. According to contemporary ethnographers, they are adaptations to life in harsh environments, but to earlier ethnographers they were expressions of the primitive nature of the Inuit. The exchange of wives for short periods or even permanently, a practice completely unthinkable in nineteenth-century Western society, was frequent among the Inuit. The best hunter, or the owner of the largest number of dogs and hunting gear, would usually get the woman he wanted for wife, even if she was married to another man; one way to achieve this was to trade wives. The exchange and loaning of wives could take place for practical reasons, as an amusement or as deference and hospitality shown to distinguished visitors. Wives could be exchanged temporarily, for example when a man might borrow his cousin's wife for deer hunting if she was a good shot while his own wife went with his cousin on a trading expedition. Usually the wives went back to their respective husbands, though sometimes the couples were more satisfied with their new partners, in which case the exchange was simply made permanent (Garber 1935: 226; Jenness 1917: 89; Kumlien 1880: 87). The exchange and loaning of wives serves important economic purposes and is very adaptive in an environment where people are totally dependent on their ability to squeeze out a living from inhospitable environments. Survival comes before any sort of morality; wife exchange was not simply an expression of the promiscuous sexuality associated with the Inuit by earlier observers.

Infanticide was another aspect of Inuit culture which early ethnographers focused on, and several reasons were put forward to explain it. First, bringing up a child entails severe hardships on the mother. She must nurse it for several years before it can endure the usual diet of meat and fish, and in semi-nomadic groups she must carry it everywhere on her back along with a heavy pack. Second, physical defects in newborn babies and multiple births might lead to infanticide. One of a set of twins was always killed; if they were of two genders, always the girl. A child born physically deformed might become a helpless dependant requiring ceaseless care yet be unable to contribute to the family's welfare. In small communities struggling to survive, there was little room for such individuals because resources were not sufficient to support unproductive members, paving the way for infanticide and other culturally approved forms of homicide. Third, infanticide leads to an increase in the proportion of older individuals in the population who can all contribute to the group's survival. Adults increase diversity and information in the population, which is crucial in a cultural system where control over resources is vested in knowledge. Fourth, infanticide was confined almost entirely to female children. Women are considered unable to hunt and hence cannot contribute to the survival of the group; they are consequently considered of little account. Female infanticide regulates the number of women in a community, and reduces the number of children born. It is a means of regulating population size in a hostile environment when conditions such as famine require it. Female infanticide also maintained a numerical balance between the sexes in a society where occupational hazards led to high male mortality (Freeman 1971: 1011–16; Garber 1935: 222, 1947: 99; Jenness 1917: 89; Kumlien 1880: 86).

Polyandry was a third aspect of Inuit culture that fascinated early ethnographers (see cover photo). As among the Australian Aborigines, however, it is difficult to define as polygamous a system in which wife-sharing is common, blurring the line between true marriage and a woman's extension of sexual services to men other than her official husband. For example, Garber describes a domestic difficulty that was 'solved in a primitive, but most logical and economical way' (1935: 223). A middle-aged man married to a young girl had one child with her after which he became sterile. He arranged for a young man of the village to live for a time at his home and cohabit with his wife, who had two boys as a result of this arrangement. The young man was paid a fee by the husband, and then settled with a wife and family of his own. In principle, it was not polyandry, since the wife was not officially married to both men simultaneously. But for practical purposes, theirs was a *de facto* polyandrous household for the duration of the young man's cohabitation with the wife. A similar practice is found among polyandrous Tibetans, where the institution of *po-rjag* allows a man to be brought in to sire a child in a sterile union. This practice is closer to *cicisbeism* (one woman having sexual relations with more than one man in a regular and lasting fashion outside marriage; see Chapter 2) than to polyandry, because such an 'imported' man is generally not married to the wife but only temporarily linked to her for a specific purpose (Peter 1963: 506).

Early on, ethnographers working among the Inuit established a causal linkage in which the harsh environment was considered to encourage widespread female infanticide, resulting in a severe shortage of women. Consequently, two men would often have to share one wife in a polyandrous marriage; a man must have a woman to sew his garments, make his boots and perform other domestic duties necessary for him to go hunting (Birket-Smith 1948; Garber 1935, 1947). Hoebel (1947: 535) counters such arguments by noting that in most Inuit communities there is in fact a small surplus of women over men in spite of the fact that many girls are killed. This is due to the high mortality of men engaged in dangerous artic hunting pursuits. Inuit polyandry hence cannot be due to a shortage of women caused by infanticide. The shortage is rather caused by widespread polygyny, where strong men monopolize the available women, and weak men are pushed out of the marriage market. This, combined with a strong principle of sexual equivalence of brothers, results in fraternal polyandry for those men who cannot find a wife of their own. Generally, polyandry is much less common among the Inuit than polygyny. One of the interesting aspects of Inuit polygamy is this coexistence of polygyny and polyandry. The fact that polygyny can coexist with polyandry among the Inuit, among polyandrous people in India (Majumdar 1962; Saksena 1962) and among some Native American peoples (Park 1937; Steward 1936) illustrates the complexity of polygamy. Usually, a society is associated with a particular polygamous pattern, but the picture becomes muddled when confronted with societies that, even on the small scale of Inuit groups, practise polygyny among the upper ranks and polyandry among lower-ranking males (cf. Balikci 1970; Yalman 1967).

Polyandry among the Netsilik and Copper Inuit of Arctic Canada, for example, may result from economic hardship for a certain segment of society, that is, polyandry out of necessity. Males who are successful and economically well off will probably practise polygyny rather than polyandry. Polyandry may have some relation to population structure, specifically sex ratio, in providing a partial solution to the problem of excess males in Netsilik and Copper Inuit populations. But there is a slight preponderance of polygynous over polyandrous unions even in these populations, showing the stronger Inuit preference for polygyny, probably as a result of its prestige value and associations of power (Damas 1975: 412–13). The gender composition and economic circumstances of Inuit populations, the traditional reasons given for Inuit polygamy, are hence not enough to explain why some choose polyandry over polygyny. Different models are needed to explain why monogamy and polygyny are more common in situations where polyandry might be more functional. The association of polygyny with high-ranking males and polyandry with low-ranking males within the same populations strongly suggests the importance of prestige and power. Sociopsychological reasons may also be involved; polygamous marriages among Copper and Netsilik Inuit often did not last long. There appear to have been many tensions in polyandrous unions, and polygynous unions were constantly challenged by the many single males seeking a wife (Damas 1975: 412–16).

To what extent various Inuit populations still wife-share, practise infanticide or polygamy is unknown, though contemporary Inuit appear to have weathered many of the corrupting influences of the West, often considered to bring doom to indigenous cultures. They are still Inuit, with contemporary economic, cultural and social adaptations (Sahlins 1999). Traditional Inuit polygamy offered people a wide variety of ways to relate to the opposite (and same?) sex, to optimize economically, socially and reproductively, and to gain power, prestige and perhaps love by exchanging and rearranging partners to everybody's satisfaction. It is an incredibly flexible marriage system, but also a textbook example of the challenges involved in describing and explaining polygamous systems.

Politics, Power and Prestige

The many explanations in modern anthropological theory concerning polygamous practices and their foundations fall, with some overlap and variation, into two main groups: production and reproduction versus power, politics and prestige. A third cross-cutting avenue of enquiry deals with gender; for a further discussion please see Chapter 7.

Politics

A classic theory about polygamy's role in society suggests that polygamy may serve a political function by cementing alliances with affines gained through a polygamous marriage. Marriage is considered part of the political organization of society, and polygamy is seen as a natural expansion of the field of political manoeuvres. Affines gained through polygamy may be directly useful as when a local chief marries the daughter of another local powerful man, and thus can count on his allegiance in the fight against common enemies, or in business dealings. Or it may be more diffuse as when a king is required to marry a woman from each local area of his kingdom in order to create symbolic, but politically important, allegiances all over his realm. In Africa, chiefs practising polygamy typically did so because of political expediency. In political terms, the more wives one had the more political alliances one could form, and thereby become a powerful broker and effective politician or tribal leader, chief or king. For example, a Bantu (South African) chief was obliged by religious and political considerations to have a large number of wives. In addition to his main wife, the mother of his heir, he had to marry two women from special clans with whom he performed certain rites considered essential to protect him, and by association his people, from danger. He secured his political position by marrying female kin of leading men, thereby making their families his political allies. In Southern Africa, marriage alliances were very important politically, because through a marriage a chief could align himself with one group rather than another. The more marriages a chief made, the more he could create potentially contrary allegiances, and therefore the chief's first marriages tended to be the most important and controlled; if he was highly polygynous, he would contract many politically unimportant marriages. A chief's polygynous marriages emphasized his exalted position: whereas a Bemba chief could have 10–15 wives, commoners rarely had more than one (Kuper 1975: 133–4, 1982: 94; Mair 1953: 10; Richards 1940: 89).

Because of its political implications in traditional Africa, 'the practice of polygamy gave ample scope for intrigue. The relatives of each wife watched jealously over her interests, and did their utmost to further the fortunes of her sons. As a result many feuds arose' (Schapera 1940: 76). Feuds were particularly prone to happen in the polygynous households of chiefs, who not only had many wives, but also many enemies and contestants to their power and position. A chief's rightful heir was traditionally the oldest son of his 'great wife', i.e. the first woman with whom he got betrothed. If his great wife did not have a son, the oldest son of his wife next in rank would succeed him. This succession rule meant that disputes regarding the relative rank of a chief's wives often broke out when a chief died, and more than one claimant to the chief's position could emerge (Schapera 1940: 74). The re-establishment of peace and security in the deceased chief's household, and hence in his realm, could then be achieved by calling on allies in the form of affines gained through the old chief's polygynous marriages.

The theory that polygamy is a necessity in multiplying alliances, thereby strengthening the unity of the group as well as securing peace, is a traditional structural-functionalist approach (cf. Fortes and Evans-Pritchard 1940; Fortes 1962; Radcliffe-Brown and Forde 1950). The structural-functionalist school of thought sees women as productive or reproductive commodities exchanged by familial groups for economic or political reasons. Polygamy is considered to be characteristic of cultures that have specific types of subsistence, being commonest among peoples whose economic welfare is a function of female production. Polygamy is also considered typical of cultures that have specific types of stratification, particularly those based on age grades or hereditary privileges, and polygamy acts as male status marker as well. Lastly, polygamy is considered characteristic of cultures with specific types of marriage systems; it is more frequently found among groups with patrilineal rules of descent and *patrilocal* rules of residence (i.e. with or near husband's family), which emphasize transmission of rights from the bride's family to the groom's group (Clignet and Sween 1981: 446–8; Wittrup 1990).

A 'structural functionalist example' of polygyny's role in creating alliances between affines is the various groups of Australian Aborigines in the Northwest Territory. They are traditionally considered to live in egalitarian social systems in which no adult controls any other adult, lacking the 'big men' characteristic of the area. Many aboriginal groups nonetheless practise polygyny, which implies unequal relations between men and women as well as between men. Women do enjoy certain prerogatives, but are subordinated to men through a marriage system that encourages polygamy and gerontocracy. It is a muddled form of polygyny, however, because polygynous males will 'lend' wives to younger men or ignore their wives' adultery. This allows senior polygynous men to forge political ties with 'brothers' who might otherwise become their rivals in their search for wives. While in principle egalitarian, the gerontocratic societies of Northern Australia allow men to secure power and prestige by passing all but two or three of their accumulated wives on to younger allies (Collier and Rosaldo 1981).

While there is agreement that polygamy can serve political purposes and does create alliances, the structural-functionalist perspective has been criticized for being reductionist. This is in line with the contemporary view of polygamy as a complex set of interdependent variables rather than as a singular institution which can be explained on the basis of a few key factors. First, marriage is considered to involve the generation and exchange of a 'bundle of rights', reducing the relationship between marriage and affinity to a linear one. This jural bias is derived from Western jurisprudence, and may not be universally applicable (Comaroff 1980: 161). Furthermore, exchanges are explained in terms of the familial groups themselves, and it is assumed that the function of institutions (including plural marriage) is identical from an individual and societal point of view. Hence, the component parts of a social institution are considered interchangeable with its totality, and whole cultures or regions are considered homogeneous in examining polygamy. Second, the approach has been criticized for not acknowledging the complexity and variation of polygamy across time and space. Frequency of polygamous marriage, for example, varies according to whether men marry additional wives in order to enhance their resources, or as symbols of wealth. A third point of critique is that it ignores the possibility of variation in polygamous lifestyles within cultures. In structural-functionalist thinking, polygynous co-wives are interchangeable and examined independently of their rank, or other characteristics such as fecundity, within households. Childbearing and -rearing patterns are expected to differ from monogamous ones, as polygamous populations are assumed to have lower fertility rates and be more likely to observe post-partum taboos (see below). Post-partum taboos and decreases in sexual relations leading to lower fertility levels may not be equally respected by all households or by all co-wives in polygamous societies, however; a husband may feel his sexual needs supersede cultural rules regarding abstinence, and wives may be unfaithful to their husbands. Fourth, the structural-functionalist approach is based on atemporal and ahistorical analyses. It ignores such issues as whether polygamy encourages divorce or whether remarriage of divorced women facilitates polygamy. It ignores differences in male and female marriage strategies: while a man has to decide successively between marriage, divorce and adding a new wife to his household, a woman must decide whether to marry monogamously or polygynously as a junior wife (Clignet and Sween 1981: 449–50).

A development of the structural-functionalist approach is the alliance theory proposed by Lévi-Strauss (1969). Where earlier theorists considered family life and kinship to be based on natural reproductive processes, Lévi-Strauss considered kinship and marriage to be social and cultural processes. He focused on how family and society define each other, and believed that 'man's deep polygamous tendency' turns women into objects whose exchange creates relations of alliance, equality or hierarchy among men. Lévi-Strauss's alliance theory, like the structural-functionalist approach before it, has been criticized for being too generalizing, because it fails to take individuals and variation within and between polygamous households adequately into account. When describing the various types of exchanges of women leading to alliances between men, alliance theorists do not explore or differentiate the contents of those exchanges, just as they assume that the relations between men who get wives, and women who become wives, are universal. While new forms of male–male relations are considered to emerge from the various types of exchanges, alliance theory does not acknowledge possible changes in the relations between women and men, because heterosexual bonds are assumed to be natural, invariant and universal (Collier and Rosaldo 1981: 315–16). Today, structural-functionalist and alliance theories, as well as numerous other schools of thought, all form part of the theoretical complex needed and utilized to understand the polygamous complex – with the modifications and qualifications required to accommodate the variable and processual nature of polygamy in a particular society.

Power

Closely related to the suggestion that polygamy serves a political function in a society is the idea that it serves as a marker of power. An influential set of theories links polygamy with power through gerontocracy, a system of social stratification in which the old, typically the old men, dominate the young. Older members of society achieve their dominant position through control over the means of production as well as reproduction, by controlling access to wives and sexual partners; they typically also control access to symbolic and religious systems, giving them added legitimacy. The classic Marxist approach, which focuses on conflicts in society and how societies are reproduced despite these conflicts, follows this line of argument by suggesting that polygamy is typically found in gerontocratic societies, where old men have power based on their control over women. Through polygyny, elders can monopolize young women and thus wield power over the younger men by hindering them from establishing independent households and hence threatening the power base of the elders. In Marxist theory, the elders' dominance over the matrimonial system allows them not only to control young people, but also to reproduce structures of dependence in society by manipulating the exchange of women. The Marxist approach has been criticized for focusing on form rather than content and for examining polygamy primarily as means of studying 'African' modes of production, and how they responded to colonization and capitalism, rather than as an institution worthy of study in itself (cf. Meillassoux 1981; Wittrup 1990). As such, it shares some theoretical weaknesses with structural-functionalist and alliance theories.

The link between polygamy and gerontocracy remains very influential theoretically, nonetheless, and continues to form the basis for many explanations of polygamy. It is argued that the distribution of power and prestige through gerontocracy is mirrored in the rate of polygyny in a society. The rate of polygyny is, in turn, related to the age of first marriage for men and women: high levels of polygyny in a society result from a large difference in ages at marriage between men and women. Polygyny, then, does not imply fewer males and more females in a society, but rather delay of marriage for men, who must remain bachelors for many years. The high levels of polygyny associated with much of traditional Africa are therefore not the result of a surplus of women, as many assume, but rather result from the difference in ages at marriage between men and women. Age systems that favour older men and delay marriage for younger men create a surplus of young women whom the older men can then marry. The age of first marriage may hence be an indicator of the level of polygyny in a society, and the level of polygyny may in turn be an indicator of the level of gerontocracy (Dorjahn 1959; Spencer 1998). One of this school of thought's important contributions has indeed been to challenge the traditional view that polygyny occurs because there is a surplus of women in the population. In most polygamous societies there is a relatively balanced gender ratio; in some polygynous societies males may outnumber females, as among some Inuit groups described above, without this fact preventing them from practising polygyny. When skewed gender ratios do occur, for example as a result of armed conflicts, it may lead to higher rates of polygyny, though the increase will probably be temporary as the gender imbalance is an effect of war rather than a cause of polygamy. Typically, in societies with normal gender ratios, men will be able to marry two or more wives only at the expense of other men, who must then marry at a later age than women do.

This form of social differentiation based on age, or gerontocracy, is on some level found in many if not most African polygynous societies, allowing the number of wives to increase with a man's age. In polygynous societies, there is a general tendency for the number of wives to increase with the age as well as power and prestige of each elder. Crucial for maintaining high levels of polygyny are thus age systems that favour the marriage of elder men and delay the marriage of younger men. This gives elders control over both younger men and their much younger wives. Nonetheless, such age-based marriage systems are in principle egalitarian, because in time all (male) members of a society could become elders and get access to this superior status through marriage. Few men will never marry, because marriage in most polygynous systems is universal. Though gerontocracy normally regulates the distribution of power and prestige between old and young men, there is also social differentiation among elders, however. Not all older members of society will be able or allowed to possess the trappings of 'elderhood', such as many wives, or any wife at all in the case of some low-ranking males. This becomes evident for younger men who pass their first test of 'elderhood' when they marry for the first time, only to remain in a relatively junior position compared to established elders with many wives. The age grade system splits the adult male population into a group of young bachelors and a dominant group of older polygynists. Among the semi-nomadic pastoral Samburu of Kenya, for example, young men – called *moran* – may remain single into their thirties, often living a separate existence as bachelors. They are trapped in a state of social suspension: they are not allowed to acquire the wisdom and knowledge of elderhood because they are not married, and they are not respected because they lack the knowledge and wisdom of elderhood. This delayed marriage and protracted bachelorhood for young men creates a surplus of young women (from the young men's age sets) for older men to marry, making a high rate of polygyny possible in Samburu society (Dorjahn 1959; Spencer 1998).

In gerontocratic systems, elders thus possess significant power and authority based on their collective superiority to younger age sets. Young men's respect for seniority within the age system is a necessary precondition for maintaining a gerontocracy, and hence by implication also a highly polygynous society. The age system and respect for seniority underpins the ranking of young men within the extended family, where the age system implants a 'queue discipline' of sorts between brothers, cousins and close male kin waiting for their turn to marry (Spencer 1998: 33). The degeneration of the age system, among other traditional social underpinnings of polygynous societies, is now contributing to the decline in polygyny levels in Africa. In urban Africa especially, migrants and city dwellers separated from their rural families no longer feel inclined to wait for their turn in the family queue for wives, but may rather marry a wife as soon as they have enough cash to do so. Young urban men may enter their first marriage, and hence their first polygynous marriage, perhaps years before they would traditionally have had the chance in rural areas. The link between polygamy and gerontocracy therefore becomes ambiguous in modern society. Traditionally, only older men could afford to marry polygynously; in contemporary societies young men, especially in urban areas, have access to waged work and make money independently of their families, enabling them to become polygynous at a much younger age than before. They may also reject traditional polygynous marriage altogether and remain monogamous permanently. In contemporary Africa it is hence impossible to determine, without a long-term study of the society in question, whether the fact that many older men are polygynous and most younger men are monogamous or single is a reflection of gerontocracy or of still more young Africans emulating monogamous Western family models. They may never become polygynous – at least not officially (Clignet and Sween 1981: 449–50). See Chapter 8 for a further discussion of modern urban African polygyny.

The social division between polygynists and bachelors in gerontocratic societies points to another theory of polygamy, which is also based on social stratification: in societies where social status distinctions are not based on control over productive resources, they are typically based on control over human resources. In some societies they may be based on both. The most direct way for a man to achieve control over many people is to expand his household by marrying polygynously and attempting to sire numerous children. In traditional African kingdoms, for example, societies were typically divided into commoners, nobles and royals. Commoners were allowed and able to marry only one wife, nobles could marry several wives according to their means, and royals could have hundreds of wives; this could give rise to the 'harem polygyny' sometimes found in despotic societies, particularly in Africa and Arabia (Betzig 1986). The fact that it is men who control human resources through social stratification in most societies entails that polygyny is much more widespread than polyandry. The social stratification theory is most clearly illustrated in societies where power differentials between high and low are widest. In Inca Peru, for example, petty chiefs were by law allowed up to seven women, governors of 100 people were given eight women, leaders of 1,000 people got fifteen women, chiefs of over 1,000,000 people got thirty women, and kings had access to temples filled with hundreds of women. The poor Indian had to take whatever woman was left, if any (Betzig 1986). In Inca Peru, then, social stratification determined the reproductive hierarchy, which allowed chiefs and kings to have disproportionate access to wives, enabling them to sire large numbers of children, and thus bolster their power base.

Prestige.   Related to the suggestion that the practice of polygamy confers political and social power on an individual is the idea that it serves as a marker of prestige. Within polygamous societies, multiple wives are typically status symbols denoting wealth and power for the husband. It signals that he has the resources to build up a large household and maintain it. This places him in an elite group within societies where most men can only afford to establish and maintain a monogamous household. In agricultural societies, the larger size of polygynists' families and households, and the labour force they contain, demonstrates their social status, as well as providing a large productive basis through which to generate more wealth. Polygyny among the Mandinka of Gambia, for example, is 'the most obvious and preferred way of accumulating prestige, especially among the urban elite ... Having four wives is valued very high on the prestige scale. Rumours about wealth, and social prestige will be limitless if each wife is placed in a separate compound' (Wittrup 1990: 135). In traditional Africa, large families brought a man pride and small families brought him shame. Small families were symbols of poverty. This association was (and is) typically seized upon by wives who wanted a new co-wife for prestige or pragmatic reasons: they would publicly ridicule their reluctant husband for being too poor to marry a second wife in order to goad him into a new marriage. It was prestigious to have many wives, and polygyny displayed status; it was unheard of for a king, for example, to have just one wife like a commoner. Among the Mende of Sierra Leone, many wives increase not only the husband's but also his present wife's social prestige. A man with only one or two wives is called a 'small boy', and his social standing is determined mainly by how many wives he will be able to marry. To marry many wives, a man must be wealthy, which makes large-scale polygyny a sign of affluence in Mende society as well (Little 1951: 141).

While the religious, political and partly economic foundations of polygyny are undergoing rapid change in contemporary Africa, it has retained its prestige value. As Phillips (1953: xiv) commented over half a century ago, 'the possession of a number of wives is normally the mark of importance and success in life and – for this among other reasons – is something which the average African man would gladly achieve if he could: in other words, monogamy is for the majority who are in fact monogamous as a matter of necessity rather than choice'. While it is conceivably many African men's ideal to marry more wives in order to increase their lineage or their wealth, most men never achieve this ideal (Mair 1953: 59). Wherever polygamy is practised, the majority of men have only one wife and are not polygamous. Furthermore, the great majority of polygynists in Africa have only two wives. A few outstanding individuals may have many wives, but there are rarely more than two wives in a traditional household (Colson 1958; Welch and Glick 1981).

Within African societies that formally prohibit polygamy, social opinion may accept certain prominent people maintaining mistresses, perhaps in the form of *de facto* polygyny. Men may also engage in serial polygyny, allowing them to continue to manage marriage as part of political power negotiations (Comaroff 1980: 179). The social acceptance stems from the fact that one of the driving forces for the men practising polygyny, as well as for the people acknowledging it, is the prestige it confers. The political and economic foundations of polygamy thus come together and express themselves in the prestige and status that polygamy confers on its practitioners. Prestige can hence be seen as an overlay, an extra dimension over and above the productive and political aspects of polygamy. The prestige dimension may be more or less prominent depending on how strong a motivating factor it is for the husband. In contemporary Nigeria, for example, urban polygynists may be keen to harness the prestige effect of polygamy and hence shoulder the costs of an additional wife who may not be able or willing to contribute to the common household economy. Rural polygynists, in contrast, may be more interested in the extra labour force generated by an additional wife and see the prestige this confers more as an automatic effect of polygyny rather than the goal in itself.

The prestige theory, like the others concerning politics and power, has also been met with criticism. According to the sociobiologist Betzig (1986: 85), prestige is associated with particular aspects of life which individuals strive for, and in polygamous societies, men strive to practise polygamy. Prestige may be more of an effect of polygamy, because prestige is automatically associated with those aspects that individuals strive for. Polygamy is thus prestigious because all men aspire to it, rather than conferring prestige on the person in and of itself. In modern urban varieties of polygyny, as in Islamic South East Asia or Africa, the idea that polygamy is an expression of prestige in a society can perhaps not be turned on its head quite as easily as Betzig suggests. A new cultural dimension added to the polygamous societies is that not all men strive for polygamy any more; a growing number choose monogamy not out of necessity, but out of choice. Along with the lessening importance of political and economic aspects of urban polygyny, the prestige aspect will probably increase for that segment of society still bent on practising polygyny. Prestige will for those men probably become the prime motive for practising it, and as such polygyny can confer prestige on a person in and of itself. This is the case among the urban Muslim elites in Malaysia, where polygamy is taking on a prestige function that moves beyond its economic or political functions; the display of wealth and conspicuous consumption is the crucial aspect. For a fuller description, see Chapter 4.

Criticizing theories of politics, power and prestige does not equal dismissing them. In most societies, polygamy is probably associated with all three elements in varying degrees. Ethnographic examples of how polygyny can serve as a direct route to politics, power and prestige are not hard to find. Among the Kapauku of Western New Guinea, for example, the ideal is to accumulate as many wives as possible. Wives tend fields and care for pigs, by which wealth is measured in Kapauku society. The man with the most wives can produce the most pigs and thus become the wealthiest man in the village. Wealth, in the form of numerous pigs, also confers tremendous prestige on a man and can form the basis of his power. So strong is the imperative for polygyny that a man's wife will encourage him to acquire additional wives, and she has the right to divorce him if she can establish that he can afford to pay the bridewealth for an additional wife, but refuses to marry again. In order to acquire wealth, however, a man must raise many pigs, which is quite complex. In order to breed pigs, large amounts of sweet potatoes – the preferred pig food – are needed. Sweet potatoes are grown in garden plots, and, as certain gardening activities can only be carried out by women, women have to generate the food for the pigs. Ambitious Kapauku men thus have to produce numerous pigs, which requires the help of numerous women. The most direct way to get women is to marry them, but this necessitates payment of bridewealth. Not all Kapauku men are wealthy enough to afford the bridewealth for multiple wives or to afford the compensation for pig care that many women would require. Kapauku men are therefore faced with the tricky problem that they need pigs, by which wealth is measured and generated, to marry wives, which are needed to raise the pigs in the first place. The significant entrepreneurship needed to operate this circular system is what produces leaders – men with political clout, power and prestige – in Kapauku society (Haviland 1983).

Production and Reproduction

Production

The economic theories regarding polygamy are built on the basic assumption that polygynous marriage systems are related to the sexual division of labour and to the economic value of women as producers for the household (see Murdock 1949). Such theories have been prominent in anthropological theory because in the majority of societies where polygamy is practised, it appears to be correlated with those political and economic systems where the most important resources are human resources. In Africa, the region with the highest levels of polygamy in the world, it has been standard practice to explain polygamy by noting that a man may increase his wealth through securing the productive and reproductive capacities of more women (e.g. Clignet 1970; 1987). In most societies where it is practised, polygamy appears to be correlated with economic status, though wealth follows different trajectories and has different significance in various systems. Thus, in most traditional rural African systems, more wives mean more social and economic powers for a man. In contrast, more wives in modern urban Africa mean expending rather than gaining economic power for the husband. Urban polygamy no longer reflects the usual association between polygamous marriage and economic and political systems where human resources are most important, nor does it necessarily involve the common age–gender stratification, where older men control the productive and reproductive resources of women and younger men. Urban polygamy nonetheless still allows African men to convert their economic capital into social capital, enhancing their prestige, as in rural Africa – and all other places where polygamy is practised.

The economic foundations of polygyny have always been a hallmark of Africa, since in pre-industrial agricultural societies, human labour is essential: the larger the family the larger the area it can cultivate, the more it can hunt, the better it can rear cattle and the more it can increase food production. By marrying several wives, a man with large land holdings can get more cost-efficient labour and create surplus for sale. As such, polygamy can produce increased wealth for the man as well as for the whole family group that he supports. The man most likely to be polygynous in a traditional community, namely the chief, had especially good economic reasons for wishing many wives. A chief often had to work as hard if not harder than his fellow villagers, and was also expected to be generous in providing food, drink and tobacco to all who visited him. The nature of the chief's position and the obligations of his office usually forced him to maintain a rather large staff; cooks and servants were particularly important in order to entertain on the expected lavish scale. Chiefs customarily recruited such a large staff by marrying them as wives; this was also the most economical way of obtaining them. A great chief may, for example, have had one wife to attend to entertainment of visitors, another to look after his farm, another in charge of his private medicines, and a fourth to valet his clothes; and then several lesser wives who could do the hard work (Colson 1958: 123; Crosby 1937: 251; Little 1951: 141; Mair 1953: 106).

One of the most influential of these theories dealing with polygamy in economic terms was formulated by Boserup (1970), who tried to detect a relationship between polygamy, economics and women's position. She argued that agricultural societies dominated by hoe farming demand labour power as their main productive input, giving men a directly beneficial reason to accumulate more wives, and hence father more children, in order to utilize them as work force in their fields. Women are therefore valuable as producers as well as reproducers, and polygamy is regarded as a profitable institution in the rural economy.[1] Theories focusing on the economic basis of polygamy have been criticized for failing to explain several facts. Boserup's arguments were quickly refuted by Goody (1973a, 1973b), who explains that female farming predominates in East Africa, whereas rates of polygamy are highest in West Africa. Goody rejects economic explanations of polygamy, instead focusing on reproduction and sexuality as key factors, as described below (cf. Wittrup 1990). The sociobiologist Betzig (1986: 83–5) points out that wealthy husbands often seclude their women as a matter of prestige and/or to minimize the risk of infidelity (see below), which may prevent them from engaging in any economic activity. Furthermore, sub-fecund women as well as women suspected of extramarital pregnancies are frequently divorced by their polygynous husbands. An economic theory that suggests that a prime reason for polygamy is to produce economically valuable children cannot account for men secluding their wives from other men or divorcing them for producing economically valuable children by unrelated men. Nor can economic theories adequately explain why wealthy men often marry prepubescent girls. It is usually done to ensure their wife's virginity, but a ten-year-old girl's contribution to the household economy is not particularly high, either in the form of work or her capacity to produce children. These various reservations challenge the economic theories that suggest that polygamy may be prominent where women contribute most to the household.

It is indeed very difficult to determine whether polygynous wives are net economic assets or liabilities. Simultaneously, the generation and expenditure of wealth by both co-wives and husbands is central to the study of polygyny, and therefore the issue needs to be addressed. In Malay polygamy, for example, a major reason why polygamy has not been widely practised in the region is probably that it is correlated with economic status. Among Malays, wealth generally forms the basis for engaging in polygamy, excluding much of the population in the process. Though as Firth remarked, 'the absence of [wealth] does not necessarily inhibit a man from becoming polygamous' (1943: 49). The generally positive association between socio-economic status and polygamy in Islamic South East Asia resembles the pattern found in sub-Saharan Africa. African and South East Asian polygamy are nonetheless very different, for while both systems are fuelled by wealth, resources flow in opposite directions. In most rural African systems, more wives mean more social and economic powers, for a man may increase his wealth through securing the productive and reproductive capacities of more women. In contrast, more wives usually mean expending rather than gaining economic power for the Malay husband. Malay wives were never accumulated for their increased productive capacities, because the structure of Malay rice production was not conducive to the appropriation of female labour by polygynous males (Stivens 1996: 194). The Malay form of polygamy rather requires the husband to have enough wealth to attract and retain more than one wife. Thus, while rural African second wives tend to be economic assets, Malay second wives tend to represent economic liabilities to the household. But this does not take into account the prestige and social standing Malay second wives generate for their husbands, as well as the children. In urban Africa, the situation parallels that in urban Malaysia.

There is probably no straightforward answer to the question of whether wealth attracts polygamous wives or whether polygamous wives augment wealth. It depends on whether one considers wealth to be required for polygamy or wealth to be generated by polygamy. The inability in most cases to specify clearly whether wealth leads to wives or wives lead to wealth rests on the fact that they are circularly linked: wealth may be needed to initiate a polygamous marriage, but the marriage may then enrich the household economically, socially, etc. As such, second wives represent 'investment opportunities' for both the co-wives and husbands, because both males and females may manipulate wealth flows in the household to secure the added productivity generated by added wives (White 1988: 547). Perhaps it is the wrong question to ask, because polygamous wives in most cases are both attracted by wealth as well as generating it on some level. The direction of causality in the relationship between wealth and polygamy, which is at the heart of many economic theories of polygamy, thus remains difficult to establish. Rank and leadership are even more difficult to quantify and measure than wealth, making explanations of polygamy based on power, politics and prestige even less secure than those based on economics.

Most economic theories about polygamy in fact deal only with polygyny, simply because this is the form most commonly encountered. But polyandry also requires explanation, and theories based on production and reproduction are the most influential in explaining why a woman would have several simultaneous husbands. One group of theories suggests that this marital arrangement can be partially understood as a response to an imbalanced gender ratio in a population, i.e. a shortage of women, necessitating the marriage of several men to one woman. Polyandry has been associated with a shortage of women due to their lower survival rates in comparison to men, particularly in societies in which female infanticide is practised. However, many researchers would now argue that this is an erroneous idea contradicted by the ethnographic record, which contains examples of female infanticide associated with societies in which polygynous marriage is practised, giving no clear causal link. One could also plausibly reverse the argument and argue that female infanticide is practised because polyandrous practices diminish the need for female children, and thus ensures that fewer women reach sexual maturity (see Chapter 7 for a further discussion of female infanticide and its relation to polyandry).

A second group of theories focuses on the economic implications of polyandry. Polyandry is generally found in areas where difficult physical environments or high population pressures create extreme stresses on agricultural systems. Polyandry limits population growth because a woman's reproductive capacity is the same no matter how many husbands she has, whereas polygyny expands a husband's capacity to father children according to how many wives he has. Furthermore, since brothers typically share a wife, their joint estate remains intact from generation to generation, ensuring coherent and viable agricultural estates. Poverty and men's frequent absence on hunting or cattle duty can also lead to polyandry; the resources added by an extra male may ensure the survival of the household (Haviland 1983: 240; Seymour-Smith 1986: 228). Berreman's (1978) study of Himalayan polyandry is a good example of the entangled nature of productive and reproductive explanations for polyandry. He interprets polyandry in terms of land shortage: by limiting family expansion through the marriage of several males to one female, the labour force is adjusted to the available land. Simultaneously, he notes that polygynous and monogamous families coexist with polyandrous ones among Himalayan Hindus, making polyandry just one of a number of possible strategies which adjust human resources and family structures to land and other resources.

Reproduction. Issues of reproduction and fertility are as central to polygamy as production and prestige. Theories of polygamy based on economic explanations, focusing on the productive aspects of polygamous households, are indeed difficult to separate from those theories that focus on the reproductive aspects, since they are two sides of the same coin. There are two main groupings within the reproduction-based explanations: theories focusing on the production of children to augment economic and social resources, and theories focusing on sexual relations between spouses. Theories involving reproductive fitness and fertility aspects of polygamy will be dealt with in a separate section below.

The desire to have numerous descendants is often the driving force of polygamy, and one of the subtle functions of polygamy is the symbolism of having many children. In traditional Africa, for example, a man's wealth was typically measured in the number of his wives and children, among other things. Furthermore, a man had to ensure that his name and his line remain in the generations after him, and he had to safeguard the names and lines of his ancestors. This was best ensured by begetting numerous children who in turn could produce offspring of their own, ensuring an adequate supply of descendants to preserve the life force of the lineage. An important obligation of kinship in many African societies is thus to give childless relatives one's offspring to adopt in order to secure their lineage (Smith 1953). The importance of reproduction in polygamous societies is most clearly expressed in the fact that barrenness of the first wife is one of the commonest reasons for taking a second wife. Because motherhood is considered such a natural and necessary part of womanhood worldwide, not being able to have children becomes a major problem for women, not only as individuals, but also as social persons. In polygamous societies, not having children opens up the possibility that a woman's husband will divorce her or marry a second wife to have children. Childlessness is seen as a great misfortune for which women are usually held responsible. This is true in most societies where biological facts of reproduction are ignored or not well known. It can have devastating effects on a woman's life (see Inhorn 1996). Childlessness in a monogamous marriage is thus one of the prime reasons for subsequent polygamy. Other solutions to sub-fertility include divorce and remarriage. In many societies, husbands who divorce a wife for barrenness are frowned upon, whereas it may well be considered acceptable for him to marry another wife in order to have children.

Because of the polygynous, or potentially polygynous, character of married life in Africa, having children becomes essential for women if they want access to their husbands' resources; sub-fertility can ultimately lead to destitution for women. The focus on children means that there is often intense reproductive competition among co-wives in polygynous households. Co-wives compete with each other to have as many children as possible, in order to secure a large share of the common husband's resources. Co-wives typically attempt to have the largest number of male children, as well as the best-educated and most successful children, because this strengthens their position vis-à-vis each other and their husband. An effect of this competition for children is that many polygynous men are reluctant to advocate birth control in their families, because they fear differentiating between their wives, thus reinforcing the high birth rates and ensuing co-wife competition. This reproductive competition can have severe implications for children, who might be resented or even mistreated by their mother's rivals. If a co-wife dies, it can spell the death of her children through neglect as well. In some Senegalese polygynous households, for example, the husband's sleeping rotation, designed to avoid favouritism and greater reproductive success for one wife, is so vigilantly upheld that children suspected of having been conceived when it was not the mother's turn to have a conjugal visit may be thrown out of the household. This happens because a very fecund co-wife breaks the unspoken rule that each wife should be on par with all others, including in number of children (Bledsoe 1995; Fainzang and Journet 1988; Madhavan 2002).

Sexuality, especially male sexuality, has also been cited as one of the foundations of polygyny. One of the most prominent theories focuses on the pattern of birth spacing and lactation in a particular society. According to this theory, polygyny emerges as a response to lengthy periods of sexual abstinence, or *post-partum sexual taboos*, that women must follow after childbirth in some cultures. In some African polygamous systems, for example, there appears to be a significant relationship between the severity of post-partum taboos and plural marriages (Clignet 1970: 29). Women may not engage in sexual relations with their husband as long as they are nursing a child, which can be up to three years after a birth. An extended post-partum taboo is associated with low protein availability and the risk of protein deficiency disease, by allowing a mother time to nurse her infant through its critical stage before becoming pregnant again (MacCormack 1982). By requiring a man to refrain from sex for up to three years with a woman who has just given birth, births can be spaced and the offspring's chance of survival thus maximized. Polygamy may then provide a solution to the sexual frustration a man may experience in societies practising post-partum sexual abstinence by allowing him to marry another woman with whom he can have sexual relations. Plural marriage may then solve a man's need for a sexual outlet. In contrast, a woman's need for a sexual outlet in the post-partum period is usually not considered equally important, typically because a woman may not be perceived to be suffering from the same level of sexual frustration as a man is assumed to be. Long periods of sexual abstinence for new mothers can also reduce population growth by serving as a form of birth control. It may simultaneously drive the husbands to acquire additional wives to meet unfulfilled sexual needs, however, which might then increase population growth. Furthermore, though abstinence is the ideal, it is not always respected, and may not constitute a pressing reason for polygyny. Tonga men in Zambia, for example, have magical means to ward off evil to an infant if they have sex with its mother; if this does not work, they have girlfriends to ease their pain (Colson 1958: 123).

A related set of theories, focusing on the sexual motives for polygamy, suggests that the desire for numerous sexual partners is built into basic human biology and that this is the basis for the universal occurrence of polygamy. In East African Mandinka society, for example, the possession of many wives is seen as an expression of prestige and wealth, which is in turn linked to a male virility complex. The male virility complex also has a direct sexual aspect, which in connection with polygamy is expressed in the proverb: 'Do you perhaps want to eat the same food everyday?' (Wittrup 1990: 126). This is reinforced by a Mandinka woman's prescribed two-year period of lactation after the birth of a child, with a resultant two-year sex taboo, which is seen as a nearly impossible abstinence period for a man. Sociobiologists have argued that, while the capacity for sexual pleasure and the propensity to seek sexual variety is probably a universal attribute of human males (and females?), powerful men who like sex may be more able to obtain it, for example through polygyny. However, explaining polygyny solely in terms of a male desire for sex and sexual variation does not take into account the many exceptions or variations that exist in polygamous sexual relations. It also fails to account for male sexual jealousy, which often results in wives and concubines of powerful men being secluded. Seclusion only makes sense if sex has a reproductive purpose, otherwise men would not need to safeguard against adultery by their wives. Sociobiologists indeed emphasize the importance of male confidence of paternity in the evolution of reproductive behaviour. Polygamous males are considered to have lower confidence of paternity than monogamous males, because as the number of wives increases, so does the probability of infidelity. Men may then attempt to increase their wives' fidelity by secluding them on some level. The crucial pay-off for women is to achieve an increased parental investment by the father in their offspring, thereby maximizing their chances of survival (Betzig 1986: 78–9; Hughes 1982: 125).

The claim that men practise polygyny because it gives them sexual gratification and diversity in mates is interpreted by some as a reflection of the fact that polygyny involves the sexual exploitation of women; polygyny is a system geared to satisfying male sexual needs rather than those of women. Another male advantage of polygyny is that it greatly increases the likelihood that there will always be at least one wife to service her husband sexually and otherwise. This becomes relevant when, for example, a co-wife dies, is visiting relatives for long periods, or completely deserts him to settle with her grown children, as is typical in parts of Africa. Such arguments have in turn led to claims that researchers often overemphasize sexuality when discussing any form of polygamy. In this view, polygyny is believed to fulfil specific functions that are unrelated, or not primarily related, to male sexuality (Kilbride 1994: 97; Mair 1971: 152). The focus on sexuality is particularly a Western bias, as Western researchers (and missionaries) have traditionally been fascinated and/or repelled by the sexual implications of plural marriages in Non-Western societies. See Chapter 6 for a further discussion of researcher bias in relation to polygamy and sexuality.

Fertility and Fitness. One area of research that has been particularly concerned with reproductive issues in polygamy is polygyny's effect on fertility. Research tends to show that polygyny lowers the fertility of individual women. The debate is ongoing, however, and centres on the so-called polygyny-fertility hypothesis (e.g. Garenne and van de Walle 1989; Mulder 1989). Several studies have dwelled on this postulated connection between lower fertility and polygyny, typically suggesting that polygyny limits individual female and community fertility through such mechanisms as post-partum sexual abstinence and longer birth intervals. For example, a study of the Amazonian Shipibo people found that polygynous women had 1.3 fewer term-births than monogamous women, primarily due to the fact that birth intervals are four months longer for polygynous women than for monogamous women. The Shipibo, who have the highest documented fertility of any human group, are now experiencing rapid cultural change, including a decline in polygyny, which will most likely lead to even higher fertility (Hern 1992). A study of a rural Arab population in South Jordan similarly found a significantly higher total marital fertility rate among monogamous wives than among polygynous wives. The husband typically decided to take a second wife as a result of his senior wife's infertility or sub-fertility, lowering overall polygamous fertility, as did the typically advanced age of the husband at his marriage to his junior polygynous wife (Sueyoshi and Ohtsuka 2003).

The polygyny-fertility hypothesis is constantly being challenged. One study suggests that the hypothesis overestimates the effect of polygyny on fertility because of the assumption that current marital status accounts for the fertility of women. It reformulates the polygyny-fertility hypothesis by arguing that polygyny is likely to depress fertility only if polygynous women have been previously married. In the absence of previous marriage, the fertility of monogamous and polygynous women is similar (Effah 1999). The longer marital exposure for individual women associated with the greater chances for marriage in a polygynous marriage system may also outweigh the fertility depressing effects which may be associated with polygyny; they include longer observance of post-partum sexual abstinence as well as higher rates of both sterility and sub-fertility. Polygyny's effects on fertility may hence be quite different on the individual level and the societal level. On the individual level, polygyny appears to reduce fertility, whereas polygyny may contribute to high fertility at the societal level. Polygynous societies vary with respect to their reproductive patterns. Some 'high-polygyny' systems favour and encourage high reproductive levels; they usually have a strong pro-natalist orientation, which encourages men to maximize their reproductive objectives by marrying several wives. At a societal level, the frequency of polygyny appears to be positively associated with early initiation of sexual and reproductive activity, early and universal female marriage and minimal interruption of marriage through rapid remarriage after divorce or death of a spouse. These practices ensure that there are enough women to make polygyny possible. This means that in polygynous societies almost all women will eventually get married, thereby maximizing the amount of children born in those societies; in monogamous society in contrast, some women may remain unmarried, and hence potentially not reproduce (Ezeh 1997; Kosack 1999: 554; Pebley and Mbugua 1989: 360–1).

In polyandrous societies, where one woman is shared by two or more men, the overall fertility of a polyandrous family will probably not be able to go beyond one child per year, even if the woman's fecundity is high. If her husbands had married monogamously, they might each have produced a child per year. If all women in the population are married, however, the particular marriage form practised should in principle not influence the population's overall fertility levels, since a woman can still only give birth to about one child per year regardless of whether she has one or five husbands (Chandra 1981). Nonetheless, it may be argued that women in polyandrous marriages have more sexual intercourse as a consequence of their many husbands than women in monogamous or polygynous marriages, resulting in more conceptions. Studies of polyandrous populations in Nepal, Kerala in India, and Sri Lanka, however, indicate that polyandrous marriage does not lead to increases in individual wives' fertility. The matrilineal and matriarchal Mosuo in Yunnan Province, China, who have been practising *de facto* polyandry for centuries, similarly do not have particularly high birth rates in individual households. The overall community birth rates were also relatively low, because the practice of polyandry actually diminished many women's chances of marrying by creating a scarcity of unmarried males and hence a surplus of unmarried women (Johnson and Zhang 1991). In polyandrous societies practising female infanticide, there would be few surplus women, and hence all women would probably get married and potentially reproduce.

Biologists and sociobiologists have also attempted to provide reproductive explanations for polygamy by applying evolutionary biology. Men gain more from reproducing polygamously than do women, and ecological and economic conditions encouraging polygamy in human populations usually favour the emergence of polygyny rather than polyandry. This process is reinforced by basic sexual differences in human reproductive physiology and behaviour. Thus, in the vast majority of human societies polygyny is the norm, whereas polyandry is found in very few societies. Sociobiological arguments focus on reproductive fitness and suggest that a crucial aspect of polygamy is the greater variation in male than in female reproductive success. Greater male variation is linked to a variation in wealth, because wealth is often decisive in securing mates in polygamous society. In the sociobiological scheme, wealth-generated polygamy, based on the control of productive resources, would serve political functions by cementing alliances with affinal relations only if they involved fertile unions, producing genetic ties between affines. Genetic ties may be crucial in establishing political bonds, as evidenced in the frequent dissolution of infertile affinal ties, or in marriages to kinswomen of infertile women in order to produce genetically related children. Political power may provide men with increased reproductive rewards by allowing them to exploit their power to make a larger pool of potential wives available (Betzig 1986: 37, 82–5; Hartung 1982: 1; Kurland and Gaulin 1984: 180; White 1988: 567)

Rich and powerful men clearly enjoy the greatest degree of polygamy cross-culturally, and there is a direct relationship between wealth, multiple mates and reproductive success. Powerful men can successfully take women from less powerful men, especially in connection with violent conflict. Where power differentials are smallest between high and low in society, successful men generally take no more than three or four wives. The concentration of women at the top of social hierarchies implies a relative deprivation at the bottom, resulting in differential reproduction. This is most clearly seen in despotic societies. In the African kingdom of Dahomey, for example, the king could in theory take any women he wanted and add her to the royal harem. The royal harem may have housed thousands of women, and their sheer number diminished their individual chances of reproducing. The women were simultaneously prevented from having children with other men, however, increasing the king's relative reproductive accomplishment. His elaborate fortifications erected for purposes of defence may hence have served the dual (identical?) function of protecting the chastity of the women of the harem (Betzig 1986: 87–90). Conversely, men at the low end of the social hierarchy may in some societies have resorted to fraternal polyandry as an alternative to not having a wife at all, since a share in reproduction may be better than none at all. In return for essential economic assistance to the household, a brother would be given reproductive rights in a wife, though he was typically not supposed to have sexual relations with the woman unless her first husband was absent. Consistent with the Darwinian theory of nepotism, polyandry is most often fraternal: investment in a niece or nephew is better in a reproductive sense than investment in a non-relative (Betzig 1986: 34–6).

Part II
Polygamy Cross-culturally

–4–

Muslim Polygyny in Malaysia[1]

Polygamous Marriage

History

The basis for polygamy in Malaysia is Islam. Islam allows a man up to four wives, and polygyny is found in all Muslim populations. However, because of legal, social and economic obstacles, polygyny is usually practised on a very limited scale in Muslim societies, including Malaysia. According to the official population census for 1991, the 18.4 million Malaysians were divided into 58.3 per cent Malays, 29.4 per cent Chinese, 9.5 per cent Indians and 2.8 per cent 'Others' (Leete 1996: Table 1.3). Ethnicity correlates closely with religion in Malaysia: all Peninsular Malays adhere to Islam, Chinese adhere to Buddhism, Taoism and Confucianism, and most Indians adhere to Hinduism. Small Christian and Muslim minorities exist among the Chinese and Indians. The indigenous peoples of Malaysian Borneo, though often grouped as Malays, practise various religions, including Islam and Christianity. Malays belong to the Shafi'i branch of Sunni Islam. Islam is the official religion of Malaysia, but Article 11 of the Constitution provides that every person has the right to profess and practise his or her religion. State laws forbid the propagation of any other religion to Muslims, however. Because of the constitutionally based equation between being Malay and being Muslim, Malays must follow Muslim rules of behaviour and Islamic law, and religion in Malaysia does not belong to the domain of privacy but is a collective and public matter. Not adhering to Muslim prescriptions can result in public accusation and punishment, administered by the state religious departments. As a Malaysian man's right to practise polygamy is based on Islam, only Muslims are allowed to be polygamous in Malaysia, which means polygamists are almost exclusively Malay. Malay polygamy, or more correctly polygyny, is regulated by the Islamic Family Law (IFL), administered by the state religious departments and implemented by the *syariah* (Islamic) courts. *Syariah* law is only applicable to Muslims in Malaysia (Bunge 1984: 110–13; Jones 1994: 1; Lie and Lund 1994: 31).

Historically in Malay society, polygamy and concubinage were largely confined to the ruling classes and were considered luxuries of the great. This pattern has continued into recent times throughout the region, where polygamy tends to be associated with the aristocracy. Another group traditionally practising polygamy are members of the rural elite, comprising schoolteachers, religious specialists, landed and titled farmers, and local political leaders, who according to Karim (1992: 137–8) may take in pretty but poor young girls as their second wives. Such marriages are acceptable since the girl's kinsmen gain social standing and economic benefits from the union and her spouse gains added prestige and glamour in taking a younger and beautiful wife. Similarly, Strange (1981: 147) observed that in the state of Kelantan religious leaders have a higher rate of polygamy than average villagers, probably as a result of the greater respect and prestige accorded to them and because of their tendency to be wealthier than average villagers. The effect of religiosity on tendency to engage in polygamy is difficult to gauge, however, since people use Islam to argue both for and against polygamy. There are reports of *imams* (leader of mosque prayers or of the Muslim community) influencing village men to remain monogamous, as men with strong religious convictions may be reluctant to marry more than one wife or may restrict themselves to two because they feel they cannot meet the commitments and responsibilities laid down in Islamic law for four wives (Karim 1992: 141; Strange 1981: 230). Among ordinary people in the Malay-Muslim world, in contrast, polygamy has not been very prevalent. The dominant marriage pattern was one of monogamy, reinforced by easy divorce for both sides, which allowed unsatisfactory polygamous marriages to be ended quickly.

In contemporary Malaysia, the wealthier urban and rural elite Malays continue to practise polygamy. Their marriages are usually limited to two wives, since economic, social and personal obstacles tend to prevent them from marrying the four permitted under Islamic provisions. Members of Malay royalty or men of great wealth and social standing often marry more than two wives. In contrast, polygamy rates are very low among the vast majority of Malays. In spite of the fact that Islam allows polygamy, all ethnographic studies have emphasized the limited extent of the practice among Malays. The general consensus in the literature is that polygamy occurs very rarely, and to the extent that it does occur, it is usually followed by the quick divorce of either the first or second wife (Carsten 1997; Djamour 1965; Firth 1943; Kuchiba, Tsubouchi and Maeda 1979; Strange 1981).

Population. Statistically, there appears to be very little polygamy in Malaysia, estimated to make up about 2–3 per cent of all marriages. But there is only scattered information available on the actual frequency of polygamy in Malaysia, and still less on its trends. Taken as a group, the numbers will be much higher among elites than among the lower social classes. Accurate information is lacking, however, because the different states making up Malaysia have different ways of registering marriages and because polygamous marriages frequently lead to divorce. One reason for the statistical underreporting of polygamous marriages is that many polygamous couples do not register their marriages in their home state or in Malaysia at all, making it difficult for the State Religious Departments or the State to create reliable statistics on polygamy. There are various reasons why a husband might not want to make public that he has taken a second wife. The chief consideration that makes it expedient for the husband to contract subsequent marriages out-of-state or out of the country is to avoid applying for permission to have a polygamous marriage. A Muslim man's right to take more than one wife is not automatically granted in Malaysia, but subject to approval from the *Syariah* court. And in many states it involves informing and getting consent from the first wife, something many men may be unable or unwilling to do. Not applying for permission to be polygamous will also minimize the risk that other people will hear about the marriage, an important consideration among the urban elites where often both husband and first wife have prominent positions and might be well known. By going abroad or out-of-state to marry a second wife, a man can have several wives while in his home state being recorded as married only to one. This phenomenon has been called 'cross-border polygyny', since it literally involves plural marriage contracted on foreign soil (Jones 1994: 275–6). As a result of this underreporting of polygamous marriages, the true extent of the practice in Malaysia is difficult to gauge. Indeed, it is difficult to obtain reliable information on the practice of polygamy in all of South East Asia. It is, however, generally considered to be quite limited.

There are several reasons why polygamy has been so limited among Malays. First, polygamy is legally but not necessarily socially sanctioned among non-aristocratic Malays. Generally in Islamic South East Asia, according to Jones (1994: 283–4), polygamy has not been fully socially approved even though Islamic law sanctions it. Malay writers have typically been critical of polygamous men, particularly those who use their wealth or religious influence to this end. Kuchiba et al. (1979: 36) reported that polygamy frequently appears to be the subject of joking in Malay society, particularly if engaged in by a man who cannot really afford it, thus reflecting an unwise lack of control over sexual drives. Another element of polygamy's ambiguous social acceptability in Malaysia is the fact that many men keep their second wives secret to all but a few good friends, as mentioned above. Not even the first wife may know that her husband has taken another wife, in fact that seems to be the case in many polygamous unions in urban Malaysia. The secrecy of the institution might again imply that it is not fully accepted by society. Clearly, it is legitimate for a Muslim man to take another wife according to Islamic law, granted he fulfils certain conditions, but whether it is legitimate in the eyes of his wife and society at large is another matter.

A second major reason for polygamy's limited distribution is women's reluctance to be part of a polygamous union. In her study of a fishing village on Langkawi, Carsten (1997: 96) relates how villagers say that it is impossible to find a woman who will agree to be part of a polygamous union. Indeed, condemnation of polygamy was almost universal among Malay women. Simultaneously, most women acknowledged a man's right in Islam to take more than one wife, granted that he meets the Qur'anic conditions for engaging in polygamy. But the acknowledgement of a Muslim man's right to be polygamous is carefully weighed against the reality of men who for the most part cannot live up to these conditions. For most women, polygamy is only a conditional, not an absolute, right in Islam, and should not be engaged in unless the man is able to live up to those conditions. Mostly, women feel that a polygamous union breaks the bond between husband and wife. It is considered an act of betrayal towards the first wife and her children, especially when, as often happens, it involves a covert second marriage that the first wife only discovers in an accidental and humiliating way.

Men's reasons for being polygamous tend to focus on the Muslim man's right to take four wives. Women rarely referred to this right as an explanation for polygamy. That right was considered conditional and next to impossible for a mortal man to live up to. The most common reasons given by men for taking a second wife included wife deficiency, whether mental, physical, social or any other reason; sexual gratification with a willing young wife as opposed to an unwilling older wife; rejuvenation when an older man marries a very young girl; childlessness where a barren first wife was replaced by a fertile young one; skewed gender ratio based on the false belief that there are more women than men in society; and finally marrying a second wife opens up her various networks to the husband. Women's motives for marrying as second wives were very different. They married for material reasons, primarily to get financial support from the husband or become wealthy; for status reasons, to be married to a powerful man; for personal reasons, such as love or particular circumstances such as pregnancy; and for temporal reasons, as some women prefer to have a husband for a few days a week only, giving them more time on their own. All in all, polygamy appears to serve some very particular needs for the people practising it, and people tend to have a very instrumental view of polygamy.

Polygamous Family Life

Arrangements

The law is quite clear on the requirements for engaging in polygamy in Malaysia. The many demands on husbands are meant to protect existing wives and make men consider carefully whether they are fit to undertake subsequent marriages. When a man applies to engage in polygamy he must typically show that he can treat all wives equally in all aspects of married life. This requirement is based on the Qur'anic injunction that if he cannot be fair to all his wives, he should not be polygamous. The requirement which receives most attention, being the easiest to quantify, is proof that the husband will not lower his existing wife or wives' standard of living upon marrying another wife. For elite men, justifying polygamy from an economic point-of-view may be less of a problem, whereas proving that it is just and necessary becomes more of a problem when married to a well-adjusted and well-connected first wife. Of all the requirements, men may dread most having to obtain consent from their first wives, and be faced with them in court, as discussed. For first wives are able to frustrate a man's application to engage in polygamy by refusing to consent to the second marriage, as well as contest any court approval of the marriage. Many men are therefore tempted not to disclose that they are already married, and so avoid having to go through a legal procedure that may end in rejection, not to mention the potential for wrecking their existing marriage. There are, of course, a myriad of personal reasons why men choose not to inform their first wives of their subsequent marriages. While only the men themselves know these, most women relate them to fear of confrontation with their first wives, but also with their wider families. A man's family often does not sanction the polygamous marriage, and may in fact side with his first wife. Moreover, men may fear their children's disapproval.

These various legal, social and personal factors make it expedient for husbands to contract subsequent marriages out of state or out of the country. Some of these marriages contracted without the appropriate court's consent are eventually registered in the husband's home state. A marriage that is not approved and registered is not legal in Malaysia. If the husband dies or divorces the second wife, she will not be recognized as his heir or dependant. That translates into such problems for the second wife as having no claim on her husband's property, no pension and the illegitimacy of her children. While registering out-of-state marriages *ex post facto* subverts the standard application and registration procedures for marriages under the IFL, the courts will usually allow them to be registered to protect the interests of the subsequent wives. In Selangor (the federal state surrounding the capital Kuala Lumpur), the errant husband will only have to pay a RM1,000 (*c.* £150 in 1997) fine upon registering such a marriage, no matter what his economic status is. As many women's NGOs have pointed out, this amount is negligible for rich men who wish to take more than one wife and in no way deters them from their endeavour. To be effective, they argue, the fine should be related to a man's income. What it amounts to is that relatively lax laws and particularly lax interpretations of the laws by *syariah* courts allow men to engage in polygamy easily. This was not the original intent of the IFL, but has become the *de facto* situation. Even religious department officials concede that the practice effectively constitutes a loophole in the law. But they also tend to argue that the men would marry anyway, and so they must try to protect the wives. Justification of polygamy on the grounds that men just follow a natural instinct, which should then be made legal to avoid sin, is very common, even among women.

Because second marriages often start out secret, arrangements for the second marriage tend to be radically different than for monogamous marriages, especially if they are out of state. First, the respective families may not be involved, since they may not be aware that the wedding is taking place at all. Commonly, the second wife's family knows about the marriage, since she may find it difficult or counterproductive to hide her marriage from her family, counting on them for advice and support. The wife's family may be involved in the actual marriage only through her father or other close male relative acting as her *wali* or guardian. The elaborate ceremonial normally associated with engagement negotiations and the marriage itself will typically be dispensed with, not least to keep the husband's own family and, more to the point, his first wife and her family from finding out about the marriage. Polygamous marriages are often hurried, hushed affairs, compared to monogamous marriages, which are accompanied by elaborate and extensive celebrations. The contrast with a couple's first monogamous marriage cannot be emphasized enough. Secret polygamous marriages tend to be completely at the husband's discretion and under his control. Only a few or none of the spouses' family members or friends may be present, denying the bride public acknowledgement of her marital status. As this status is of critical importance to Malay personhood, the secrecy surrounding polygamous marriage has a natural life span that ends, if for no other reason, when a wife needs to assert that status. That usually happens at the latest when she becomes pregnant and has a child. Of course, if the second marriage is not secret, marriage celebrations can be held as normal, though they are typically on a smaller scale than a first monogamous marriage.

Polygamous residential arrangements are quite fluid. Customarily, each wife should have a separate residence, with the husband usually sharing a main house with his first wife. As Djamour (1965: 84–5) observed among Singapore Malays, it was considered humiliating for a woman to have a co-wife and even more humiliating for them to live under the same roof. In order to avoid friction between wives, most polygamous men maintain separate establishments if they can afford to, or one wife might stay with her parents and be visited there. Malay co-wives rarely cohabit, because separate residences are considered necessary to counteract the assumed inherent quarrelling, jealousy and favouritism. Conflicts are greatly lessened when co-wives do not cohabit or live in separate villages or towns, perhaps unaware of each other's existence. Co-residential houses appear to have existed primarily among the nobility, whose wealth enabled wives to be kept in separate quarters, even though they were in the same house (Firth 1943: 52–3; Geertz 1961: 131–3; Jones 1994: 278; Karim 1992: 141; Strange 1981: 142–9). But even among nobility co-residence appears to have been rare, for as Gullick noted, 'royal wives submitted reluctantly to polygamous marriage as a price to be paid for their privileged position. To relieve the inevitable jealousy between wives, and because convention required it, a ruler usually accommodated his wives in different places' (1987: 52). Co-residence of wives in upper-class polygamous houses is at the husband's discretion and presumably depends on how the wives get along and accept each other's presence. Even among upper classes, co-wives prefer their own home if they have the choice. Indeed, when co-wives appear to be on good terms with each other or live peacefully together under the same roof, the husband may be suspected of applying magical means to achieve such unlikely harmony. A man who manages to keep two women in the same house is considered to use special powers to hypnotize them into accepting a situation which, viewed from outside, is untenable (Banks 1983: 99).

The tendency among rural polygamous men to maintain wives in different villages does not seem to be regularly practised in urban areas. Polygamous men living in the capital Kuala Lumpur (henceforth K.L.), for example, tend to keep second wives within easy reach. They are able to do so because K.L. offers the anonymity of a big city in which people do not know each other, unlike in villages. Furthermore, second wives in K.L. may have their own house and income when marrying. They will then remain in their houses, which might be close to the house of their husband and his first wife. Second wives who have no income or are still living at home may be set up in new houses by their husbands. Husbands typically place them in apartments located within easy reach so they can visit them regularly, without having to travel great distances that might arouse the suspicion of their first wives. Some men go to what is considered rather unscrupulous lengths to make it convenient for themselves. A typical scenario might involve a man with three wives, who lives with his first wife in their mutual house, and then has bought an apartment for each of his other two wives in the same building close to his main house, making it easy for him to move between wives. Certain apartment complexes in K.L. and Selangor have indeed become infamous for housing secret second wives. Expatriates and polygamous wives alike usually patronize such complexes, often luxurious by Malaysian standards, as both groups enjoy above average incomes. Living among expatriates rather than locals also lessens secret second wives', and their husbands', chances of being 'exposed'.

Management

Closely related to the customary rule that each polygamous wife should have her own house is the rule that a man should spend equal time with each of his wives. Equal treatment of wives is a Qur'anic prerequisite for polygamy and, as such, an ideal that both men and women refer to. Few polygamous unions see such fair sharing of the husband's time, however. It represents the ideal rather than the practised reality. In fact, feeling neglected is the most common complaint from polygamous wives about their marriage (excluding comments about the institution as such). As Firth noted, 'the equal distribution of time is not always followed and inequality in this respect is a common cause of friction between a man's wives' (1943: 52–3). How a man manages his duties towards his wives is closely connected with the circumstances of the secondary union. If it is official, it is easier for a man to distribute his time between his wives, since both would presumably insist on it. Secret second wives, in contrast, usually have to agree to a 'schedule' that allows their husband to maintain an officially monogamous marriage to their first wife. A man can then dictate the terms of his time commitments since a second wife has little leverage over a man to whom she is not officially married. Indeed, she may quickly land in the classic situation where after some initial months of 'equality', the husband starts spending more and more time with his first official wife and their children.

Typically, a polygamous husband's allegiance is with his first wife and their children, and second wives are more likely to lose out eventually to first wives in polygamous unions. Some second wives fight back, however, and may indeed achieve the ultimate goal of most polygamous wives, namely to make their husband divorce their co-wife. One strategy is to spend as much time as possible with the husband, so that the first wife feels neglected. It appears to be uncommon that the husband will actually divorce his first wife even if he spends more time with his second wife, however. If he had such intentions, it would have been easier for him to divorce her right away and marry another woman without the trouble of contracting a polygamous marriage. In such cases, it might rather be first wives requesting a divorce than husbands initiating it. Trying to augment one's share of a husband's time as a strategy to oust a rival co-wife revolves around the assumption that equal sharing of time is of such paramount importance to co-wives in polygamous marriages. In the same vein, polygamous men who attempt to bring their wives together at certain times break the fiercely guarded customary rule that each wife gets certain days allocated. Violation of these rules was felt by polygamous wives to be a serious infringement of their rights. Husbands attempting to bring together their wives may not just be trying to maximize their own comfort, however, they may also be attempting to come across as model polygamous husbands, able not only to retain several wives but also to maintain harmony between them.

Of polygamous husbands' requirements for equal treatment of wives, most women find financial sharing as important as time-sharing. They both constitute highly visible indicators of a woman's relationship to her husband, whereas emotional support is more private and less quantifiable. Financial support becomes paramount in most polygamous wives' minds, the direct sign of their husband's affection for them and their relative position vis-à-vis their co-wives. First wives are concerned because they used to be their husbands' sole beneficiaries, whereas second wives are concerned because they may have married for financial reasons. It is difficult to generalize about the economic basis of Malay polygamy, however, because it varies according to individual circumstances. Many Malay women work and take care of themselves financially, so if they become second wives, they may look for husbands who offer other support than financial. First wives who have independent incomes may also be satisfied financially if their husbands keep paying the bills, especially children's education, so at least their standard of living is not lowered. They can then pay for their personal consumption themselves.

Financial sharing is particularly contentious if all wives in a polygamous marriage are dependent on their husband. First wives who have obliged the common request from Malay men to be housewives are left vulnerable in case of divorce, abandonment or polygamy. That is part of the reason most elite parents today insist that their daughters get an education, so they can take care of themselves 'in case their husbands should let them down'. For first wives, the arrival of a second wife may spell destitution as the husband concentrates most of his support on his new wife. Middle- and upper-class women, though, are less likely to suffer dramatically as they usually have families that can help them out financially if they have no personal source of income. Second wives who marry partly for money may not always get what they bargained for or were promised by their husband before the marriage, since their husband's allegiance may remain with his first wife and her children. The competition between co-wives over their husband's financial support can therefore be very fierce. Firth (1943: 57) similarly observed that bad feelings between wives often stemmed from economic concerns, particularly the sharing of the husband's income, perhaps reflecting the underlying personal hostility between co-wives.

In many systems of polygamy, co-wives' rights and obligations are carefully defined and guarantee a certain amount of equality between the wives. The senior wife is usually given special powers and privileges, distributing the workload among the co-wives, dividing all monetary rewards from the husband, and being consulted by the husband when he wants to take a new wife. Senior wives usually have greater authority over their co-wives and over all their husband's children (Clignet 1970, 1987). According to Banks (1983: 99), there are also accepted patterns of behaviour between Malay co-wives. The older should receive the respect of the younger and be addressed as *kakak* [older sister]. But in urban polygamous unions there is little evidence of such regulated systems of deference, and systems of seniority do not appear to be in operation. First wives may enjoy some privileges, such as being brought to official functions and receiving their husband's title, but cannot expect preferential treatment from their husband in financial or emotional matters. Generally, a Malay first wife does not have any authority over her co-wives, nor does she have any responsibilities towards them. Urban co-wives tend to live completely separate lives, to the extent that they are sometimes unaware of each other's existence. The typical absence of relations between co-wives is probably a function of the fact that there is no socially accepted framework for polygamous family life in urban Malaysia. Polygamy is not universally accepted in the Malay community, as mentioned, and this translates into a lack of rules and regulations which could reduce co-wives' insecurities by guiding them as to what to expect and what was expected of them vis-à-vis their co-wives, as in other polygamous systems. Some first wives nonetheless feel that their senior position entitles them to more than equal treatment from their husband, and some husbands do defer to a senior wife's position and give her preferential treatment. That requires, of course, that the first wife knows that she has a co-wife.

To sum up, being equal to all wives entails a polygamous husband spending equal amounts of time with each wife, as well as sharing equally of his emotional, physical, social and financial support. Of those, equal financial sharing is usually seen as the most important, as mentioned. Maintaining the first wife financially but neglecting his other duties is not acceptable, however. But polygamous husbands are generally seen as unable to share their love fairly. Simultaneously, love is not always the basis for Malay marriage. While some women may accept living with less love in a polygamous marriage, for the many women who feel that love has grown between them and their husband, the appearance of another wife might be a serious setback, one that directly channels most or all of their husband's love to the new wife. It does appear, particularly to first wives, that second wives get the lion's share of their husband's attention, at least initially. Many second wives feel entitled to it, especially those who work and are not dependent on financial maintenance, for they often marry under the assumption that their husband married them for love. It reflects a strategy used by some men to engage in polygamy and the devastating emotional effects it can have on their wives: they convince their girlfriends that they no longer love their first wife or have any relations with her as a way to make them marry as second wives. This strategy is also commonly employed by men in monogamous societies, when attempting to secure or retain mistresses.

Polygamous Sex Life

Reproduction

A Malay polygamous family starts out, in the vast majority of cases, as a monogamous family consisting of one husband and one wife. Men seldom seem to contract a second marriage at the same time or shortly after their first marriage, whereas second, third or fourth wives may more commonly be married closely in time. The first wife in a polygamous marriage will in most cases have started married life as a monogamous wife and remained an only wife for some years. When a man marries a second wife, polygamous reproduction begins. What reproductive decisions the spouses make in a polygamous union are influenced by various factors, such as whether the woman has been married before, whether she is past childbearing age or whether one or both spouses have children from previous unions. For young childless women marrying a man who is already married, childbearing in polygamy seems to be as natural a consequence of marriage as for any other woman who starts married life as a young and never previously married official wife. Reproduction for such women seems not to be particularly influenced by polygamy, but may follow the normal pattern of three to four children, spaced and timed regardless of the reproductive status of co-wives. In short, polygamy does not lead to specific childbearing patterns; the spouses' individual circumstances upon marriage seem to play a more important role.

For purposes of planning polygamous families, husbands can be roughly divided into two groups – those with and those without children from their first union. A childless man may typically marry a second wife in order to have children of his own. One may assume that his second wife will have agreed to have children with him regardless of whether she has children from a previous union. If, on the other hand, the husband already has children from his first union, he might want his second wife more for his enjoyment than to have his children. Polygamous wives, in contrast, come in many significant categories – first, second, third or fourth, never married or previously married, divorced or widowed, with or without children, still capable of bearing children or past childbearing age, financially independent or dependent on their husband. It seems that some husbands find women who do not want children attractive as second wives precisely for that reason, freeing them from the normal expectation that marriage entails parenthood. Women who are still in their childbearing years and marry a man because they need his financial support may find it important to have children with him to cement the relationship and stake a claim on his property, whereas women who are financially independent may not need children for such reasons and thus opt not to have them. This is particularly so for older career women who may have remained single for so long that they have come to accept that they will not have children and may be satisfied with just having a husband. It is important to remember that, in some cases, polygamous unions remain childless involuntarily. What appears as a pattern based on choice may be a result of biological obstacles faced by older women, who make up a significant portion of second wives, or by (relatively) older men, who make up the majority of polygamous husbands. Polygamous wives who are unable to bear children may then face the same kind of problems as sub-fertile monogamously married women (described below).

A polygamous wife's likely reproductive career is also affected by the secrecy surrounding many secondary unions. In most cases, it is the husband rather than the second wife who is keen to keep the marriage secret and thus opts not to have children, because the identity of a polygamous husband is more easily identifiable when a child is born to the union. Sometimes, it is second wives who do not want children in order to keep the marriage secret. Giving birth in a culture where having children out of wedlock is completely unacceptable would alert people to the fact that an apparently single woman is probably someone's second wife. For such wives, maintaining the secrecy of their union takes precedence over the spouses' desire to have children together. So a second wife may enjoy her freedom from a Malay woman's 'reproductive duties', having a husband without having children. Women who marry as second wives today are therefore much less 'predestined' to have children than second wives a generation ago. It is likely, then, that a number of secondary marriages will be childless to protect their secrecy, particularly if both spouses have children from previous unions and so feel more at liberty to choose whether or not to have children together. Husbands typically opt for second wives as companions rather than mothers when the second wife is secret and when they already have children with their first wives and do not want any more, though this may conflict with their second wife's wish for children of their own – and vice versa.

If the spouses later do have children, they may find that the birth of a child provides them with an opportunity to make their marriage public.

Sexual Relations

The expression and control of sexuality within or outside marriage constitutes one of the crucial domains of cultural ideas and practices that shape reproduction. Contemporary Malay women's control over their own bodies and their sexuality is limited, as attitudes to sex are tied to expectations that women become mothers and associated ideas of chastity and purity. This is not least due to the increased importance of Islam in Malays' everyday lives: Islamic discourse represents women's active sexuality as a disruptive potential and disorder, which requires that women be controlled so as not to tempt men. Curbing active female sexuality is at the basis of many of Islam's family institutions (Nicolaisen 1983: 5–6). But alongside the strengthening of rigid sexual morals brought about by Islam's increased influence in Malaysia, there is a relaxing of taboos through Western influences that are increasingly overtaking traditional moral attitudes. Media coverage of non-Malay, especially Western, gender relations and sexuality, particularly in television series, has penetrated and shaped local discourse on sexual relations and male–female relations generally (Peletz 1996: 122). What has not been affected is the norm that premarital sex is completely unacceptable for a Muslim woman. It brings shame not only to the woman herself, but also to her entire family. Even parents who are liberal in religious matters tend to enforce strict measures to avoid exposing their daughters to 'risks', because of the strong sanctions against physical intimacy between unmarried adults. A pivotal issue in Malay sexuality is this strong religious taboo associated with premarital sex. It would be impossible for women to live with boyfriends before marriage for social and cultural reasons, as well as for religious and legal reasons: they could be arrested under the *khalwat* law where unmarried Muslims caught in 'close proximity' to each other can be fined or jailed for adultery, whether or not it has taken place.

In marriage, allowing a husband sexual access is not just a matter of personal choice for wives. If a Muslim woman refuses to have sex with her husband, it constitutes grounds for divorce, and she could lose maintenance if divorced. Sexual access is also important because permission to engage in polygamy can be granted precisely because marital relations have ceased between spouses. When a marriage turns from monogamous into polygamous because of dysfunctional marital relations, the stage is set for problems. At issue is husband-sharing, a polygamous husband's prescribed equal sharing of his physical attention between all his wives. As Mernissi (1987: 48) suggests, polygamy may be seen as a way for a man to humiliate his wife sexually, expressing her inability to satisfy him. The sexual relationship between husband and wife is one of the most contentious aspects of polygamous life, one that can cause great strife and misery among co-wives. As with other aspects of polygamy, however, there is a difference in the perspectives of first and second wives, as well as in how their husband tends to treat them. First wives, by the time their husband marries a second wife, may have ceased having relations with their husband, or have them less frequently. In fact, having regular sexual relations is often cited as a reason why men might want to marry a new wife, even by first wives themselves. In some cases, the first wife presumably stops having sexual relations with her husband precisely because he has married another woman. For second wives, sexuality in polygamous marriages is often viewed and experienced very differently than for first wives. Whereas a man's first wife may offer him stability, family and children, his second wife may know and accept that she is more of a companion. In such relationships sex typically constitutes an important ingredient.

Rather than seeing 'husband-sharing' in all aspects of marriage, many polygamous unions see different wives getting different treatment. The first wife may remain the husband's official wife, sharing in his public and social life, whereas the second wife may get his emotional and physical attention, leaving the first wife with a husband in name only. Second wives are so associated with sexual relationships that they are often accused of marrying as second wives because they 'need a man' or 'crave sex'. So much so that they don't care about hurting another woman whose husband they 'steal'. Men are also seen as marrying a second wife for sexual gratification, but somehow this is less shocking and more understandable. Divorced or widowed women in particular are considered 'man-eaters'. Since they previously had legitimate sexual relations in marriage, they are considered in special need of resuming them. Strong social sanctions against premarital sex mean that even divorced women may find it necessary to marry, often as second wives, to have sexual relations with men. Another group of women typically marrying polygamously are older unmarried career women, and for them sex also forms a natural part of the marriage, since engaging in legitimate sexual relations might be the only pressing reason why an otherwise independent woman should marry at all. Polygamous marriages are not all about sex, of course, and second wives can just as easily as first wives become neglected by their husbands when his interest in them wanes. Being a second wife does not mean automatically being showered with all your husband's affection and attention. Sometimes, he returns to his first wife, sometimes he marries a third or fourth wife, and neglects his other wives. In ideal cases, where a husband is able to share himself equally among all his wives, the emotional and contentious nature of shared sexual access to one man can still cause grief among co-wives, however, no matter how well they cope.

Polygamous Social Life

Social Relations

Living in polygamous families is ideally regulated by various customary rules and norms regarding how the husband should treat and interact with his wives, and how his wives should interact with him and each other. But in the Malay reality, there is little respect for such rules and norms, as mentioned. Generally, how a woman copes emotionally and socially with being in such fluid polygamous families depends on her individual circumstances and resources. There are no particular cultural or religious guidelines, though some virtues ideally possessed by Malay women are considered important in dealing successfully with polygamy, such as being 'very patient' or 'very religious'. One coping strategy that first wives might use is finding acceptable reasons why the husband should take another wife. One of the commonest justifications is to prevent the husband from engaging in adultery. A wife, it is argued, may prefer that her husband be married to another woman rather than have a mistress, as this is less morally compromising. Another common justification for polygamy is childlessness. Many women argue that the only situation in which a woman might accept polygamy is if she cannot have children, and so accepts that her husband takes another wife to have children of his own. Infertile married women might have rather different views, however. Finding legitimizing reasons for their husband to engage in polygamy might therefore work less well than simply accepting that polygamy is a 'circumstance' that Malay women must be ready for in marriage, no matter what their personal feelings are about it.

Because of the rigorous separation of co-wives typical of Malay polygamy, relations between co-wives are often extremely cool. Particularly when the second wife starts out in secret, first wives often harbour strong antipathy towards the woman who 'stole' their husband, and have no wish to have anything to do with her. A polygamous husband will often not interfere in the wives' battles with each other, for they tend ultimately to benefit him, as each wife will try to cater to his whims in order to achieve his preferential support and attention. This can create great tension in the marriage by shifting relations between spouses from the complementarity, which traditionally exists in monogamous Malay marriages, to competition, resulting in stress and insecurity for the wives. Some husbands do attempt to make their wives coexist or at least accept each other. This makes life easier for themselves and their wives; it also approaches the Islamic requirement of equal treatment and the Islamic ideal of a harmonious polygamous family. If a husband achieves harmony between his wives, whether directly as a result of his fair behaviour towards them or because the wives themselves accept each other, he is generally praised for what is considered his extraordinary domestic ability. But even more praise is lavished, at least by women, on the first wife who can accept new wives into her marriage, for this is considered an even more extraordinary ability, which goes against basic human instincts. Her sacrifice and patience, her indulgence and acceptance will usually earn her the highest accolade that a modern-day Malay can aspire to, that she is 'a good Muslim'. The message seems to be that women, or men, who can maintain a harmonious polygamous family, are seen as particularly good Muslims because they seem able to emulate the Prophet's marriage, which was polygamous.

While co-wives may not have any relations to each other, they must have relations to the families involved. Usually, the husband's family places its primary allegiance with the first wife if she married according to traditional customs and with their approval. Often, the husband's family is as shocked and bewildered when he takes a second wife as is his first wife. Among Singapore Malays, Djamour (1965: 87) found the same pattern of parents rebuking their sons for contemplating polygamous unions when their daughters-in-law had been good and dutiful wives for many years and did not deserve such treatment. It is of course not just the husband's family that a polygamous wife must deal with, but also her own. When a married woman becomes a first wife, either voluntarily or involuntarily, her family will usually look upon her with sympathy and pity, and if angered enough on her behalf may choose to more or less sever relations with the husband and his family. Only rarely would they blame the first wife for the polygamy. But when a woman chooses to marry as a second wife, there is often little understanding for her choice even in her own family. Exceptions may be made if she is older, widowed or divorced, or if young girls from poor families marry rich men as second wives. In some cases, second wives choose not to tell their families that they have married, perhaps because they know and fear their family's reactions. It is probably rare that women who become second wives do not tell their families, since Malays live lives deeply enmeshed in familial networks and rely on their support for everything from financial help to childminding to social identity. For various reasons some choose to remain secretly married for a time, and if second wives live away from their families in another state they may keep up the charade longer. But sooner or later the families will find out, since their lives are so intertwined. Once a child is born it will usually be impossible to hide the fact any longer. That is a reason why second wives may choose not to have children, as discussed.

Friendships, like familial ties, do not necessarily guarantee that a second wife will be accepted by those close to her. Friends and acquaintances of polygamous spouses, like family members, have to contend with the pragmatic difficulties and tricky etiquette of knowing the husband and often both wives. For example, how does one decide which wife to invite whenever one invites the husband, if one knows all people involved? One challenge for polygamous husbands is indeed how to handle the social commitments of being married to several wives. Within his own family and with his close friends, he may feel at liberty to bring whichever wife he wishes and expect his choice to be accepted by those close to him. But when it comes to more distant acquaintances and official social functions, stricter rules of etiquette apply with respect to which wife to bring. Different wives are brought to different functions. First wives will usually be brought to official functions because they are the senior wives and get their husband's title if he has any. They may also themselves hold prominent public positions. Furthermore, the second wife may be secret or unofficial. If a husband were to bring both his wives to an official function, it would most likely cause talk and so rarely occurs. To avoid any public confrontation between different wives of the same man, a hostess may discretely let it be known that she will only accept first wives in attendance. Husbands might then bring second or younger wives to more fun and unofficial events, as when he is among (male) friends and therefore feels entitled and safe in bringing her. The customary rule that husbands bring their first wife to official functions is bent when husbands feel that their second wife is more suitable. Some men marry a second wife because they feel they lack an 'equal partner' in their first wife, and so may bring their second wife to official functions. Their first wife might then be pushed into obscurity by her new co-wife and so lose social prestige. Sometimes, a second wife completely takes over as the main wife.

Children born into polygamy will mostly know that their father has another wife and other children. But a major problem faced by spouses in polygamous unions is whether, when and how existing children should be told of the polygamy. Children of first wives are often not told of their father's second marriage, even if their mothers know about it, to spare them potential trauma. A wife may also agree to keep it secret for strategic reasons. Sometimes children of first wives discover their father's second marriage in traumatic ways, often with little help or guidance from their parents, who may be unsure of how to approach the very emotional subject with their children. Children of women who become second wives usually know about the polygamous marriage, because second wives are often keen to have their children accepted and perhaps adopted by their new spouses to secure them socially and financially. Children are sometimes used by their mothers as 'pawns' in their strategies to oust rivals, strengthen their relative position, or hurt offending husbands or co-wives. A disgruntled first wife may use her children to negotiate the terms of polygamy with her husband, who is well aware of the potential consequences if she tells them about their father's new wife and how unhappy she is. Even if first wives agree not to tell their children, the threat that they might can still work to their advantage. This use of children only works, of course, if the father is close to his children. But it is not just disgruntled wives who use their children against errant husbands; polygamous husbands may find equally powerful uses for their children. Through them they may seek to gain acceptance of secondary marriages or establish the seniority of one wife. It would therefore 'not be amiss for a husband to proudly introduce a child by his first wife to a third person in front of his second wife' (Kuchiba et al. 1979: 36). It is common in polygamous families where co-wives maintain separate houses that their children mix, mostly in the first wife's house, once wives know of each other's existence and regardless of their relationship.

Divorce

In Malaysia, polygamy is commonly expected to lead to divorce, usually when economic support or emotions become problematic. It is unclear whether more husbands than wives, or more first than second wives, tend to seek divorce because of polygamy (Karim 1991: 76–7). Although, theoretically, a Muslim woman may petition for divorce (see below), it has traditionally been the exclusive right of a Muslim husband to dissolve his marriage by pronouncing the divorce formula in the form of one, two or three *talaq*, through which he repudiates his wife. Such a divorce used to be effective whether or not there were witnesses to it, and it could take place anytime or anywhere. In order to take effect the only other step necessary was to report the divorce by *talaq* to the local *iman*. The divorce rules have now been modified to counteract the ease with which men could and did divorce their wives. If a Malay man wants to divorce his wife today, he cannot simply pronounce the *talaq*, but must under new Islamic Family Law regulations present a written application and, among other things, state why he wishes a divorce. If the wife does not agree to a divorce, the couple must go through a counselling process in order to attempt reconciliation (Cederoth and Hassan 1997: 41–2). The IFL also gives women access to divorce, but women are generally hindered by a low level of knowledge about divorce and marriage rights under Islamic law, and so do not act on them. For a woman, the first step in initiating divorce proceedings would be to go to the *syariah* court. Once an application for divorce has been filed, her husband is called in for counselling, and there will be consultations between the spouses. However, the courts make it very difficult and time-consuming for women to get a divorce because of the extensive counselling required. The problem is compounded by the fact that there are far more male than female counsellors, and that there are no female *kadis* (Islamic judges). The *syariah* court is seen by most women as working for men only, since judges are thought to be more inclined to take men's needs into consideration than women's.

For women determined to obtain a divorce, however, there is a list of grounds on which women can apply for divorce from their husbands. Polygamy is included on this list, but only if the marriage is not accepted by the court. Women normally cannot get a divorce simply because of polygamy, especially if the husband can prove that he can still support the family. Upon marriage, men must pronounce a pledge that they will maintain their wives, the implication being that if they fail to do so wives can get a divorce. Specifically, if a husband does not maintain his wife for four months, she can claim divorce from him. Similarly, according to Islamic law, if the spouses have not had sexual relations for three months, the marriage can be ended. Refusing sexual relations with a husband is not grounds for divorce if he still wants to maintain them, however. Indeed, not being compatible is not admissible grounds, even though a main reason why Malay women choose to divorce their husbands is personal incompatibility (cf. Firth 1943). While there are many legitimate grounds for women to seek divorce, the problem arises in proving those grounds to a judge's satisfaction. This burden of proof makes it very difficult to use grounds such as cruelty, mental abuse or abandonment, because a woman must prove her husband is at fault, prove his absence, and she needs witnesses to prove that he treats her cruelly. But the court has the power to grant a divorce if the husband is cruel to his wife, and cruelty can include polygamy. The court can similarly pronounce a divorce for a woman without adequate proper grounds if counselling fails, in effect taking over the powers of the husband. It is considered contemptible to hold a wife against her will, and a husband who is reluctant to pronounce the *talaq* may be goaded into doing so by his wife shaming and insulting him in public. This has always been a feature of Malay divorce, driven by women's difficulties in obtaining a divorce from husbands unwilling to grant them one (Banks 1983: 100; Djamour 1965: 66).

Women who choose to divorce their polygamous husbands face not only all the obstacles faced by women wanting to end monogamous marriages, but also some problems particular to polygamous unions. Women who have engaged in 'cross-border polygyny', secretly marrying as second wives abroad or out of state, face the major procedural complication of having had a civil marriage or a religious ceremony, or sometimes both, abroad or out of state, both of which may require termination without their husband's cooperation. A marriage that is not approved and registered in one's state of residence is not legal and therefore there can be no divorce, making divorce in polygamous marriages a double jeopardy for many women. It may pit foreign civil law against Malaysian *syariah* law, and women are caught in between. Another deterrent to divorce is the feeling among many women that polygamy is part of a Malay woman's life, something she must be prepared for in marriage and accept as a Muslim woman. Women might, of course, have personal reasons for staying in polygamous marriages even if unhappy. There are first wives who still love their husbands and wish to remain their wives. Women might also fear the financial and social fall from grace, or indeed the loneliness, that being without a husband might entail. First wives, however, know that polygamy can be even lonelier than being divorced, as they might not get any attention from their husband and are unable to form new relationships because they are still married. The perception that remarriage is implausible for a middle-aged divorcee seems to be a strong reason why older wives tend to stay in polygamous marriages.

Among women determined to obtain a divorce are those who cannot accept being in polygamous marriages, either because they find polygamy unacceptable or because their polygamous marriages do not function. Especially among young people, divorce is more tightly linked to polygamy. Among young men today, economic issues make polygamy less attractive: it is too expensive to pay for several wives, and so they will probably divorce the first wife before marrying the second. Young women today also tend to accept polygamy less, partly as a result of changes in attitudes to marriage, having become more of an individual choice and considered less sacred, less inevitable. A young woman who chooses her own partner because she wants to marry, not because she has to, is less likely to accept her husband behaving according to his own whims. The likelihood that divorce follows upon polygamy is indeed age-related. Younger women who believe they can remarry and have the means of supporting themselves may be more likely to divorce their husbands if they do not approve of his polygamy than older women who do not believe they can remarry and do not want to lose the financial and social security they have been enjoying. In contrast, young urban women today know that they can build an existence without husbands. Furthermore, women have the option of putting a decree in their marriage contract to have the marriage annulled if the husband should do something they object to, like marrying a second wife. Such forms of prenuptial contracts are gaining ground among women who do not want to face perhaps years of anguish in obtaining a divorce from recalcitrant husbands.

–5–

Christian Polygyny in the USA

Polygamous Marriage[1]

History

The Mormons are a religious body founded in 1830 by the American Joseph Smith, the first Mormon prophet. Contemporary American Mormons live primarily in the state of Utah, in Southwest USA, where 70 per cent of the 2,500,000-strong population belongs to the Mormon Church. It is estimated that there are 40,000–60,000 Mormons who continue to practise or condone the principle of plural marriage today, despite opposition by local and federal government and the mainstream Mormon Church.

The Mormon faith originated in New England, where Joseph Smith had a series of religious visions in which he received a set of gold plates from an angel; based on his translation of the plates he founded Mormonism. Smith and his followers believed that their movement was a restoration of primitive Christianity, and hence adopted the designation Latter Day Saints, following the New Testament's use of 'saints' to refer to members of early Christian communities. They took the name Church of Jesus Christ of Latter Day Saints (henceforth LDS), and considered it the New Testament Church, formed again in these latter days. The Book of Mormon established America as a chosen land destined to receive the fullness of the everlasting gospel, but it gave no details about how its peoples should observe the particulars of Old Testament law. It neither stated nor presumed any religious practices or laws similar to those in the Old Testament. This 'problem' was addressed through revelations, and early Mormons structured their Church as specified in revelations given through their prophet Smith (Charles 1987: 49; Delaney 2001; Shipps 1987; Smith and Kunz 1976: 466; Van Wagoner 1989: ix–1).

In the process of re-translating the Bible, Smith claimed to have received a revelation from God regarding plural marriage and a commandment from God to take more wives. The LDS Church believed plural marriage was instituted and practised by the earliest prophets of the Old Testament, and was restored anew to earth for the Mormon people in the nineteenth century by direct revelation from God to their prophet. Mormons considered the practice to be a requirement for entry into the highest heaven after death, which they call the 'third degree' of the Celestial Kingdom. More specifically, Mormons believed a man must marry at least three wives in order to ascend to heaven. Mormon plural marriage was in effect polygyny, with rare cases of polyandry. Most plural marriages involved sexual relations between husband and wives, though some plural marriage relations were celibate. Despite urgings from Church leaders, and the fact that no laws existed banning polygamy when Mormons announced its practice, it was only practised by a minority within the LDS Church during the mid to late nineteenth century. It is estimated that less than 10 per cent of Mormon adults in Utah entered into plural marriage or were ever part of polygamous families. The surveys further suggest that the majority of Utah polygamists in the nineteenth century had only two wives. The popular idea that nineteenth-century Mormon husbands had a large number of wives does not correspond with reality, where men very rarely had more than three or four wives. Therefore, the typical Mormon family is not and never was a polygamous family; Mormons began as monogamists, and are again (mostly) monogamists (Anderson 1937: 601; Christiansen 1963: 167; Nimkoff 1955; Rockwood 1987: 11; Smith and Kunz 1976: 471; Van Wagoner 1989: 19).

Joseph Smith was the first who practised what he called plural marriage or spiritual wifery, perhaps as early as 1833. Smith's many revelations, and the growing power of the Mormon Church, led to increasing hostility from the surrounding New England society, and so in the 1840s the majority of Mormons moved to Nauvoo, Illinois. Here, Smith secretly introduced the doctrine of plural marriage to select individuals and instituted the practice among a group of his closest associates. Some Mormon leaders at the time voiced their objection and left the Church. Most early Mormons, many with strict New England Puritan backgrounds, found polygamy as sinful as adultery in breaking the monogamous Christian covenant. For dissenters who voiced their reservations in public, punishment was often excommunication. Growing public antagonism against Smith led to charges against him, and while imprisoned, a mob rushed the jail and shot him. After Smith's assassination (or martyrdom, as Mormons see it) in 1844, the Mormons were evicted from Nauvoo. The Saints followed the second prophet Brigham Young to the Rocky Mountain Great Basin, in the present US state of Utah, then Mexican territory. In 1847, they settled in the Valley of the Great Salt Lake, now Salt Lake City. Here they established Zion, which they believed would be God's kingdom on earth and where they hoped to practise their religion without interference from the US government (Christiansen 1963: 167; Smith and Kunz 1976: 466; van Wagoner 1989: 19, 64–70).

In 1852, the Mormons had become securely established in Utah, allowing Brigham Young to publicly acknowledge and proclaim the doctrine of polygamy and urge its practice. The announcement that polygamy was being instituted as a plan to prosper Zion came as a shock to the country, but also to lay Mormons, most of whom were completely unaware of the 'celestial principle'. Many justifications were offered for the practice, such as helping widows who lost their husbands while crossing the plains to Utah, but for Mormons there was really only one reason for it: God had told the Mormons to do it. Not all Mormons could see the hand of God in the revelations, however, and suspected more earthly reasons for Smith's new doctrines. The harshest critics suggest that Smith committed adultery with Fanny Alger, a young maid in the Smith household, and later invented the doctrine of plural marriage to legitimize his immorality. To his detractors, Smith's licentiousness was illustrated by the fact that he propositioned several more women than his more than forty wives, including women who were married to other men (Anderson 1937: 602; van Wagoner 1989: 41–2).

The general opinion in the rest of the country was indeed that the practice of plural marriage was offensive. On 8 July 1862, President Abraham Lincoln signed the Morrill Anti-Bigamy Law, which forbade the practice in US territories. The law was not enforced, however, until after the civil war, where immigrants to Utah who were not members of the Church began contesting for political power. In 1871, Church President Brigham Young was indicted for adultery due to his marriage to fifty wives (which resulted in at least fifty-seven children). In 1879, the Supreme Court upheld the Morrill Act in *Reynolds vs. US* (see Chapter 9). In 1882, the Edmunds Act was passed, amending the Morrill Act by revoking the right of polygamists to vote or hold office, and allowing them to be punished without due process. In 1887, the Edmunds–Tucker act further extended the punishments of the Edmunds Act of 1882. In the same year, the US Attorney General filed a suit to seize the Church and all its assets. The Church had now lost control of the territorial government, and members and leaders of the Church were being actively pursued as fugitives. But Mormons continued to challenge the US government by refusing to obey anti-polygamy laws, arguing that their faith dispensed them from non-Mormon marriage laws and federal legislation. It was a moral and political battle that Mormons could not win, however. In 1890, Church President Woodruff and the Quorum of the Twelve Apostles (the governing body of the LDS Church) issued a statement to the press, which became known as the Manifesto. It banned the practice of plural marriage and ordered Mormons to cease polygamous relations. Those who were already in plural marriages were not forced to end them, but no new ones could be entered. The Manifesto allowed for the restitution of all Church members' rights, as well as paving the way for the statehood of Utah in 1896; Utah could not ascend to statehood as long as polygamy was permitted in the territory. Church leaders who continued to seal polygamous marriages quickly undermined the Manifesto, however. Other leaders interpreted the Manifesto as allowing polygamy anywhere but in the USA, and established polygamous settlements in Mexico and Canada, where laws prohibiting polygamy where not enforced. The settlements still exist today and remain in contact with their American counterparts (see Chapter 9). The Church was accused of disingenuousness, leading Church President J.F. Smith to issue the Second Manifesto in 1904, declaring that anyone who participated in additional plural marriages, and those officiating, would be excommunicated from the Church (Christiansen 1963: 167; Gordon 1996: 819–22, 837–9; Smith and Kunz 1976: 466).

Many Mormons left the Church when it formally began to excommunicate polygamists in the early twentieth century. They formed small isolated communities, mostly in the Rocky Mountains area, where they felt free to follow what they saw as the true principles of Mormonism. These various settlements of like-minded people coalesced into a formal organization in the late 1920s, and from then on the so-called fundamentalist movement developed into the several groups that are active today. Like their nineteenth-century forebears, contemporary Mormon fundamentalists consider the practice of plural marriage to be a requirement for entry into the highest heaven. The mainstream Church was particularly hostile to fundamentalists in the 1930s to 1950s, where their movement took form, encouraging arrests and legal action against them. In 1935, the Church was decisive in making the Utah legislature pass a law making 'cohabitation' a criminal felony. This law was used in many polygamy prosecutions in the 1930s and 1940s. The Church has continued to support enforcing laws against polygamy, vigorously disassociating itself from the practice of plural marriage, and continues to excommunicate its polygamous members. Moreover the Church has attempted to convince the public that the term Mormon fundamentalist is misrepresenting reality, because in their view polygamists are not fundamentalists in the sense of upholding the fundamental doctrines of the Church, which is opposed to polygamy. Mormon fundamentalists, however, consider themselves to be the faithful followers of Joseph Smith and his original theology. Nonetheless, the mainstream Church feels only it represents Mormonism, an argument underscored by the fact that there are about 9 million Mormons worldwide who do not practise polygamy, whereas fundamentalists number only about 40,000–60,000 (Altman and Ginat 1996; van Wagoner 1989: 191).

In the period from the 1950s until the new wave of anti-bigamy prosecutions at the turn of the twenty-first century, polygamists were rarely prosecuted. This was in line with the increasing tolerance of variant lifestyles, and the view that polygamists were religious fanatics rather than criminals (Van Wagoner 1989: xi). But the climate is changing for polygamists, who are coming under increasing pressure from the authorities and the general public, not least because of the increasing public awareness of child abuse and paedophilia. In some groups it is considered acceptable for older men to marry under-age girls as young as 13–15 years old. This practice, which apart from polygamy itself is illegal in most states, has generated public controversy. The Utah government has taken action by raising the age of consent. The 2006 arrest of Warren Jeffs, a fundamentalist leader, on charges of sexual conduct with a minor, conspiracy to conduct sex with a minor, arranging marriages between older men and under-age girls, and several other charges, signals a tougher new stance against polygamy. Warren Jeffs, the second son of his late father's fourth wife, was placed on the FBI Ten Most Wanted list and was arrested after he had been on the run for two years. Along with such recent high-profile cases as that against Tom Green, who was sentenced to life in prison for bigamy and statutory rape of a minor in Utah in 2001, federal and state prosecutors are beginning to target America's polygamous communities. But polygamists have also turned to the law and are lobbying for their right to practise plural marriage as part of their First Amendment rights. For a full discussion of the future of polygamy in America, see Chapter 9.

Mormons have endured persecution for their beliefs ever since the religion was founded in the early nineteenth century; they have been derided for their religious beliefs, their secrecy, their hierarchical organization and their unquestioning obedience to self-proclaimed prophets. For many converts, acceptance of Mormonism meant being cast out by family and community. Their common violation of conventional behavioural and religious norms unified the Saints, however, who early on became convinced of the peculiarity of their ways. Mormons today continue to feel distinct from non-Mormons. They cultivate their exclusivity by a tendency to orient themselves more towards the norms of nineteenth-century American family life, as they understand it, than towards contemporary norms. Today's polygamists frame their struggle as a continuation of their nineteenth-century forebears' opposition to a federal government bent on preventing the Lord's chosen people from practising their God-ordained right and consider it, as they did, a badge of courage and honour. Polygamists continue another tradition by establishing new polygamist communities in remote locations in the American West when they outgrow or become disaffected with their settlements of origins. In the late nineteenth century, when anti-polygamy persecution and prosecution were at their height, Church leaders established settlements in remote areas they thought were beyond the reach of government harassment, and these settlements became havens for fleeing polygamists (Anderson 1937: 601–3; Raynes 1987: 230–1; van Wagoner 1989: 102, 125).

For fundamentalists, there is an unbroken link between the Mormon past and present, for the beliefs on which they base and legitimize their polygamous practices are the same. This allows for the use of 'old' material to describe contemporary polygamists who base their beliefs and behaviours on nineteenth-century precedents, a necessary exercise as today's polygamous Mormons are, for obvious reasons, secretive communities. The following chapter will be a zigzag through time, mixing what is known of contemporary practices with descriptions of nineteenth-century Mormon polygamy. Contemporary practitioners see themselves as descendants and defenders of earlier polygamists; their belief in the practice as both Church doctrine and Mormon tradition, as well as the persecution they suffer because of it, act as self-perpetuating forces. Unlike other forms of contemporary polygamy, which in most cases have developed as part of cultural processes stretching over generations, Mormon polygamy was 'man made' from the start, proclaimed by a named individual at a given time in history. It was presented as a revealed doctrine, but it was imposed upon a group that had no cultural or religious premises for accepting and understanding it. This is still the case today, where many polygamists are new converts. Contemporary Mormon polygamy is hence the same sort of cultural reinvention as it was for nineteenth-century Mormons.

Population

The 40,000–60,000 fundamentalist Mormons live primarily in polygamous communities scattered across Utah, Idaho, Montana and Arizona. The precise numbers are impossible to establish, as many of the communities are isolated. Not all Mormon fundamentalists practise plural marriage; many old members as well as new converts are attracted to fundamentalist groups because they feel the mainstream Church is too 'liberal'. Mormon fundamentalists are divided up into several groups, none of which are associated with the official Church of Jesus Christ of Latter Day Saints. The largest polygamist group in the USA is The Fundamentalist Church of Jesus Christ of Latter Day Saints, commonly called FLDS. It is estimated to have 8,000–10,000 members. Large concentrations of members live in the twin cities of Colorado City, AZ and Hildale, UT. The FLDS tend to be very conservative in dress and lifestyle. Another large group is the Apostolic United Brethren, commonly called AUB, estimated to have about 5,000–9,000 members. The AUB is one of the more liberal groups practising plural marriage and does not authorize plural marriage for people under eighteen. The Kingston clan, also known as the Latter Day Church of Christ, may include up to 1,500 members. Several members have been charged and convicted of polygamy, not least because the Kingston clan allows marriage of under-age girls (see Chapter 9). In addition to these large groupings, there are hundreds of small polygamist clans, with memberships in the tens or hundreds, located in many parts of the USA, Canada and Mexico. The many internal splits and the emergence of new groups stem partly from political power struggles and partly from the religious underpinnings of Mormonism. Because of the belief that any individual can commune with God and experience a 'revelation', there have always been dissident groups splitting off from the main Mormon Church. These new groupings, comprising anything from a few families to several thousand people, can then decide to re-establish polygamy as a guiding principle. This tendency to fission is seen in the large number of independent Mormon polygamists who practise the principle of plural marriage based on individual revelation rather than through a Church or sect regulating the principle. It is estimated that there may be as many as 15,000 independent polygamists, many more than in any one formally organized polygamous group (Altman and Ginat 1996: 443).

Not all Mormons practising polygamy have been formally excommunicated from the Church, but they would be if discovered. Critics argue that current LDS policy is insincere, however. First, plural marriage is still a seminal doctrine to Mormons even though the Church does not teach about plural marriage except to say that it is banned and will be punished with excommunication. Joseph Smith's concept of eternal marriage, in which families can be together forever, lies at the core of salvation and thus remains central in Mormon doctrine. Although plural marriage is not essential to salvation or 'exaltation' any more, Mormon doctrine maintains that polygamy will commence again after the 'Second Coming of the Son of Man' and the 'ushering in of the Millennial Reign' and will, of necessity, be sanctioned by God. The belief that a marriage contracted with proper authority extends into the afterlife hence provides a basis for those Mormons who wish to practise polygamy today. Spouses in contemporary plural families further claim that they practise polygamy to continue meeting 'the fullness of the gospel'. By having several wives in a family, all members become 'saved'. Therefore, co-wives may 'marry' each other at marriage ceremonies to underscore the commitment all members of a plural family make to each other, a commitment that has to last into eternity (Altman and Ginat 1996: 99; Christiansen 1963: 167–9).

The process by which a woman joins a family as co-wife varies across fundamentalist groups. It is typically a communal decision to add a new wife to a family. In urban communities, the participants themselves – a husband, his wife or wives, and a prospective wife – play an active role. The group leader must approve of the union, but individuals have considerable space to pursue possible relationships, in which personal compatibility plays an important part. In rural communities, the prophet plays a stronger role in arranging marriages, sometimes without consulting the partners or families in advance. Religious doctrine has always been a major reason for plural marriages, and a Church leader may disapprove of a marriage if a man seems interested in a new wife primarily for personal reasons, for example. Courtships are generally brief and in rural communities often non-existent. They may involve husband–potential wife only, husband–current wife/wives–potential wife or indeed in some cases current wife/wives–potential wife only. The courtship phase usually emphasizes the importance of the husband–potential wife developing an intimate and unique relationship with each other so as to preserve some feeling of privacy in a communal setting. There are strong norms against physical intimacies prior to marriage, however, as there are among mainstream Mormons. Unlike mainstream Mormons, most fundamentalist courtships involve some combination of couple and family courting. For the established wives, a new courtship is often a time associated with feelings of jealousy, loneliness, personal neglect and a desire for the husband's attention and support. To minimize these frictions, current wives in a polygamous family will almost invariably be involved at some stage in the courtship. This 'family courtship' underscores that the bonds between wives are as important as the bonds between husband and wife in a plural family (Altman and Ginat 1996: 89, 109–19).

Fundamentalists tend to aggregate in communities where all share their specific religious basis for polygamy. Fundamentalists therefore typically find their additional spouses from within their own communities or networks of similar communities. Those who are geographically separated from other polygamous groups must use personal networks or, increasingly, the Internet to find additional spouses. Several websites now exist where polygamy partners can be found, although their most sought after profile, the young single woman wanting to become a second wife, is in short supply. The site *2Wives.com*, for example, 'Where Good Pro-Polygamy Families

Find More Wives', proclaims itself to be a non-religious site providing polygamy personals. It aims to help people wishing to be part of a 'totally-committed marriage of a husband with two wives or more, where all the wives agree 100%'. Several sites promoting polygamy have also appeared in recent years, such as *Polygamy.com* and *Pro-polygamy.com*, which beyond personals provide mission and support statements such as how polygamy benefits women, as well as advice on practical aspects of polygamy. As the polygamists become more visible, not least on the Internet, so does the anti-polygamy movement. They also have websites promoting their views, such as *polygamy.org*. This is a site for Tapestry against Polygamy, an organization that works to help under-age girls forced into polygamy, among other things (see Chapter 9).

Polygamous Family Life

Arrangements

Mormon polygamy, unlike plural marriage in other cultures, was developed within a relatively short period and without any coherent set of guiding principles for its practice. For example, the number of wives permitted was never defined, as in Muslim polygamy, which allows only four wives. There was also no set pattern of living arrangements, which were administered by individual families to fit their particular circumstances. Joseph Smith practised the principle, but was more interested in discussing its theological implications than practical arrangements. To Smith, marriages sealed by civil authority were for 'time' only, binding a husband and wife together on earth but no longer valid in the hereafter. In contrast, marriages sealed by the priesthood were for 'time and eternity', extending into the hereafter forever. Such 'celestial' marriages were considered sacramental covenants rather than secular contracts, which allowed religious leaders to perform plural marriages within the Church and hence bypass the civil system. Mormon circumvention of secular marriage was legitimized by claims that plural marriages were acts of God. Following this doctrine of eternal celestial marriage, Young and select members of the Quorum of Twelve began secretly marrying the widowed plural wives of Smith after his death. It was a common benefit of polygamy cited by Mormon leaders, namely that it allowed older women and widows to achieve security and support through new marriages for 'time', that is, in earthly life, while remaining sealed to their original husband 'for eternity'. Mormons leaned on the old biblical custom of the levirate, whereby a man should marry his deceased brother's wives in order to take care of them, while the wives remained socially married to their deceased husband. Contemporary Mormon fundamentalists still adhere strongly to these principles and maintain that several priesthood holders were secretly commissioned to continue the practice as individuals rather than as Church representatives after the Second Manifesto banned polygamy once and for all. This allows plural marriages to be performed today by special dispensation of priesthood authority independent of the Church organization (Altman and Ginat 1996; van Wagoner 1989).

Modern fundamentalist weddings are by nature very flexible, depending on the particular fundamentalist Church involved, as a concession to their illegality and the many years of arrests and persecutions, which encouraged hurried, secret and simple weddings. Generally, fundamentalist weddings follow the format of Western Christian marriage ceremonies, but vary according to where ceremonies are held, who officiates, who attends and what role co-wives play. The first marriages of Mormon polygynists are often civil marriages, whereas subsequent plural marriages take place within the fundamentalist Church. Because they are illegal, they cannot be performed by publicly authorized officials or documented in civil records. Ideally, all wives of a polygamous husband should attend the wedding ceremony of his new wife. In some cases, established wives actively participate in their husband's plural wedding, which primarily formalizes the bond between him and his new wife, but also allows wives to make wows to each other. Co-wife sealing is more common in urban communities, whereas in rural fundamentalist communities wives may not be present. The formalization of bonds between co-wives symbolizes the communal nature of weddings and plural family life, as well as reflecting early Mormon times, where women were also crucial parts of each other's lives. The concept of 'sisterhood' was popularly applied to the official organizations for Mormon women, and Mormon co-wives were and are still known as 'sister-wives' (Altman and Ginat 1996: 126–36; Derr 1987: 154–68).

Living arrangements of polygamists reflect the variable, 'experimental' nature of much of their culture. In the nineteenth century, a diversity of arrangements emerged as Mormons struggled to come to terms with this new and radical marital principle. During the half century in which the practice was officially encouraged, no one living pattern emerged (Raynes 1987: 229). Among wealthy and powerful nineteenth-century Mormons, like Brigham Young, all women might live together in one large house. Cohabitation often led to jealousy and frustration, however, so Mormon husbands typically tried to accommodate their wives in separate houses (van Wagoner 1989: 89–90). Among fundamentalists today, co-wives live in a variety of residences, either alone, in pairs or in family groups. Their living arrangements tend to change in response to changes in family composition and financial circumstances, and such factors as work requirement, childcare, personal desires and interpersonal relationships between wives. The flexible living arrangements of Mormons used to be a reflection of their fear of prosecution or discrimination, though this does not seem to be a prime consideration any more. Many contemporary polygamists are still reluctant to admit that they are part of plural families, however, and still register their children under the mother's maiden name and address to avoid exposure. Mormons who are not worried about being exposed often opt for large communal family houses, or several smaller houses next to each other to allow the family to remain close (Altman and Ginat 1996: 183–94).

A prime motivation for communal living is the financial struggle many contemporary polygamists appear to face. There are few well-to-do families, most belong to the lower or middle classes, and husbands as well as most of their wives have to work to make ends meet in the often large families. Simultaneously, living with the whole family under one roof satisfies the deeply rooted value of contemporary fundamentalists of a harmonious, unified and integrated plural family, led by a husband or father patriarch. This will prepare the plural family for its life together throughout eternity in its own heavenly universe in the hereafter. Communal living is commoner in the rural fundamentalist communities, where Church ownership of land permits larger homes for plural families. In urban areas, communal living is not always practical or possible, as houses large enough to accommodate a husband, several wives and often a very large number of children may be difficult to find or too expensive. In the city, each wife typically has her own residence. This creates a sort of 'bicycle polygyny' (Mair 1971: 154), also known from other parts of the world, where husbands are constantly on the move between different wives. Typically, husbands have no space or room of their own in any of the homes, but rather try to integrate into their respective wives' space in order to strengthen bonds and not show favouritism by living primarily in one wife's home. They may, for example, have some clothes located in each wife's cupboards, sometimes making the logistics of dressing rather complicated. The difficulties involved in living the ideal communal plural family life are a constant source of frustration for many urban fundamentalists, who often feel part of 'plural monogamy' rather than polygamy. Rural fundamentalists living in communal plural families have the opposite problem. Here, wives who must share everything with each other have a strong need for privacy, insisting on some personal and independent space and time in their daily routines. Neither urban nor rural plural living arrangements are static, however, alternating between various forms in order to accommodate both religious ideals and pragmatic realities (Altman and Ginat 1996).

Management

The greatest challenge facing contemporary plural families is that Mormon polygamy developed quickly and without firm traditions or cultural guidance as to its practice, as mentioned. In urban areas, many fundamentalists are converts who joined the fundamentalist movement as adults or when their parents joined. Converts who grew up or lived in monogamous families usually enter plural marriages with little or no personal experience of how to live a polygynous lifestyle. They hence have to experiment their way to solving all those everyday issues facing them both as individuals and as a family. Familial adjustment problems are often compounded by personal adjustment problems faced by the many converts who were raised as mainstream Mormons, and now not only have been rejected by their parent

Church, but perhaps by their natal families as well. Converts must, in other words, attempt to live a lifestyle that is not only completely unfamiliar, but also contradicts everything they were brought up to believe about family life. Converts, like all other fundamentalists, must create their own plural family style and find idiosyncratic solutions to such problems as balancing a household budget that must accommodate and satisfy perhaps thirty people. There is consequently great variation in how plural families manage their financial resources. As in all polygynous (and monogamous) societies, financial issues are a prime source of tension in the family and need to be dealt with constructively in order to ensure smooth family living. Plural families may have completely communal finances, with each adult family member contributing towards a joint budget and getting out an approximately equal share, while in other families wives prefer to manage their own budgets. Plural families typically operate with some combination of these two systems, thereby acknowledging both their collective and individual selves. As with other aspects of their lives, such systems tend to change as familial circumstances change (Altman and Ginat 1996).

Such problems have always formed part of Mormon polygamous practice. The problem was that polygamy in the period from 1852 to 1890, when openly advocated by the Mormons, was never really an integrated cultural institution but rather a symbol of status and inclusion in the inner Mormon circle of power. Polygamy had allowed Joseph Smith to create an exclusive fraternity of men, among them his successor Brigham Young. Mormon men who wanted to scale the Church hierarchy felt pressured to live polygamously; their willingness to engage in plural marriage was considered a reflection of their loyalty to Joseph Smith and the teachings of the Church. Church leaders would threaten monogamous men with excommunication, or at least admonish them that they would lose not only their place in the hereafter but also their one wife to more obedient polygamists. Many men with monogamous backgrounds probably practised plural marriage without believing in the principles because of such pressures; some men were probably willing to bend their personal principles in order to advance in the Church hierarchy. There were widespread doubts among the early Mormons as to the 'worthiness' of more than a few exceptional men and women to live in polygamy. Doubts could also divide families into husbands who may have come to terms with polygamy and wives and children who may not have. Many polygamous Mormon men probably had guilt feelings over their violation of monogamous mores, but they received only little help or guidance from fellow practitioners. Instead, polygynists found strength in the higher status they mostly enjoyed in their local communities as well as in the anticipation of the extra glory awaiting them in the celestial kingdom. Mormons who could convince themselves of the world's sinfulness and the Saints' moral high ground were also better able to ignore the vigorous and often virulent opposition to polygamy from the rest of the country (Altman and Ginat 1996: 28; Hullet 1943: 279–82; van Wagoner 1989: 97).

With most contemporary fundamentalist Mormons pursuing some version of nineteenth-century family life, tensions are as inherent in polygamous marriages today as they were 150 years ago. There is consequently the same wide variety of polygamous family patterns in today's plural marriages as there was in the nineteenth century. The variation is partially a result of, and reinforced by, the social isolation polygamous families often live in; they are ostracized from the mainstream Mormon Church and from American society at large, and in some cases from rival polygamous communities as well. This makes fundamentalists highly dependent on each other for social and emotional support, and often for their economic well being as well. This support is crucial as individuals or families struggle to live a plural lifestyle, but also subjects people to strong pressures to be completely loyal to the norms and values, as well as the leaders, of their fundamentalist communities. For rural fundamentalists, all aspects of their lives are intertwined with their Church: religious affairs, civil government, education, public services, work, business, home and social life. Rural communities are often very conservative and isolate themselves from the surrounding society. In urban areas, the Church has less direct influence on fundamentalists' way of life, even though allegiance to Church doctrine remains strong; the communities are less conservative and engage more with the surrounding society. This gives more room for experimental lifestyles (Altman and Ginat 1996: 61–7).

Polygamous Sex Life

Reproduction

When Brigham Young brought up to 60,000 Saints to Utah, he told his followers to be strong or be overwhelmed by their enemies. This called for a rapid birth rate and every woman was expected to do her duty. Mormon women have lived up to this duty ever since; in the early twentieth century a Utah woman had over eight children on average (Anderson 1937: 601–7). The birth rate in 1970 was 27 births per 1,000 population while the national birth rate was 14 per 1,000 population, giving Utah the highest birth rate in the nation. Utah's population is 70 per cent Mormon and, apart from higher birth and marriage rates than the rest of the country, it means lower divorce, illegitimacy and abortion rates as well (Raynes 1987: 230, 240). The prime focus for a Mormon woman from babyhood onwards was and still is children. A good mother was expected to devote all her time to having all the children possible and raising them. For Mormon women, bringing up children by Church rules was a full-time job, and very few women were able or willing to avoid this Church-ordained duty; failure to have children gave a husband a legitimate reason to marry a second wife in order to have children (Anderson 1937: 605–6). Surveys suggest that women in childbearing years were attracted to Mormonism, as there were more women than men in this age group among early Mormons. Polygamy was seen as a practical and honourable route to marriage and motherhood for thousands of women who might have remained unmarried in a monogamous society. But Mormon emphasis on procreation went further than providing new members for the Church. It became the basis for the Mormon concept of humanity's progress to divinity. Salvation became a family affair revolving around a husband whose plural wives and children were sealed to him for eternity under the 'new and everlasting covenant' (van Wagoner 1989).

The continuity of the Mormon family is thus vastly extended into the celestial world. Marriage is a tie that outlasts this life, and the family continues and grows in the next existence; the father is the ruler of a constantly expanding kingdom, which recruits its members by birth and by post-mortem baptism of forebears. Joseph Smith taught that Saints had spiritual obligations towards unenlightened dead ancestors and friends, and introduced the concept of 'baptism for the dead'. With this bond between the living and the dead, every family in the next life becomes a tribe, with the father at the head like a patriarch in ancient Israel. The status of the Mormon father is also elevated in earthly life. He is the priest or high priest of the family, holding the 'keys of salvation', and it is only through him that the family can be saved. Furthermore, every man or woman is great in direct proportion to his or her offspring, encouraging large earthly families: the more children, the more salvation. Women are responsible for children's upbringing and socialization, and children are very important to women for personal, religious and status reasons. Children can therefore be a source of competition and conflict between wives in plural families (see below). Today's plural wives maintain the earlier Mormon pattern of very high birth rates, partly perhaps because of the competition that can exist between co-wives. Very large numbers of children are not unusual in plural families, with some women giving birth to ten to twelve children each (Altman and Ginat 1996: 373; Anderson 1937: 607; Hullet 1943: 281; van Wagoner 1989: 27 n.10, 56).

The early Mormon emphasis on women's childbearing and rearing role reflected general American attitudes of the time, but Mormons went further in emphasizing children at the expense of other aspects of marriage. Church leaders, recognizing the emotional trauma that polygamy could induce, encouraged plural wives to focus their attentions on their children rather than on their husbands, as well as on Church and community activities. Mormon children were considered as 'stars in a mother's crown', 'her glory in heaven and honor on this earth'. The focus on children meant that plural wives should attempt to distance themselves emotionally from their husbands, for love 'should have no existence in polygamy'. Love leads to jealousy and heartache, something most sister-wives probably experienced on some level (Derr 1987: 167; van Wagoner 1989: 101–2). Children are still highly valued in Mormon communities, but one major change is that love and affection are now central features of marriage for modern plural families. Their nineteenth-century counterparts downplayed love and emphasized religious duty as the basis for plural marriage. Today, love runs parallel to religious commitments and is emphasized in the importance accorded the relationships between a husband and his individual wives. Ideally, sister-wives should also love each other (Altman and Ginat 1996: 343).

Sexual Relations

Mormon sexuality, today as in the nineteenth century, labours under the paradox that sex is God given and therefore good, yet sexual drives are instinctual and carnal, and therefore bad. The debate about whether sex has lawful functions beyond procreation has been intense. In articles and speeches on sexuality, general authorities, Church leaders and lay members stress that sex is God ordained and positive in marriage but sinful outside marriage. Contemporary Mormons have markedly lower rates of premarital sexual intercourse and their premarital sexual norms are strikingly more conservative than the rest of the country, particularly compared to non-Mormon populations in the same areas. Mormon conservatism in sexual matters is quite resistant to change, and sexual conservatism is actually increasing among Mormons, who are becoming more restrictive in their sexual norms as the outside world becomes more liberal. This was not so in early Mormonism, where many verses in the Doctrines and Covenants are devoted to the issue of adultery. Adulterers were to be forgiven if they repented and severed from the Church if they did not. However, women who had married under the new and everlasting covenant and then committed adultery were to be destroyed, while a man only suffered the penalty of having his wife transferred to another worthier man, without consulting the wife. Many Mormon men apparently lost their wives as punishment or were 'tested' by being asked to give up their wives. The seemingly astonishing number of Mormons who were unfaithful to their wives, including polygamous wives, was seized upon by anti-polygamists, who claimed it gave further evidence that polygamous men did not respect marriage. But to Mormons, adultery could be eliminated through plural wifery, which allowed a man who lusted after a woman to marry her. Contrary to the corrupt sexual practices in the rest of the country, they had a mandate given by God, through a revelation, commanding faithful Mormon men to marry more than one wife (Charles 1987: 46–7; Gordon 1996: 844; Raynes 1987: 231–41).

Joseph Smith, who introduced the principle of plural marriage to his followers, revealed in many of his statements a basically positive attitude towards sexual expression, and the difficulty he sometimes had in keeping his own sexual impulses in check. Smith declared sex to be eternal in the form of eternal marriage, eternal procreation and 'eternal lives'. When polygamy was instituted, he emphasized its positive features, though he did on occasion acknowledge the practical difficulties of living with several marriage partners, as he confronted them at home with his first wife, Emma (Raynes 1987: 237). Mormon marriage was not primarily about sex, however, rather sex was necessary to beget children. 'Contrary to popular 19th century notions about polygamy, the Mormon harem, dominated by lascivious males with hyperactive libidos, did not exist. The image of unlimited lust was largely the creation of Gentile travelers to Salt Lake City ... Mormon plural marriage, dedicated to propagating the species righteously and dispassionately, ... was essentially puritanical' (van Wagoner 1989: 89). The contemporary Mormon alignment with nineteenth-century family life models remains in evidence not just through the continuation of the tradition of high birth rates, strict morals outside of marriage and very low premarital sex rates, but also by the enjoyment of sex beyond procreative functions. Among fundamentalist Mormons living in plural families, sexuality appears to be as natural an element of their marriages as among monogamous couples, with the difference that husbands have to accommodate the different needs of the different wives according to some rotation system. Sexual jealousy is an ever-present problem in plural families, which needs to be addressed.

The family management experimentation among contemporary polygamists is most clearly seen in the rotation process by which husbands visit their wives. A functioning and mutually satisfying rotation system is crucial for family stability, as conjugal visits have the greatest potential for creating tension among sister-wives. Some families follow inflexible systems where visits are organized around a rigid schedule, others opt for a very loose and unstructured system where visits are organized *ad hoc* according to the wishes of the husband and his wives, while some operate a flexible system whereby the husband visits his wives according to a schedule which can be changed to take special circumstances such as birthdays into consideration (Altman and Ginat 1996: 277). The Mormon husband is the family patriarch and leader, and can in principle follow whatever system he sees fit without consulting his wives; in reality wives have great or equal influence on the running of family affairs (Derr 1987: 232). A husband's insistence on unilateral decisions would in most cases be counterproductive, as this invariably leads to accusations of neglect and favouritism. Families operating very loose rotation systems typically suffer from such problems.

Polygamous Social Life

Social Relations

Contrary to popular stereotypes, nineteenth-century Mormon women generally endorsed plural marriage in line with their husbands and their Church. Among the early converts, women in their childbearing years outnumbered men in this age group. Here was a problem and polygamy was the answer! Despite warnings from family and friends, women were not afraid of Mormonism, and much less of polygamy, and they defended plural marriage. 'Another prevalent 19th century misconception about Mormon polygamy was that women were dehumanized by the practice' (van Wagoner 1989: 89). Nonetheless, there were undoubtedly women who did not enjoy becoming part of a plural marriage and suddenly having to share their husband with a sister-wife. Much of the suffering plural marriage may have caused for individual women would not have been made public in the nineteenth century, however. Unhappy plural wives could not publicly admit their antipathy out of loyalty to the Church and fellow Saints. Church members, acknowledging non-Mormon feelings towards polygamy, might have tended to present a 'storybook polygamy' rather than exposing the difficulties involved in trying to live such a complex and challenging lifestyle. Among twentieth-century Mormons, two out of three respondents in a study said they could not love their spouses as much in polygamous relationships as in monogamous ones. The same feelings may have been behind strained relations in early Mormon polygamous marriages (Anderson 1937: 602–3; Christiansen 1963: 169; van Wagoner 1989: 94).

Today, as in the nineteenth century, a sizeable proportion of women appear to enter polygamous marriage involuntarily under pressure, and for them polygamy can become a burden. But just as many or even more contemporary Mormon women, as their nineteenth-century forebears, appear to strongly support the practice of plural marriage. Women who become plural wives know that the role requires both spiritual commitment and emotional suffering; as sister-wives they become part of a sisterhood whose underlying principle is the individual and collective conviction that plural marriage is a 'holy principle' (Derr 1987: 164–7). In a study of women in an AUB polygamous community, Bennion (1998) describes how plural wives achieve economic security and personal autonomy through their female networks. Rather than being subjugated and helpless victims of a male-dominated culture, as they are often portrayed to be, women in these polygamous groups were quickly integrated and enjoyed upward social mobility. This explains why so many female converts join this group and stay there; the women are typically attempting to improve their socio-economic status and in the process leave behind their marginal status in the mainstream Mormon Church. Increasing numbers of mainstream Mormon women are starting to consider polygamy as a solution to such difficulties as single-motherhood, spinsterhood, poverty and loneliness. For the women already 'living the principle', often in isolated polygamous settlements, new wives are seen as new companions to socialize with, friends who will help you cope with an often hostile outside world, and co-workers who will help you run the household. As such, sister-wives can be important and cherished parts of each other's lives (Altman and Ginat 1996: 99).

Some contemporary proponents of plural marriage have even gone as far as suggesting that polygamy could help today's working mothers, who often find it hard to balance work and family life (see Kilbride 1994). For many career women it has meant not having children: having a sister-wife would permit those women keen to pursue a career outside the home also to have children, as they could leave them in the hands of women they trusted. Similar suggestions were made in the nineteenth century, when women were encouraged to participate in economic activities designed to make Mormons economically independent of surrounding non-Mormon populations (van Wagoner 1989: 102). It is a system that works well in traditional polygamous societies, where co-wives rely on each other for childminding and various domestic tasks in order to pursue other activities. Many contemporary Mormon families practise this system already, as economic circumstances force wives to work to make ends meet in often very large families. For some it may work, for others it can become a source of tension and jealousy when one wife is pursuing a career outside the home, while the other in effect becomes reduced to a housemaid and childminder (Merrill 1975). Tensions also typically arise over budgetary issues when housewives spend money earned by working wives. Moreover, today as in the nineteenth century, Mormon women's extensive mothering duties mean that few are able to pursue full-time outside careers. Most contemporary polygamist Mormon women subscribe to some version of the nineteenth century's strictly circumscribed gender roles, which would rule out professional careers for most of them. Mormons today thus have to contend with contrasting messages of expansive, public female roles from the larger society versus constrictive, domestic roles from the Church. For example, Mormon teachings suggest that husbands should head the family but modern couples generally feel that both partners should jointly steer the marriage. This paradox causes considerable tension for many Mormon women today, and will probably continue to do so (Raynes 1987: 233–6).

Tensions may similarly exist among children in fundamentalist polygamous families. Despite religious and communal ideals of a harmonious plural family living together in one household, and the closeness of half siblings in polygamous families, feelings and affections between full siblings are much more pronounced in most families. Fathers may try to instil in their children that they are all part of a single family and should not think about siblings of a different mother as 'half' brother or sister. In the nineteenth century, outside observers noted that in close-knit plural families it was often difficult to determine which children were the biological offspring of which wife because of strong bonds of affection between children and their 'aunts', as sister-wives were called. Such harmonious feelings might have been particularly dominant in polygamous families where the wives were blood sisters or even mothers and daughters, or where families were striving to live up to the ideal of a large communal household. However, this principle of sibling equality is difficult to adhere to for mothers, who almost invariably love their own children more. The mother–child bond is exclusive in virtually all polygamous populations, including those practising 'group marriage', where all 'fathers' share the paternity of children. The biological mother of each child will invariably be known and socially recognized within the family, even if the child refers to all its fathers' wives as 'mother' (see chapters 2 and 6). Generally in polygamous populations, the difference between full siblings and half siblings is socially important (Radcliffe-Brown 1950: 5).

The mother–child bond is indeed emphasized in Mormon plural families, where children are taught to distinguish between their own mother and the other wives of their father, whom they traditionally refer to as 'aunts'. For mothers, the husband's perceived differential treatment of children by different wives is often a source of great tension. Mothers are very sensitive to how fairly their husband treats their children as well as how their children are cared for and disciplined by other wives. The husband/father is the central figure in establishing acceptable family patterns, but is often challenged by the very large number of children in plural families, perhaps as many as sixty or seventy. When directly asked, many polygamous fathers do not know how many children are in their family, what all their names are or how many children each wife has (Altman and Ginat 1996: 423–30; Derr 1987: 166–8; Jankowiak and Diderich 2000). The ideal of harmonious plural family life can hence easily be threatened by husbands' perceived transgressions involving children and may sometimes lead to marital break-up.

Divorce

Mormons who have married in a Mormon temple must have a 'cancellation of sealings' granted by the Church if they want a divorce. Such divorces are colloquially referred to as 'temple divorces'. Utah's divorce rate is equal to the national average, whereas the rate of Mormon 'temple divorces' is only one-fifth of the national average. Utah women marrying in a temple are on average two years older than those marrying in civil ceremonies, and higher ages at marriage and marriages performed religiously typically lead to a lower divorce rate. There are for obvious reasons no statistics on divorce in polygamous marriages, as they are technically illegal and hence cannot be undone if they have not been registered in the first place. In the nineteenth century, divorces in polygamous marriages were common, and granted solely by the Mormon religious courts because plural marriage had been declared illegal after the 1862 Morrill Anti-Bigamy Law banned the practice in US territories. Presumably the same process is at work in polygamous communities today, where the Church leaders who feel they have a legitimate right to marry people polygamously also have the authority to divorce them. How often this happen remains unknown, though there do not appear to be many divorces in fundamentalist communities today. One reason may be that people are willing to endure both external pressures to give up their lifestyle as well as the internal pressures it generates because they believe in the religious righteousness of plural family life (Altman and Ginat 1996: 439; Gordon 1996: 843; Raynes 1987: 230).

Present-day Mormon fundamentalists follow the nineteenth-century Mormon divorce system, which was based on Joseph Smith's view that civil marriages not sealed by his blessing were invalid. He had the authority to release a woman from her earthly marriage and seal her to himself or to another man with no stigma of adultery. A woman could also obtain a divorce if a temple blessing had occurred, following appropriate divorce proceedings. If she wanted to be sealed to a man of higher standing and authority in the Church hierarchy than her present husband, however, no divorce proceedings would be required. It clearly benefited Church leaders, as their high rank in the priesthood automatically allowed them to marry any woman, even those already married. This flexible divorce system was created to facilitate quick civil divorces for converts whose spouses had not become Mormon so they could remarry within the faith. It was primarily aimed at, and used by, the many female converts married to non-Mormon men, allowing them to leave such marriages behind, marry Mormon men and produce Mormon children. The suggestion that non-Mormon or lay Mormon husbands could not take their wives to the highest degree of the Celestial Kingdom sometimes resulted in the creation of complex polyandrous trios, however, which could only be legally resolved when the first husband sought a divorce. In 1846, Zina Jacobs, six months pregnant by her husband Henry, was resealed by proxy to the murdered Smith and 'sealed for time' to Brigham Young. Her faithful first husband Henry Jacobs stood as an official witness to both ceremonies. Effectively, Zina had two husbands here on earth with whom she could have sexual relations. Brigham Young had already been 'sealed' in 1843 to another woman who was already married, Augusta Adams Cobb. Her first husband was less tolerant than Jacobs and divorced her in 1844. To Young, they would not have been polyandrous unions, because to him and other Church leaders civil marriages were not legitimate and he could claim to have married a single woman. From a federal point of view, they were illegal polygamous marriages, however (van Wagoner 1989: 42–7).

Mormons used to be infamous for what appeared to be their frequent divorces. Utah's divorce statute was the most permissive in all of the USA in the nineteenth century, and it was considered another example of Mormon disrespect for marriage by the American public. As Utah was one of the few 'consent divorce' jurisdictions in the USA, it attracted numerous divorce petitioners after the completion of the transcontinental railroad in the 1870s. Late nineteenth-century anti-polygamous rhetoric often seized upon the ease of divorce in Utah, whereas Mormons argued that Easterners practised 'consecutive polygamy' by divorcing and then remarrying several times. By the late nineteenth century, Utah had become a virtual divorce mill, allowing anti-polygamists to use divorce as a tool in their political and ideological persecution of Mormons (Gordon 1996: 835–43; van Wagoner 1989: 92). Today, the protection of children and under-age girls has replaced divorce as a driving force in these persecutions (see Chapter 9), and the USA remains as intolerant of Mormon polygamy today as it was 150 years ago.

–6–

Hindu Polyandry in India

Polygamous Marriage

History

In Hindu India, polygamy is legally, morally and religiously prohibited. There are nonetheless small pockets of polyandrous people in the Himalayas; Hindus who based on centuries-old tradition continue to practise polygamy despite it being prohibited by the Hindu Code Bill (Sharma 1980: 199). The polyandrous peoples described in this chapter live in the lower ranges of the Himalayas from south-eastern Kashmir across northernmost India and through Nepal, and are collectively called Paharis, literally 'of the mountains' (Berreman 1962). The focus will be on the inhabitants of the Jaunsar Bawar region of the Dehradun district in the Central Himalaya area of Uttar Pradesh. The Jaunsar Bawar region is particularly interesting because monogamy, polygyny and fraternal polyandry, including a combination of polygyny and polyandry approximating group marriage, appear in the same villages and even in the same families. It thus offers a unique glimpse into Hindu polygamy.

There are few sources that can illustrate the history of Jaunsar Bawar polyandry; it is generally believed that peoples emigrating from the Himalayas brought the practices with them to India and thus spread the custom. Traditional religious practices and cultural norms appear to have made the people of Jaunsar Bawar accept polyandry in spite of opposition to the practice from the neighbouring monogamous peoples of the plains. The present distribution of polyandry in the Himalayas appears to reflect regional divergence from a common source, which also affected other areas of society such as language, dress and forms of worship. The cultural patterns of the Western Himalayas differ in a number of ways from those of the Central and Eastern Himalayas, a differentiation caused and supported in part by the relative regional isolation of the societies; regional isolation appears to encourage the development and maintenance of polyandrous practices (Berreman 1962; Parmar 1975; Raha 1987).

Polyandrous systems are characterized by diverse forms and functions, which may vary from population to population within the same general area. Some of the societies in the area may be polyandrous, while others practise monogamy and polygyny. Polyandry, like polygyny, is not a unitary institution with similar functional attributes or perceived benefits wherever it is found; it is hence not possible to establish exactly what gives rise to polyandry in some areas but not in others (Berreman 1962: 72). Where polyandry is practised in India, there are always nearby populations living under similar socio-economic circumstances, which do not tolerate fraternal polyandry or wife-sharing. Marital relations very similar to those practised in polyandrous marriages are nonetheless found over a wide area of India (Peter 1963: 574). To the east of Jaunsar Bawar, for example, in the Garwhal region, people are vehemently opposed to polyandry, but the sexual relations within families are actually quite similar to those within the polyandrous families of Jaunsar Bawar. In Garwhal, brothers have rights of sexual access to each others' wives, but every man has his own wife and her children are his only; children are only passed on to another brother through the levirate upon their father's death. This disqualifies it as 'classic polyandry', which is based on one wife being married, at least *de facto*, to several husbands, and is rather a form of 'wife-sharing'. In the Himalayan Hills, however, polyandry and *monandry* (having only one husband at a time) are both based on the central principle of 'equivalence of brothers': a group of brothers constitute a socio-economic unit holding various rights and property in common, including wives. Marriage is a group transaction, in which the family's collective payment for a woman entitles the whole family to make collective use of her economic, sexual and reproductive services. In Jaunsar Bawar, all her services are shared, whereas in Garwhal only her economic and sexual services are shared, while her reproductive services are exclusive, even if the specific biological father of a particular child can rarely be established. Whether social fatherhood is shared or exclusive thus represents a major difference in values between polyandrous and monandrous systems in the region, if less in practice (Berreman 1962: 66).

The Jaunsaries have undergone a number of classification and developmental changes. At present, they are a scheduled tribe, and have been so since the Jaunsar Bawar area was declared a scheduled tribe area in 1967. The Jaunsaries have also experienced great changes in their matrimonial patterns in recent years. In India, polyandry was generally practised in the interior of states where the peoples' relative isolation was maintained until the first decades of British colonial rule. These regions are now being integrated into modern India by the opening of roads and railways as well as access to education and modern communications. Various developmental programmes are also altering the socio-economic foundations of polyandry, a process occurring in all regions of India where polyandry is practised. Development in Jaunsar Bawar has meant the growing denudation of forests and their denial to the people, the growing impact of the monetary market economy, trade and commerce, cash crops, education, party politics and the growing administrative integration of the region. These factors have all helped create an improvement in people's financial conditions, educational facilities and employment opportunities, which in turn has created new cultural and social norms. Polyandry is now losing out to monogamy. Indian development policies, either through legislation or administrative measures, undermine the social economy of polyandrous peoples, and they have generally not enforced any policies that aim to protect the peoples' particular social organization while attempting to improve their living standards. If monogamy is enforced, either through legislation or social reform, the partition of property following from monogamous family structures will destroy the economic foundations of people who have arranged their economy on polyandrous family structures. Several studies have thus highlighted that traditional cultural patterns centring on polyandry are rapidly disappearing, and today monogamy dominates in Jaunsar Bawar. This process is particularly evident among Jaunsaries who have an education or have travelled, because the increasing contact with neighbouring non-polyandrous societies of the plains has made them shameful of, and negative towards, polyandry and its associated practices. Since independence, India has also been swept by various social reforms, and there have been many proposals on how to change what most Indians see as the backward and un-Hindu (and in fact illegal) polyandrous customs to bring them up to what is presumed to be modern and Hindu level. The existence of polyandry in a country that is overwhelmingly Hindu, and in a region considered sacred by Hindus, causes great resentment among mainland Hindus (Majumdar 1963; Parmar 1975; Raha 1987; Saksena 1962; Samal, Chauhan and Fernando 1996; Samal, Farber, Farooquee and Rawat 1996; Tyagi 1997).

Population

Why do people in Jaunsar Bawar become part of polyandrous families when monogamous or polygynous family forms are also practised and socially acceptable? If one looks at individual reasons, Jaunsaries tend to focus on polyandry's role in maintaining harmony and solidarity in the family. In fact, reducing quarrels among brothers was the reason given by most people for practising polyandry, followed by avoiding sisters-in-laws that could create conflicts between brothers (i.e. their husbands). Many Jaunsari women prefer to have several men maintaining them and their children because it gives them greater security relative to having only one husband, in terms of both standard of living and physical protection. Both men and women emphasize that one of the crucial advantages of having several men in a household is the protection it affords to the wife in a dangerous country when her husband is away. A woman's and her offspring's chances of survival are greater in Jaunsar Bawar when she has a group of brothers maintaining her, leading to the perpetuation of this lifestyle. The principle of 'equivalence of brothers' in economic and sexual matters in patrilineal societies is clearly illustrated when a husband leaves his wife for extended periods: his brothers will take his place, protect their common wife, and if she becomes pregnant during her husband's absence, it is in keeping with the shared paternity of the co-husbands in polyandry. Wife-sharing within monandrous systems may provide similar benefits, though the reproductive exclusivity required may create different expectations and behaviours (Berreman 1962).

Regarding Pahari people's personal inclinations towards polyandry, some have suggested that women want to have several husbands in order to be happier and have a better sex life (see below), as well as to increase their prestige in the family and community. Just like men in polygynous societies may acquire more wives for prestige reasons, so women in polyandrous societies strive for the prestige that many husbands confer (Peter 1963: 526). The argument has been met with criticism, not least because it implies that women are free to choose whether to join polyandrous families; this argument will be explored in Chapter 7. It has also been suggested that men's disinclination towards polyandry is part of the reason why it is so rarely practised: the natural desire in most men is to be in exclusive possession of their wives (Peter 1963: 570, citing Westermarck 1891). Examining Tibetan polyandry, Trevithick (1997) argues that humans everywhere prefer monandry (one husband only), based on the facts that, first, polyandry is extremely rare; second, polyandry is never the only allowed marital form; third, when polyandry is fraternal, it is often functionally monandrous; fourth, when polyandry is non-fraternal, it is also non-residential and tending towards monandry; fifth, polyandry is always apt to 'fission' into monogamy. For Pahari men practising polyandry, such 'natural desires' to possess their wives exclusively must be suppressed, or may in fact not exist anywhere else than in the Western researcher's mind (cf. Levine 1988: 266). This would suggest that a condition for practising polyandry is the absence of factors that almost universally prevent it. Only very few peoples have no cultural norms that hinder the adoption of polyandry; most societies do not officially allow several men to have sexual access to one woman simultaneously. A male typically has the monopoly over matrimonial relations in his household, though he may in some cases have to share his sexual privileges with other, usually related, men. In polyandrous societies, this male monopoly is weakened, in part through pressure from unmarried brothers who can make communal claims on the women and thus override the dominant male's exclusive rights (Steward 1936).

The various more or less formally acknowledged polyandrous practices in the Himalayan Hills indeed all involve a community of brothers maintaining a community of wives among a community of other goods. Marriage is a 'group contract' based on the principle of 'equivalence of brothers' who share labour and property in common. Such 'equivalence of brothers' may predispose a society toward formal polyandry, but must be supported by other factors for polyandrous practices to be adopted. Economic reasons are by far the most commonly suggested. A traditional explanation for the practice of polyandry is that it emerges in inhospitable areas where an arid or unfertile natural environment is hard to exploit, and where there is consequently a constant struggle for survival. The economic circumstances make it difficult for many men to maintain a family through the fruits of their own labour, and force them to adopt a way of life that ensures the exploitation of several subsistence sources. Brotherhood loyalty provides the ideal foundation for setting up the joint family form on which polyandry is based; adelphic polyandry is by far the commonest form in the world. Polyandry allows one brother to cultivate joint land, another to breed cattle and a third to engage in trade, all to the benefit of the collective. In Jaunsar Bawar, polyandry hence allows poor men who cannot afford to marry and maintain a wife separately to combine their resources with those of their brothers, enabling them to maintain a common wife and children in a joint household. A further benefit of polyandry is that it maximizes the number of working adults in the family, while minimizing the number of children. This in turn results in fewer heirs, thereby decreasing the chances of fragmenting the patrimonial estate, a serious problem in areas like Jaunsar Bawar where there is great scarcity of land. Reducing the numbers of heirs and keeping estates undivided is another traditional explanation for the practice of polyandry. Limiting offspring and maintaining estates unpartitioned may be a consequence rather than a cause of polyandry, however, and such functional explanations must form part of a larger explanatory model in order to understand Pahari polyandry. In patriarchal Jaunsar Bawar societies, the control of male property by keeping it intact in the family remains crucially important, nonetheless (Berreman 1962, 1975; Chandra 1981; Levine 1988; Parmar 1975; Peter 1963; Saksena 1962).

Polygamous Family Life

Arrangements

In Jaunsar Bawar, marriage is predominantly polyandrous. A woman is married to the eldest of a group of brothers, and as he represents all his brothers, she is by extension married to the whole group of brothers, who are all her official husbands. The most common and preferred marital arrangement in Jaunsar Bawar is fraternal polyandry with multiple wives. A new wife customarily gets married to the eldest brother, but is, like the first wife, shared by all brothers. Several wives can be added to the household, resulting in a form of fraternal group marriage that combines polygynous and polyandrous arrangements. The basic polyandrous nature of the marital relations remains no matter how many wives are added, however. Brothers who share a wife always have the same set of fathers, in line with the patrilineal Jaunsari kinship system, but if their fathers had multiple wives, the brothers may have different mothers. This means that co-husbands could have completely different fathers and mothers, and hence in principle be classificatory rather than full or even half biological brothers. This differentiates Jaunsar Bawar polyandry from other fraternal polyandrous systems, were co-husbands are typically uterine brothers. A married woman is called a *ryanti*, and all the brothers who share her as a wife are called by the single term *khawand*, meaning husband. As paternity is shared, children born of the polyandrous union call all brothers *baba* or father. Children may only differentiate between brothers/fathers according to the function they perform in the household, such as the *baba* looking after goats or cultivating fields (Berreman 1975).

Jaunsar Bawar families are very unstable, constantly shifting between different forms as a result of frequent marriages and divorces, and occasional deaths. Thus, fraternal polyandry as well as monogamy and polygyny are found within the same villages and within the same families; non-fraternal polyandry does not occur. Surveys conducted in Jaunsari villages reveal that about 50 per cent of the marriages were polyandrous (four-fifths of which contained more husbands than wives and one-fifth an equal number of husbands and wives), 10–15 per cent were polygynous and 35–40 per cent were monogamous (Berreman 1962; Bhatt and Jain 1987). The commonest polyandrous pattern is two husbands sharing two wives, followed by two husbands sharing one wife, then three husbands sharing two wives, and so forth through various less common combinations of husbands and wives. In polygynous marriages, the norm is one husband with two wives. Most polygamous families are rather fluid, whatever their original composition, as new marriages, divorces or deaths change their composition over the years. In other words, the family might go from a classic polyandrous pattern of three brothers with one wife, then reach a stage with three brothers and three wives, then after several permutations be reduced to a polygynous pattern of one brother and two wives, only to end in the classic monogamous pattern of one brother and one wife. The presence of several wives and husbands in a household, where all have sexual access to each other, means that many of the Jaunsar Bawar families actually practise a form of fraternal group marriage, as discussed in Chapter 2. They contain all ten 'required' kinship relations: wife, co-wife, husband, co-husband, mother, father, daughter, son, brother, sister. One contrast to the 'classic' group marriage as formulated by Morgan is that while paternity is shared in Jaunsar Bawar, maternity is exclusive, as mentioned (Berreman 1975).

The Jaunsar Bawar polyandrous family typically lives in a large house where all members reside, the husbands, their wives, all the children, and sometimes the husbands' remaining fathers and their wives (usually but not necessarily the brothers' mothers) as well. Landless people typically have smaller families and less wives because of the reduced need for agricultural workers as well as their general poverty, leading to 'classic' polyandrous households with one wife only. Upon marriage a Jaunsar Bawar woman will settle in the house of her husband/s, where as a wife, she has very low status within the patrilocal and patriarchal Jaunsari society. Saksena vividly describes the drudgery of a wife's daily life in her husbands' house:

> she has to work from early morning till late in the night. She gets up early and brings water from distant water holes or springs. Then she does the cooking before she goes to the field to do each and every kind of work. She pounds paddy, breaks up clods of earth,

transplants paddy and reaps the harvest. She goes to the forests and climbs steep slopes of the mountains to cut grass. When she returns in evening, she again brings water for the whole family and does all the cooking. She is the first to get up in the morning, usually long before sunrise, and the last to go to bed. Over and above that she has to meet the sex demands of all the brothers. She is denied all rights to own property. If she is divorced, she has to leave all her ornaments and other jewellery behind. She is strictly prohibited from taking any kind of liberty with any other member of the community except her husbands. The slightest disloyalty or slightest slip will be finalized by divorce (*chut*) or lifelong ill treatment from her husbands' family. (1962: 28)

In addition to her economic and sexual duties, a Jaunsar Bawar woman of course has reproductive duties, and is expected to produce numerous, ideally male, offspring. Childbearing and rearing as well as domestic duties in the household have to be performed parallel to her economic and sexual services. A polyandrous Pahari woman's hard life in the Himalayan Hills puts into perspective the common argument that polyandry implies a higher status for women, as will be discussed in Chapter 7.

Management

In polyandrous Jaunsar Bawar households, it is the main husband (i.e. the eldest brother) who manages household affairs. He presides over all the other members, whereas his wife has some informal influence. While the wife is obliged to provide productive and reproductive services to her husband, and remain faithful to him, a husband is obliged to provide similar services to his wife in order to ensure her adequate subsistence and security. In households with several wives there are different management requirements. The main or first wife is called *ghariawi*, and has certain rights and privileges not shared by her co-wives. For example, she holds the key of the wardrobe where all garments and ornaments are stored, and she makes the decisions as to when and by whom they can be used. She manages the women and children, and exercises similar power over her co-wives as the eldest brother (her husband) exercises over his brothers. As such, she is entitled to respect from family members (Saksena 1962: 28–9). The eldest wife's dominant position is often resented by her co-wives, resulting in family tensions; co-wives are typically considered to be sources of potential strife. Quarrelling co-wives tend to create quarrelling children, as the relationships between half-siblings often reflect their mothers' relationships to each other. As adults, half-siblings may have little contact, and may consider each other rivals. Half-brothers hence typically divide their fathers' property after death and go their separate ways. Fraternal polyandrous arrangements, in which both men and women can own and inherit property, usually help reduce conflicts and strengthen solidarity between siblings: when several brothers share only one wife, their only heirs would be children of that wife. In contrast, if the brothers have several wives (shared or individual), as is common in Jaunsar Bawar, their children would have individual economic interests, increasing the chances of fragmentation of their fathers' estate (Berreman 1972: 176; Leach 1955: 185). The same phenomenon of co-wife jealousy transplanted into half-sibling rivalry has been observed in polygynous families, for example among the Nuer (Evans-Pritchard 1951).

A Jaunsari polyandrous wife is expected to treat her husband with devotion, service and respect. She refers to him as *malik*, meaning owner or simply 'man'. While Jaunsari women, and especially secondary co-wives, have low status and limited freedom within their husbands' household, a curious 'double standard' applies for women when they return to their parents' household. A woman typically visits her parents during festivals and fairs, and while there, she can enjoy herself without any restrictions. She is in fact free to do whatever she pleases and nothing she does would be considered an offence unless it is specifically prohibited. In her parents' village she is known as a *dhanti*, which changes her status from a married woman to a temporarily unmarried one. This gives her substantial freedom to pursue amorous affairs, which will be ignored as long as she is in her own village. Once a woman returns to her husbands' house, she must again accommodate herself to her circumscribed and inferior position. Nonetheless, most Pahari women do enjoy a certain amount of freedom even within their married world. Unlike many Hindu women, Pahari women are allowed to work without male companions, they can move freely around the village and talk to everybody except strangers. They do not live in separate quarters or under *purdah* (seclusion). A woman's inferior position is also softened by her ability to divorce and remarry, if she is not satisfied with her present union (Berreman 1972: 169–70; Saksena 1962: 28).

Polygamous Sex Life

Reproduction

The importance of reproduction in Jaunsar Bawar polyandrous families is illustrated most clearly by the fact that subsequent wives can and will be taken if the first wife is unable to have children. Usually a second wife is added to the family if the first wife does not give birth to a child within a reasonable period of time, suggesting that she is sterile. The addition of a second wife because the first one was unable to have children can create great tension between the co-wives, and conflicts often grow out of the threat that a fecund second wife poses to the status of a barren first wife. A woman's natural duty in Jaunsar Bawar is to give birth to children, and a childless woman consequently has a very low social status. Her inability to bear children may in some cases lead to her being branded a witch, as a barren woman is supposed to possess knowledge of witchcraft and sorcery. Childless women are accused of causing misfortunes in their villages and are blamed for whatever disasters strike their fellow villagers. The 'witches' are forced to produce counter-magic or prove their innocence, otherwise they are likely to be mistreated or be thrown out of their husbands' family. Sterility is hence a frequent cause of divorce in Jaunsar Bawar. A barren woman may, if the family is divided, be able to demand a share in the children of her co-wife (Bhatt and Jain 1987: 416–17; Saksena 1962: 29).

In polyandrous families, the eldest brother has a dominant position vis-à-vis his brothers with respect to the shared wife in the conjugal group; all wives added to the group after the original wife are normally all married to the eldest brother. The eldest brother has no exclusive sexual or reproductive rights over the wife/wives, however. The woman considers all the brothers of her husband to be her husbands as well, just as the children recognize the whole group of brothers as their fathers. In families with several husbands and wives, the biological mother of each child is always known and socially recognized, even though children address and refer to all their fathers' wives as 'mother'. In contrast, the paternity of children is regarded as shared by all brothers, and children call them all father. Children inherit from all husbands and wives as a group without regard to particular paternity or maternity. The shared paternity means that no brother can claim exclusive rights to a wife or particular children in the joint household, and if he left the household with one of the shared wives and her children, the entire joint family would most likely break up as its foundation had been challenged. If any brother wants to have his own separate wife, he is normally obliged to leave the joint household and forfeit any rights to the shared wives and their children, even though he may know that he is the biological father of some of them. He is then free to marry a new wife and set up his own monogamous household (Berreman 1962, 1975).

Sexual Relations

In Jaunsar Bawar, a married woman is expected to uphold the principles of poly-androus family life in sexual matters. Family loyalty is essential in keeping the family's property united and ensuring its economic survival. There are of course women who violate those principles as a result of their inclination towards one particular husband or another man, and hence face divorce or familial sanctions. In a polyandrous marriage, sexual adjustment between husbands and wife/wives is essential to the smooth running of the family; maladjustment leads to divorce and potentially family dissolution. A wife is required to oblige her husband's request for sex, officially to produce children and preferably male children. A husband is obliged to have regular sexual intercourse with his wife, as a woman is believed to have seven times more sexual energy than a man. As the official husband, the eldest brother has a sexual prerogative over his wife or wives. His privileged position entitles him to be with his wife whenever he is home in the joint family house. The other co-husbands typically have access to the wife when the eldest brother is away from the joint residence; since he manages household affairs, he is frequently absent from the house. A wife is expected to gratify not only her main husband's sexual needs, but his brothers' as well, at least occasionally. There are usually implicit understandings among brothers to defer to each other's access to the common wife, and sexual jealousy is consciously repressed (see below). A husband tolerates his wife's relations with his brothers as long as he is given priority and is not denied his own sexual rights, and as long as their unions take place discreetly, away from the house or in his absence. A husband might be less tolerant if one of his brothers pays too much attention to his wife (Berreman 1972: 169–73).

In polyandrous families with several wives, sexual access to the wives is arranged according to a system of priority among the brothers, such that the 'sexual hierarchy' mirrors the status hierarchy within the patriarchal family. The eldest brother has privileged sexual access to all his younger brothers' wives, who may sometimes be married to the individual younger brothers rather than as usual to the eldest brother only. Younger brothers have access to their eldest brother's wife if the age difference is not too large. As generation constitutes a crucial boundary in sexual relations, it is considered unacceptable for a very young man to have relations with a much older sister-in-law. If there is a large age gap between the eldest brother's wife and his youngest brother, for example, a second wife may be added to the family to accommodate the young man's needs. The new wife may be married to the eldest brother according to tradition, or the younger brother may himself marry her; in both cases the eldest brother will have access to the new wife. The addition of wives to a Jaunsar Bawar household does not entail that polyandrous relations stop, and the eldest brother retains preferential sexual access to all wives in the household. Younger brothers then have access to the wives according to their place in the household hierarchy. To avoid conflicts and jealousies, however, they generally try to avoid a wife in her husband's presence. Typically, a brother in need will follow a wife to the field where she works, and there have relations with her. He may also wait till her husband has left the house, as mentioned, and then attempt to have relations with his wife. A brother/co-husband is able to insist on intercourse even if the wife is not interested or objects, as it is his right. Forcing oneself on an unwilling woman is considered wrong, however. Women who have been forced to have sexual intercourse against their will may report it to their co-wife or their main husband to avoid it happening in the future; some may keep it secret to avoid strife in the family (Berreman 1972: 172–3).

Outside the confines of the extended family, both men and women in Jaunsar Bawar do enjoy some sexual freedom. Most people of the same general age and caste status in their village can and do have relations with each other, and in some cases these relations lead to marriage. For example, people generally expect that if a man and a woman meet alone in the jungle, they will have sexual intercourse. It is hence easy to suspect a wife working in the jungle of having an affair, and to protect her from the advances of non-family members, her mother-in-law or elder sister-in-law may send one of her husband's young unmarried brothers to work with her. This is done not only to protect the wife, but also to encourage relations between her and her young brother-in-law. It is also a typical way in which boys are initiated into adult sexuality. A wife is expected to have at least occasional relations with her husband's brothers, real and classificatory, but is never allowed to have relations with people of her own lineage or clan: lineages and clans are strictly *exogamous* (i.e. marry outside a given group) in Jaunsar Bawar. For men, the wives of brothers and parallel cousins are permitted sexual partners, whereas the wives of sons, of brothers' sons, and of fathers' brothers are not. Sexual relations across generational lines are not permitted, and are regarded as unacceptable and deviant. Relations between unmarried but potential spouses, such as a husband and a wife's younger sister who can marry according to the sororate, are acceptable however (Berreman 1972: 172–6; Parmar 1975; Saksena 1962).

Polygamous Social Life

Social Relations

To most people unfamiliar with polyandrous practices, one of polyandry's most exotic features is several men's sexual access to one woman. In most societies that have instituted formal marriage, a husband's exclusive access to his wife is the foundation of husband–wife relations, because marriage allows men to protect their wives' sexuality and reproductive capacities. Formal marriage has little meaning if it does not entail some form of boundary around sexual access to the marriage partners. In polyandry, boundaries are also present; a wife may usually only have sexual relations with her husbands or with a certain defined group of men. The boundaries are nonetheless much more fluid in polyandrous than in polygynous or monogamous systems. The focus has therefore been on the apparent lack of sexual jealousy, which enables a husband to accept his brothers' or, in some cases, other unrelated men's access to his wife's sexuality and reproductive potential. Earlier theorists argued that a 'repression' of sexual jealousy is essential for several men to accept sharing a common wife or wives; polyandry is typically practised in inhospitable areas where survival depends on the cooperation and interdependence between several men. In order to ensure that the survival of their families has higher priority than their individual needs, men must repress whatever natural aggression or jealousy may be present towards their fellow husbands, otherwise the close association between males that polyandry entails is not possible. In fraternal polyandry, this repression is assumed to be based on the principle of equivalence of brothers (Peter 1963: 567–8).

This ability to suspend natural but disruptive feelings has been associated with the emotional make-up of people in polyandrous societies by Peter (1963: 526), who notes of polyandrous Tibetans that they 'are remarkably devoid of jealousy, but they do not seem to be moved by love either'. It may seem logical to Western eyes that lack of jealousy must be correlated with lack of love, since they both entail a suspension of strong emotional bonds between marital partners. Levine (1988: 4) argues that this view represents a male bias, since Western researchers have tended to assume that sharing a spouse is impossible for men (hence the rarity of polyandry), but not for women (hence widespread polygyny). The (male) arctic explorer Knud Rasmussen, for example, believed that two women would be more compatible in sharing a husband than two men sharing a wife (see cover photo). This interpretation thus says more about Western conceptions about gender than about the society in question's view and handling of spouse-sharing. Whatever their basis, Jaunsari men's coping mechanisms for living in polyandrous families are now being challenged by changes in local cultural norms; this will be discussed further in Chapter 9.

The inability or unwillingness to control feelings of sexual jealousy is nonetheless a challenge all polygamous spouses, regardless of their gender, face. In those polyandrous families where members follow the rules of the patriarchal society and respect the higher status ascribed to the eldest brother, sexual jealousy and other sources of conflict that may result in family dissolution may be successfully suppressed. Those families in which members cannot control their feelings will often break up into component parts; it is impossible to live together in joint families if one member attempts to establish an exclusive relationship with another member. Any signs and symptoms of jealousy or feelings of exclusiveness must be eliminated quickly in order to ensure smooth family living, but if it persists the offending party must be punished or thrown out of the family. In practice, it is difficult to eliminate such emotions altogether, however. In polyandrous families in Jaunsar Bawar, as elsewhere, conflicts typically arise over property, inheritance or the way communal work is distributed, and sexual tensions between brothers or co-husbands may be channelled into conflicts in their economic relations (Mandelbaum 1938). Shared economic interests that are considered beneficial by all normally reduce fraternal strife over a shared wife or wives. In India, the dissolution of joint families is typically not blamed on fraternal strife, but rather on sister-in-law jealousy (such as resentment against the elder sister-in-law's domination), or on quarrelling wives who force their respective husbands to take sides against their brothers. Assigning wives the blame for a family dissolution is often an attempt to hide fraternal conflicts, however. The principle of equivalence of brothers presupposes a respectful and harmonious coexistence, and if brothers are unable to live up to this principle, it may be more acceptable to blame the conflicts on their wives, because wives do not influence family reputation as directly as the brothers do (Berreman 1962, 1972: 174–6).

Divorce

In Jaunsar Bawar, divorce is known as *chut*; both husband and wife are free to separate and divorce is quite common. There are several reasons for the frequent divorces in Jaunsar Bawar. There might be problematic personality issues, as in all marriages, which make the spouses incompatible, or the wife may prefer to have another (set of) husband(s). Divorces are often directly related to the presence of several wives in the household, as mentioned. The main husband may decide to marry a second wife, but his first wife might not accept it, even though it is socially legitimate. First wives may resent a new wife who usurps part of their influence and position. Co-*ryantis* (wives) have rights and obligations toward each other, but tensions often arise in their communal and intertwined lives. Conflicts may develop over such issues as preference and hence competition for a particular husband, attempts to avoid certain hard and unpleasant work tasks, or a husband's preferential treatment of, and attention to, one particular wife. Such co-wives' conflicts often end in divorce for the aggrieved party. Second wives, whether joining polygynous or polyandrous marriages, have a different status than first wives, and this status difference is particularly obvious in a family partition. When a household breaks up, perhaps but not necessarily because of a divorce, the first wife typically stays with the eldest brother in the communal family home. Polyandrous relations may continue despite the partition, as the younger brothers may retain their sexual access to the first wife, though no longer in the main house. Additional, often younger, wives may take up residence with the younger brothers if agreed upon, particularly if they have been married to the younger brother(s) rather than to the eldest brother. The joint family then breaks up into monogamous units. If a joint family is dissolved because of the main husband's death, the first wife is entitled to choose which remaining husband she would prefer to live with (Berreman 1972; Bhatt and Jain 1987: 416–17).

A Jaunsar Bawar wife is normally divorced through the system of *reet*, through which a woman can buy back her freedom from her husband. A woman's ability to dissolve an unsatisfactory marriage is hence based on her ability to pay compensation to her husband for some of the expenses he has incurred in the marriage, such as the marriage celebrations. In practice, it is the woman's parents or her new husband who will pay her former husband(s) whatever monetary compensation (*reet*) they demand. A wife may have very little with which to pay herself, as she is not allowed to own property; she does not even own the ornaments given to her by her husband's family, as mentioned. There has been a great increase in the size of compensation claimed and granted in recent years. This partly reflects the rising costs involved, but it is also a function of the widespread speculation in the *reet* system. Expenses incurred when marrying a young girl are not very high, so an established husband can marry several wives in addition to his main wife. As there is a pronounced gender imbalance in the region in favour of men, however, the result is a further decrease in available unmarried women. This creates a profitable opportunity for the husband who will divorce one of his wives and allow another man to marry her if he pays him compensation. This 'business' has resulted in increases in both polygyny and divorce rates in Jaunsar Bawar. The speculation has been able to develop to its present stage because women in Jaunsari society are assigned extremely low status in their husbands' household. The rising amount of compensation demanded to execute a divorce has further depressed women's status because it basically amounts to selling women in the name of *chut*. Contemporary women are very aware of, and suffer under, this problematic development, as it is becoming too expensive for women to buy back their freedom. Though changes in social attitudes in Jaunsar Bawar have helped step up attempts to counteract the speculation in the *reet* system, women are mostly still left to plead for their right to dissolve their marriage without having to pay compensation to the husband they are divorcing (Bhatt and Jain 1987: 417; Parmar 1975; Saksena 1962: 29–30).

Part III
Living Polygamy

–7–

Polygamy and Gender

Gender Dimensions

Gender Relations in Polygamy

Polygamy is, by its very nature, a gender issue. Polygamy as marriage forms part of a society's sex/gender system, and as such it is important to address the gender dimension of polygamy. A major aspect of polygamy's gender dimension is the asymmetry it implies. First, in polygyny a man can marry several women, whereas a woman can marry only one man. In polyandry, the reverse is usually the case. Second, in polygyny a man can make a second choice, he can marry a second wife for his own pleasure whereas the first wife might have been chosen as a concession to familial obligations. A woman can only marry one man at a time, and has no second choice unless she gets divorced first. Third, gender asymmetry is inherent in the often significant age difference between husband and wife, who may belong to different generations. In traditional Africa, for example, a polygynist's youngest wife may be as much as fifty years her husband's junior (Solway 1990: 46). This age discrepancy, with its concomitant prestige, power and status differences, renders gender equality in polygamy 'an impossibility' (Crosby 1937: 262–3). Differential marital privileges pave the way for potential conflict between the sexes. In polygynous societies that have seen the emancipation of women through education and new economic opportunities, polygamy's creation of status and power differentials has become a key aspect of contemporary gender relations. Particular attention must therefore be paid to power relations between husbands and wives as well as women's access to divorce in polygynous marriages. Issues of gender and power run like undercurrents through the whole discussion of polygyny, because to most women it implies unequal relations between men and women, as reflected in men's ability to take several wives versus women's one husband.

Wittrup (1990), in her study of the Mandinka of Gambia, argues that polygamy is part of a cultural logic in which gender plays a crucial role and suggests that polygyny is an arena of potential conflicts between the sexes. The problem involved in examining polygamy within the domain of cultural constructions of gender relations is whether this domain is best placed in the conventional realm of kinship and marriage, or within the political and economic spheres of society, or within its 'prestige structure' (cf. Ortner and Whitehead 1981). That is, one must first establish which realm best expresses gender relations cross-culturally. Wittrup (1990), who favours the 'prestige structure model', considers polygyny to be a cultural symbol representing Mandinka concepts about the relations between the sexes. Men who have several wives reflect Mandinka ideals of prestige and wealth and hence occupy a higher position in the social hierarchy. A strong male virility complex, which has not only sexual but also powerful political, social, economic and reproductive aspects, further encourages polygynous practices in Mandinka society. Gender relations are organized around notions of virility, associated with maleness, and lack of discipline, associated with femaleness, and this provides the cultural basis for polygyny (Wittrup 1990: 126–38). Such gender dichotomies, providing institutionalized differences between men and women, are found in many cultures and lend themselves eminently to legitimizing polygyny.

In a theory relating the intensity of the so-called pre-industrial male supremacy complex to the intensity of warfare and reproductive pressures, Harris (1983: 255) suggests that polygyny increases conflicts not only between the genders, but also within the same gender. The widespread preference for male offspring has in many areas created a shortage of women. The lack of marriage partners led to the development of systems in which access to sex and marriage was granted on the basis of being a fierce warrior, and males were forced to be aggressive in combat to get wives. Logically, this might encourage polyandry as sharing a wife might seem an easier way to obtain one than fighting for her. Instead, strong men tended to marry several women in pre-state societies with widespread warfare. Hence, men competed for women rather than sharing them, and polygynous practices created an even greater shortage of women. This resulted in sexual tensions and conflicts between men and women, as well as between junior men with no wives and senior men with several wives. The gender dimension of polygamy hence not only involves the relations between the sexes, but also very much concerns the relations between members of the same sex. Men's competition for wives has ramifications in all aspects of society, not just in how they organize their domestic arrangements. For women in polygyny, the dynamics of co-wives' relations constitute an important gender dimension. It is, for example, meaningless to discuss women's subjugation or autonomy in polygamy without specifying which wives are referred to as well as their internal hierarchy. Senior and junior wives in the same household may have radically different experiences and life conditions, such that senior wives may enjoy quite extensive autonomy, whereas the most junior wife may be little more than a house slave.

Researchers, and particularly feminist researchers, have typically correlated polygyny with the subjugation of women, because much of the research on polygyny represents it as detrimental to women. One major problem is that Western analyses and explanations of polygyny tend to focus on men and their power in a polygynous marriage. For example, Western analysts often focus on the potentially troublesome sharing of a husband's sexuality, whereas the people involved may not necessarily find 'drinking from the same cup' strange (though some might resent it, of course). Senior wives in traditional African polygynous households will typically encourage and help choose new wives for their husband, often partly to avoid having sex with him any more. Among the Marachi of western Kenya, it is considered inappropriate for a wife to have sexual relations, and hence potentially children, with her husband once her grown children marry and start bearing children of their own. This typically leads the husband to take a young second wife; she may in turn be inherited by his oldest son, typically her agemate, when he dies (Whyte 1980: 138). Researchers may also overemphasize what they consider the special qualities of men, such as exceptional economic resources, as being the basis for polygyny. Control over economic resources gives men power over women and makes women willing to share a polygynous husband with other women. To many researchers, however, the question of women's subjugation in polygyny cannot be examined without focusing on the women themselves and their internal relationships. To a woman in a polygynous marriage, the bond to other adult females, including both the husband's female kin as well as her co-wives, may constitute a more critical relationship than that with her husband for her productive, reproductive and personal achievements (Anderson 2000). Several studies have indeed demonstrated the potentially cooperative nature of polygynous relationships. It is therefore not possible to generalize as to whether polygyny is by nature competitive or cooperative. It depends on the particular polygynous context, in which co-wives may negotiate their relative statuses within the domestic group through both competitive and cooperative strategies (Solway 1990; Madhavan 2002).

It is thus essential to examine both inter- and intra-gender relations in polygamous unions in order to examine the postulated association between polygamy and the subjugation of women. The association is traditionally formulated in two ways: polygyny as primarily associated with male dominance and polyandry as primarily associated with female autonomy.

Competition or Cooperation

The nature of co-wife relations is a crucial element in relations of gender, power and status in polygynous unions, just as co-husband relations would be in polyandrous unions. One of the most salient features of co-wife relations is their internal ranking. The ranking of polygynous wives within a marriage determines not only how a wife relates to her husband but also to the other wives. The wife's ranking typically dictates her specific rights and obligations in the household as well. The commonest way wives are ranked within a household is by order of marriage to their common husband, and the one married to him longest becomes the senior wife. This is practised by the Hausa of Nigeria, for example (Smith 1953). A wife's rank may also be based on her achievements in the household, or her husband's preferences. In some polygynous systems, there are significant status differences between senior and junior wives, and high rank entails control over lower-ranking wives. In such systems, senior wives will usually organize and distribute the work load among their co-wives, divide all monetary rewards from the husband, supervise his sleeping rota, and be consulted when the husband wants to take a new wife. They also have greater authority over their co-wives and over all children. There will usually be significant age differences between high- and low-ranking wives as well, reinforcing their status differences. The co-wives, depending on their rank, will thus perceive the integration of a new wife into a polygynous household differently. An older high-ranking wife might feel less threatened by the addition of a new young wife than a low-ranking one will, as her position is more secure. In societies practising the levirate, a special problem may arise for senior wives who become widows and have to be integrated into the household of their husband's heir. They may be given special status because their previous seniority may not fit into the hierarchy of co-wives already present in the heir's household. In some leviratic societies, the widows may be allowed to remain in their deceased husbands' home in an attempt to reduce such conflicts (Clignet and Sween 1981: 453–9; Whyte 1980).

In most African systems of polygyny, co-wives' rights and obligations are carefully defined and guarantee a certain amount of equality between them, though the senior wife is usually given special powers and privileges. In other polygynous systems, senior wives may be less privileged or even worse off than junior wives. A study of polygyny among Palestinian Muslims showed, among other things, that senior wives felt they had more economic problems than junior wives did. Overall, junior wives were less dissatisfied and had higher self-esteem than senior wives (Al-Krenawi et al. 2001). Among Muslim families where all wives do not necessarily participate in domestic economic production, as in most traditional African polygynous systems for example, the younger wives may be their husbands' favourites and thus get a larger share of the resources than their older counterparts. Where a senior wife has no economic function or responsibilities towards her co-wives, she has little leverage over her husband. In African polygyny, where women usually make important economic contributions, as women age and 'work their way up' to a privileged position as senior wives, they can exercise considerable control over their junior co-wives. The power of seniority is mostly domestic, for wives in polygynous societies generally have limited control over resources and/or political authority. However, when they are geographically close to their kin and have sisters as co-wives, i.e. have female 'allies', they tend to have greater resource control and power (Yanca and Low 2004).

A second important feature of co-wife relations is therefore their backgrounds. Some polygynous husbands and wives prefer when co-wives have similar backgrounds, as this is seen as conducive to harmonious relations between them. This is most clearly seen in populations practising sororal polygyny, which presumes identical co-wife backgrounds. It is typically found in matrilineal societies, but does not necessarily increase women's autonomy vis-à-vis their husbands; sororal co-wives may be permanently subservient to the males of their natal family (Clignet and Sween 1981: 453). As mentioned, some populations condone sororal polygyny, because they believe that women who have similar backgrounds can function better together as co-wives, whereas some populations believe quite the contrary and specifically prohibit sororal polygyny. The Bulsa of northern Ghana, for example, practise a form of sororal polygyny involving a preceding female kin fostership. Through a *doglientiri* relationship, an older married woman incorporates a younger woman of her lineage into her household in anticipation of the young woman's later marriage to her husband or one of his (classificatory) brothers. The institutionalized *doglientiri* system is based on the structure of Bulsa kinship relations, where women are ritually responsible for their brothers' children and therefore have the right to adopt their daughters (Meier 1999). Here the ritual and kinship systems give women some autonomy with respect to marriage, but not necessarily in other areas of their lives. Bulsa sororal polygyny also illustrates that polygynous relations can be cooperative. Co-wives helping and being fond of each other is a feature of many polygynous unions. Little (1951: 165) describes some traditional ways in which Mende co-wives gain advantages by cooperating: co-wives may collectively, through many small nuisances, strive to make their husband's life so intolerable that he agrees to some general demand. Furthermore, a man with numerous wives can usually not control the movements of every one of them, and his wives may then cooperate in keeping each other's secrets and covering up each other's illicit affairs.

Nonetheless, studies of polygyny often focus on rivalry, antagonism and jealousy between co-wives (e.g. Fortes 1950: 281). In modern polygynous families in East Africa, the competition between co-wives is centred on access to limited resources. In a family with four wives and twenty-eight children, for example, the husband may not be able to afford school fees for all his offspring. This creates intense rivalry between the wives, who become locked in a constant struggle to secure enough funds for their own children's needs. Present economic conditions in Africa thus mostly make it impossible for co-wives to live up to the ideal of working together towards a common goal. Furthermore, the general cultural ambiguity toward polygyny in modern East Africa may also contribute to increasing co-wife conflicts, as there is little positive reinforcement for polygynous families (Kilbride and Kilbride 1990: 201–5; Meekers and Franklin 1995: 322; Solway 1990; Whyte 1980). The chronic competition between wives over resources appears to enhance the husband's dominance (e.g. Levine 1980: 287), which in turn supports the proposition that polygyny is associated with the subjugation of women. Lamphere (1974) thus suggested that polygyny is inherently competitive, because women will typically attempt to build their own nuclear family within the polygynous household, often at the expense of their co-wives and their co-wives' children. The position of women in polygynous unions does not allow them to collaborate, and women must work through men to gain power.

In contrast, Madhavan (2002) argues that polygamous households are often more cooperative than conflictual and that female empowerment can happen through cooperative strategies among women in polygynous unions. Women in polygynous families can acquire power and status through seniority, children and other culturally prescribed achievements, and they can gain freedom, mobility and autonomy from sharing productive, reproductive and domestic responsibilities with other women. Co-wives in Mali, for example, negotiate their relative statuses within the domestic group through both competitive and cooperative strategies, thereby reducing or avoiding potential conflict. Jealousies also tend to be reduced when co-wives share domestic tasks, such as cooking and childrearing responsibilities, as well as when there are strict rules regarding domestic arrangements, especially the husband's sleeping rota. Some degree of jealousy probably exists in all co-wife relations, but this does not make cooperation impossible. The degree of cooperation and competition within the household, as well as how successful a polygynous marriage is, is basically determined by how co-wives get along with one another. This in turn depends on individual personalities and personal circumstances as they are shaped by their particular cultural and socio-economic contexts. Whether a polygynous household is characterized by cooperation or competition can therefore only be revealed by an in-depth examination of individuals within these contexts (Madhavan 2002: 69; Meier 1999: 100).

In a study of female choice and male coercion models of polygyny in an Australian Aboriginal community, Chisholm and Burbank (1991) suggest that sororal co-wives were better able to reach their reproductive goals than non-sororal co-wives. Sororal polygyny hence appears to constitute the best compromise between male and female reproductive interests. This seems to support the cooperative model of polygyny developed by researchers working primarily in Africa, where co-wives in such systems as the Bulsa *doglientiri* clearly gain advantages in term of power and autonomy by collaborating. The authors nonetheless reject the female choice model. They argue that the Aboriginal women seem to have little choice in their marriages, and that the lifetime reproductive success for women in polygynous marriages was significantly lower than for those in monogamous marriages. This is precisely the conundrum facing researchers trying to argue for female empowerment through female cooperative strategies in polygynous unions. While women in a polygynous union may be able to optimize their living conditions by helping each other, can they be empowered in a situation where they might have been forced into the marriage at fourteen, as a fourth wife of a 64-year-old man? Do they have the right of divorce and access to their children if they want to leave their husband? And who decides how they spent their time, themselves or their husband? What authority and autonomy do women have if they can decide on the food schedule in the household but may not be allowed to leave the household to get an education or a job? Furthermore, are all co-wives empowered by the cooperation, or just the senior dominant ones? It may, in other words, not be enough to have power in certain domains if one is disempowered in others; not being able to freely choose or reject a spouse, for example, would seem to invalidate any power held or acquired in other areas of social life. As such it is difficult to accept polygyny as empowering to women. A similar conundrum arises in polyandrous systems such as the Nayars', described below.

Male Dominance

Power Relations in Polygamy

The matrix gender–power–polygamy is woven into the very fabric of the institution, because there is a fundamental inequality in one person having the possibility of marrying several spouses, whereas these spouses can only marry one person in return. And where there is inequality there is power. When examining power relations within polygamy, however, one cannot automatically assume where this power is located, or what indeed its substance is. As was the case for marriage, there are numerous definitions of power (e.g. Connell 1987). Here, Max Weber's (1948) classic definition is used, namely that power is the likelihood that a person within a social relationship will be able to execute his will even if others resist it.

Several researchers have grappled with the question of whether polygyny enhances female autonomy or ensures male dominance. The question is a pertinent one, because it guides how one sees polygyny at its most basic level: does polygyny involve two matricentric families attached to the same male or two patriarchal nuclear families sharing the same husband/father (Clignet and Sween 1981: 466)? While many researchers believe that polygyny suppresses women, as mentioned, others believe that polygyny may give some women considerable independence. One can find studies to support both positions, and it comes down to the particular group being studied and the particular researcher involved. Most studies seem to suggest that polygyny enhances male dominance and that polygyny clearly affects the gender hierarchy and relations within the family. For example, a study of polygyny in Ghana, where women and their domestic roles are seen as easily replaceable, revealed that there was significantly more gender inequality within families regarding such issues as reproduction and family planning in areas with high levels of polygyny than in areas with lower polygyny levels (Agadjanian and Ezeh 2000) (see Chapter 8).

A logical implication of the polygyny/male dominance theory is that polyandry would be more prevalent in societies where women have higher social status and enjoy some autonomy (cf. Stone 2006) (see below). This is clearly not always the case, as described in Chapter 6, where women in polyandrous populations in the Jaunsar Bawar region of India are assigned an extremely low status in their husbands' household, and are treated as little more than slaves. On the other hand, polyandry among the Native American Shoshone is related to a high status assigned to females. Generally, a woman's social status is not a function of the number of husbands she has. Female status and autonomy may be higher in societies that allow for non-conventional marriages for women and/or allow them to assume male roles either temporarily or permanently. For example, among the Lovedu of Southern Africa women can assume a ruling position on a par with men, including marrying other women as wives (see Chapter 1). The Nuer of Sudan similarly practise woman–woman marriages in which a (typically barren) woman may marry one or several wives. The Nuer also practise several forms of 'ghost marriages', usually involving a man marrying a wife in the name of a deceased, childless patrilineal kinsman, in order to beget children in the name of the dead man (ghost) (Evans-Pritchard 1951: 108–10). Another form of ghost marriage involves a wealthy and powerful Nuer woman marrying a dead man's ghost in order to maintain control over her resources. Had she married a living man, she would have had to relinquish her wealth and power to him as is customary for Nuer wives. Socially, she is a widow, and any children she may give birth to are the children of her ghost husband, such that the children will inherit in the name of their father but actually receive the property of their mother. Among the Mende of Sierra Leone, a chief's senior wife, rather than as normal one of his male relatives, may be placed in a position of trust in the chiefdom, in effect ascribing her a dominant male role. Other high-ranking women, such as sisters of chiefs, may similarly be ascribed the same social status as the 'big men' of the chiefdom (Little 1951). A similar pattern is found among the Lovedu of South Africa (Kuper 1982). High-ranking Mende and Lovedu women may thus have autonomy and social dominance as a result of their close association with dominant males, rather than through their own achievements or positions as wives. For low-ranking women this means low levels of autonomy and lower social status than their husbands.

Clignet and Sween (1981) have dealt extensively with the question of whether polygyny leads to male dominance or female autonomy. They have created a 'road map' of features to look for in order for researchers to answer that question. They suggest using what they call an 'interactionist' approach, which acknowledges the interdependence of marriage choices and individual behaviours in polygynous arrangements. Such interdependence varies within and between cultures, as well as between members of the same household. The distribution of power in polygyny similarly varies within and between cultures, as well as between members of the same household. Variation in women's power, and by implication their autonomy, vis-à-vis their husbands and co-wives is related not only to the privileges assigned to their rank in the household, but to other sources as well. It is important to examine whether access to female autonomy and power is shared by all co-wives in a particular household or just granted to some wives at the expense of their co-wives. Furthermore, is female autonomy and power a feature of all polygynous households in a society, or just certain households within that society? One cannot speak of women's empowerment in polygynous arrangements within a specific society if it only applies to certain women in certain households.

Clignet and Sween's (1981) 'road map' can be thought of as four cornerstones in the attempt to establish whether a particular polygynous arrangement leads to female autonomy or male dominance. It also involves examining the distinct manifestations of whatever power women may have, because it is not always possible to identify a direct connection between the sources of co-wives' power and their effects.

First, it is necessary to distinguish male and female perspectives, because men and women will make different cost–benefit decisions regarding whether to enter or leave polygynous marriages. From a male point of view, a large number of wives may be desirable to increase his agricultural labour force, give him more sexual partners or to confer him social prestige. From a female point of view, several wives may be undesirable because it will decrease each wife's individual access to the husband and other resources, and thereby create tensions with co-wives. It is therefore also necessary to distinguish between the perspective of senior and junior wives, as the roles of co-wives are not interchangeable. Tensions in polygynous marriages are not just products of individual maladjustments, but also of the co-wives' internal hierarchy. As mentioned in Chapter 6, junior co-wives typically resented the dominant position of the senior wife, and this often led to divorces in the family. A woman's level of power and autonomy hence stems in part from her position within the household hierarchy.

Second, it is necessary to distinguish individual women's mode of access to various roles within the marriage and household from the performance of such roles. Women's autonomy vis-à-vis their husbands and co-wives is influenced by their productive, reproductive and sociopsychological contributions to the household, but it is also influenced by their individual backgrounds. A woman from a high-ranking family may enjoy more autonomy in her polygynous marriage than her co-wives from low-ranking families, as illustrated by the Mende above. However, co-wives' differential backgrounds are only relevant if they result in differential domestic roles; if domestic roles are distributed according to an egalitarian system, co-wives' birth privileges will be meaningless. Similarly, women's autonomy vis-à-vis their husbands and co-wives is, as mentioned, influenced by their matrimonial rank, but again this will only be, or at least be more, relevant in societies where the hierarchy of co-wives is highly institutionalized. The marriage histories of individual women must therefore not only describe who is expected to do what, but also who in fact does what.

Third, it is necessary to distinguish polygynous arrangements along contextual lines. Polygynous arrangements may vary along ethnic lines within a community, and are influenced by the ethnic group's organizational structure, history and exposure to social change. The more complex the context in which polygynous households are located, the more alternative lifestyles are possible for individual co-wives. Female autonomy and power is indeed related to a wife's opportunities outside as well as inside the household. If a wife has few obligations towards her husband and his kin in a polygynous marriage, then polygyny may increase the autonomy of all co-wives. In a context where a husband has few rights over his wives, polygyny simply offers him a way to maintain domestic and economic services at a socially acceptable level. The same polygynous arrangements allow his wives to seek economic, social and emotional benefits outside his kin group and maintain close ties with their own kin group. Polygynous systems vary tremendously with regard to how close a contact wives are able to maintain with their family of origin, as well as with regards to wives' ability to leave their husband's household for extended or even short periods. Within individual households, co-wives may also experience variation in their freedom of movement.

A wife's autonomy and power is influenced not only by her private but also by her public involvement in activities that are considered important and valuable by her husband or society, such as having many children or making a profit on trade. Wives who work and earn money outside the home generally have more power, particularly if they are on the same occupational level as their husband. This naturally requires that the husband permit his wives to leave the household to seek employment, indicating that the wives already have some autonomy. Permission to leave a polygynous household to work is often related to a wife's matrimonial rank. In contexts where there is little differentiation between co-wives, the opportunities presented to married women by modern waged work, particularly in urban areas, may allow co-wives to gain power collectively in relation to their husband. However, while a husband may allow one or several of his wives to create and control their own economic resources, he may retain control of their social resources, deciding why, when and whom they visit. Once again, female autonomy may not necessarily be characteristic of all aspects of co-wives' lives.

Fourth, it is necessary to distinguish the effects of time and space on polygynous arrangements. Female autonomy within polygynous households does not only vary on the micro-level of individual life cycles, but also on the macro-level of historical events affecting polygynous arrangements in the society as a whole. Time is an important factor because power and autonomy can increase and decrease as wives move through various roles and statuses in the developmental cycle of their families. For example, children are usually highly valued by polygynous husbands, and reproduction will affect the power of each wife. Co-wives may, as mentioned, compete with each other to produce as many children as possible for their husband. The most fecund wife, or the one who gives birth to most boys, may then become the husband's favourite, and hence potentially most powerful, wife. A powerful wife may be able to transfer power on to her own children by giving them opportunities, such as access to secondary schooling and elite positions, denied her co-wives' children. While formal education typically bolsters the benefits that senior co-wives' children gain from their mothers' matrimonial rank, education can also give the children of junior or less powerful wives upward social mobility if they can get access to it. Education might allow them to move beyond their mothers' social status over time.

Furthermore, the effects of space on polygynous arrangements are most clearly seen in the territorial organization of domestic groups. A polygynous wife will have more autonomy if her residence is separate and independent from that of other members of the union. Her economic and social autonomy will increase with increased scattering of houses or landholdings, because scattered co-wives make it difficult for the husband to control their daily lives. With the above considerations in mind, Clignet and Sween (1981: 466) conclude that both male dominance and female autonomy vary over time and space with the life cycle of each spouse, and to resolve which one is pre-eminent would require the reconstruction of the matrimonial history of each member of the polygynous household!

Subjugation or Emancipation

The notion that polygyny subjugates women led to the idea that women's emancipation, following upon social and economic development, would eradicate polygyny. The notion has a long history and tradition in Western thought, where it forms part of a Western progress-oriented world-view. For example, socialist states typically built their constitutions on the ideology that all men are equal and that men and women are equal before the law. This gives women access to the same education and work as men. It has also meant that many socialist states have banned polygyny (or bigamy) as contrary to women's emancipation and equal rights (Moore 1988: 137). Such ideologies, which often remain thought ideals rather than acted out realities, were shared by many (early) Western observers of the non-Western world, such as missionaries and anthropologists. They typically believed that man's inevitable progress as a consequence of economic development, and its concomitant processes of social and cultural change, would destroy traditional customs like polygyny as inconsistent with the modern world. Polygyny levels have indeed been decreasing in almost every country in Africa as a result of the combined effects of urbanization, industrialization, education and the influence of Christianity. But simultaneously, informal polygamous practices such as 'outside wives', whereby a man may have both an official and unofficial wife, thus not registering as practising polygyny, is increasing in many urban areas (see Chapter 8). Modernity has not eradicated polygyny, quite the contrary: traditional ways, themselves products of adaptations to changing circumstances over time, are simply adapted to the modern world, and offer practitioners new benefits from old but reworked forms (cf. Piot 1999).

The idea that women's emancipation through development would wipe out polygyny and end its subjugation of women took its most crystalline form among Christian missionaries in Africa. The missionaries early on focused on women in polygynous marriages, whom they saw as powerless victims of an oppressive and heathen African tradition. They took on the role of women's advocates, preaching women's 'liberation' from what was considered their enslavement by polygynous males. They saw it as one of their main missions to free women from polygyny and reinstate their dignity. The only way forward for subjugated women was through Christianity, which offered women not only liberation but salvation as well. While missionaries primarily used biblical arguments to condemn polygyny, they also emphasized the absence of respect and equality between spouses. They believed that polygyny would disappear when women's status was raised, and women experienced a greater awareness of their own selves, as well as a greater awareness of marriage as a sharing reciprocal relationship rather than a subservient relationship. This change in the status of women was considered a prerequisite for Africa to move into the modern world. The closer African countries would identify themselves with countries of the Western industrial world, the closer they would necessarily come to monogamy. Polygyny was to have no place in modern, independent, ideally Christian, African nations (Notermans 2002; Reyburn 1959).

Missionaries, through their work, their sermons and their writings on polygyny, appeared to voice African women's interests, but the majority never really attempted to understand the women and their concerns and circumstances as individuals, nor attempted to include their voices in the debate (Notermans 2002: 342). Among researchers and activists today, the debate about the pros and cons of polygyny is often criticized for being tied to a Western/non-Western agenda. African (and African American) feminists criticize Western feminists for their overemphasis on gender oppression in their discussions about African polygyny and for their rudimentary understanding of the conditions and concerns of African women. Western feminists in turn criticize African feminists for often wilfully ignoring the negative aspects of polygyny; African feminists are quite divided on the issue of polygyny. To many Western feminists, polygyny is inherently oppressive to women, and as Madhavan (2002: 70) points out, many African women would probably agree. Just as many African women might not, however. The 'problem' with an analysis based on the assumption that development will bring about change and demise to the 'outdated' and oppressive practice of polygyny is that many women in Africa appear to choose polygynous over monogamous marriages even when there is no external pressure to do so, for example from relatives. Modern women do not necessarily question whether polygyny as an institution is oppressive and subjugates women, rather they choose to become part of a polygynous marriage because they consider it advantageous, and have new tools at their disposal for manipulating it. For African women, polygyny can be a way of gaining economic power, for example. For African men, polygyny still has huge prestige value; it creates power over life and of life, and thus remains very important. While some of the reasons behind polygyny may have changed, the institution is still going strong, albeit in modified forms, as will be discussed in the next chapter.

This adaptation in form rather than in content is nowhere clearer than in Cameroon, where Christian missionaries have been trying to remove polygyny from the marital repertoire for over a century, and where monogamy is a prerequisite for baptism and acceptance into the Christian Church (see Chapter 2 for a fuller description). The missions have only been partially successful, for while people in Cameroon generally consider themselves Christian, they do not see any need to abandon polygyny in order to be good Christians. In fact, quite the contrary may be the case for Cameroonian women who, as mentioned, successfully combine their polygynous lifestyle with their Christian identity. They use Christianity as a moral guide to deal with polygyny and especially with co-wife conflicts, which helps them create harmonious conditions within themselves and their marriages. Rather than challenging or opposing polygyny, the women feel that polygyny offers them a chance to show their 'true Christianity' through their handling of the inevitable tensions in their polygynous marriages. By fusing ideals and behaviours from different cultural domains into new constellations, they have developed a local variant of Christianity that supports rather than rejects polygyny. The aim of the women in Cameroon, according to Notermans, 'is to integrate Christianity in their polygynous way of life. The workable outcome of this interaction between tradition and modernity is the proliferation of the traditional in a totally new understanding of polygyny, that is Christian polygyny' (2002: 352).

Men in Cameroon have been equally reluctant to abandon polygyny, not least because it continues to be advantageous for them. In the 1950s, when land was plentiful and trade barriers low, the state encouraged men to plant cash crops. A man typically subsisted by working a plot with his wife and children, but in order to switch to cash cropping, he had to increase his holdings. This in turn created the need for more co-wives, as the many tasks involved in producing coffee, cocoa or tobacco greatly increased women's workload and hired labour was unavailable. Modern times and economic development in the form of cash cropping, introduced in colonial times, and expanded in the post-colonial period, thus created a need for more wives and more children, further reinforcing polygynous patterns. So did the extra money men received from the State for each extra child, as many children were best obtained by marrying many women. Women who suddenly got a greatly increased workload because of cash cropping would most likely be positive towards or even encourage their husband to take another wife. A co-wife to share her work burden will give a wife more freedom to pursue her own activities. She may suddenly have time to bring produce to the market, sell it and spend money on herself or her children, or to return to her home village for a visit (Reyburn 1959). Modern uses of polygyny in Cameroon illustrate that African women, whether cash cropping in rural areas or seeking emotional harmony in urban areas, may still find advantages in polygynous practices, and this makes the eradication of polygyny through women's emancipation and modernity rather unlikely.

Female Autonomy

Status Relations in Polygamy

The question of female autonomy in polygamy is nowhere better addressed than in the discussion of women's status in polyandry. It has often been assumed that polyandry implies female autonomy and hence is practised in societies where women have a high status (i.e. a high position in the social structure) and/or are matrilineal. This idea arose among nineteenth-century evolutionists who thought polyandry so strange and repugnant to men that it must have developed in ancient times when females had not yet been tamed, and would only be practised today in areas where females had considerable power. It was also a reflection of the assumed fact that polygyny is practised in societies where men have high status and/or are patrilineal. Bachofen (1861) had suggested that matrilineal descent and maternal rule emerged out of an initial and universal state of promiscuity, paving the way for polyandry. McLennan (1865, 1876) further argued that the earliest form of marriage must have been polyandry, an institution closely associated with matrilineal descent and maternal authority, because they provided solutions to paternity uncertainty at early stages of human social evolution. Such evolutionary schemes are now discredited, as mentioned, not least through studies showing that fraternal polyandry is very strongly represented in patrilineal societies, such as those in Jaunsar Bawar (see Chapter 6). While most researchers still believe that women have a higher status in matrilineal social systems, there is more disagreement about the status of women within polyandrous societies with a patrilineal social system. Patrilineality is often ambiguous in polyandrous societies, because such societies may also sanction *matrifocal*, or female-centred, marital arrangements and inheritance through females. Where marital arrangements are patrilocal, women may surrender their claims on ancestral land but receive a dowry of moveable goods as compensation instead, strengthening their status. Women are typically considered to have a higher status in societies that allow them some measure of economic independence and control over domestic economy. In pre-literate societies this is typically linked to matrilineal descent and inheritance, as well as *matrilocal* domestic arrangements (i.e. with or near the wife's family). Even in matriarchal societies, however, men almost universally dominate economically and politically, and female leaders are the exception (Leach 1955; Levine 1987a; Levine and Sangree 1980b; Nandi 1987; Peter 1963).

There is thus no simple connection between polyandry and women's status, even within matrilineal social systems, because polyandry as an institution as well as polyandrous practices are themselves ambiguous, as mentioned. Several arguments have been put forward, nonetheless, to try to establish a causal link between them. First, there is the argument that women must have high status if they can marry several husbands, whereas men in polyandrous systems usually can marry only one woman. Native American Shoshone society (see Chapter 2), for example, contained some of the classic elements which might be seen as encouraging the practice of polyandry: a sexual equality in which men did not have higher status than women, allowing women to have several husbands; a sexual division of labour which acknowledged the economic contribution of both sexes and conferred no exclusive property rights to either sex; and last but not least no moral bias against any form of marital union. The question is, however, whether marrying several men actually is a result of, or creates, high status. Or indeed whether it is a result of, or creates, low status! Returning to the Jaunsar Bawar region of India (see Chapter 6), the particular form of fraternal polyandry practised in the region actually contradicts the argument because it appear to be based on women having lower status than men. Jaunsari men can enter into several marriages without dissolving their first marriage, leading to a form of fraternal group marriage involving several husbands and wives. In contrast, a woman can only be married to her one official husband (and by extension all his brothers as her co-husbands) at a time and must divorce him (and by extension his brothers) before being able to marry another man (Berreman 1975).

A second line of argument relates women's social status to their multiple sexual partners in polyandrous unions. It is argued that married men in polyandrous societies have a restricted choice of sexual partners, whereas married women have a much wider choice of legitimate sexual partners. This appears to give a woman a privileged sex life, she can enjoy a variety of husbands, and she is not resigned to only one partner throughout her life. The availability of multiple sexual partners is not usually considered sufficient to ascribe high status to women, however, and it must be supported by social and economic factors that promote sexual equality in the particular society. There are indeed several problems with arguments that consider women's higher social status reflected in their multiple permitted sexual partners. Returning to Jaunsar Bawar (see Chapter 6), a wife cannot freely choose with whom she wants to have sex as long as her husband is in the house, since this customarily prevents his co-husbands from approaching her. Some wives do attempt to 'punish' their husbands for some transgression by going to sleep with one of their co-spouses while their husband is still in the house; if the husband is annoyed with his wife he may similarly ask her to go and sleep with one of his brothers. Second, co-husbands can demand sex from their common wife whenever circumstances allow it, night and day, inside and outside the house. Women are thus required to be available for sex whenever one of the men wants it. If there is a large group of brothers, this can be quite a strenuous affair, not least because it does not absolve her from all her other domestic duties, including rearing children. It would seem as if women in polyandrous societies hardly have time for the pure enjoyment of so much sex, with all their domestic, productive and reproductive work. It might hardly feel like a privilege for a woman that she has to make herself sexually available at any time to any co-husband (and perhaps their classificatory brothers as well), and it is hardly the setting to explore her sexuality. Especially not when sex is accompanied by pressures on her to become pregnant as often as possible and with male progeny. Third, a wife's sexual freedom is curtailed by her obligation to remain faithful and loyal to her husbands; a wife's infidelity normally results in the dissolution of the marriage (Bhatt and Jain 1987: 417–18; Nandi 1987: 428).

Polyandrous wives' so-called sexual privileges can therefore equally be considered to lower women's status. The view that polyandry gives women a superior sexual outlet to men might rather be a male fantasy reflecting a belief that polygyny provides this sort of sexual outlet for men! The male anthropologist Berreman (1975: 137, n.2) notes that the male fascination with polyandry probably stems precisely from its exotic sexual element (cf. Levine and Sangree 1980b: 389; White 1988: 547). Perhaps only a male anthropologist would suggest that a woman would really enjoy all that sex after a hard day's work in the fields, where incidentally she is also a legitimate sex target. Servicing several men sexually in addition to working, cooking, cleaning, nursing, giving birth to and taking care of children would appear to this female anthropologist to constitute quite a burden for a tired woman. This is not to say that some polyandrous wives do not get a heightened sexual pleasure and a more rewarding sex life through the variety offered by several husbands. It certainly does not seem to raise their status to be communal sex partners, however, especially as they are subjected to demands of strict fidelity and loyalty to their husbands. Indeed, Jaunsari women's resentment against the sexual sharing of wives is increasing. In many contemporary marriages, spouses now agree upon entering the marriage whether or not this sexual sharing should be allowed. If a wife is then forced to be shared contrary to the agreed arrangement, she can leave the marriage (Bhatt and Jain 1987: 417–18). The breakdown of polyandrous structures in Jaunsar Bawar is further discussed in Chapter 9.

Polyandrous sexuality does not happen in a vacuum, of course, but is related to reproduction; children are extremely important to the survival of the often small-scale polyandrous communities. While there must be a certain number of children to carry on societal institutions, there is also a strong need to restrict the number of children because of the often harsh economic conditions. As in most traditional cultures, boys are wanted and girls discounted. Women's lower status is thus already apparent and exercised at birth. Levine (1987b) poignantly describes how differential childcare in Tibetan polyandrous societies leads to many deaths among infant girls. This amounts to covert female infanticide and continues to be practised because parents only really welcome economically valuable sons. This indifferent attitude to girl children's survival is perhaps the lowest status a woman can have! Tibetan women who reach adulthood, however, can marry several husbands and gain status through these marriages. They may also gain some power in their households by being responsible for assigning paternity to their children, thus creating strong bonds with certain husbands or 'hiding' illegitimate children (Levine 1988: 200). This dichotomy in women's status in polyandrous societies is also found among the Lachenpa communities in the Indian Himalayas, bordering Tibet. Lachenpa women have a significant influence in the domestic sphere and some sexual privileges, but it is Lachenpa men who dominate all other facets of life. Descent and inheritance is patrilineal, decision-making in the communities is in the hands of male elders, males control the economic sphere and male children are more welcome (Nandi 1987: 430–1). It would hence be difficult to argue that women have an equal, or indeed superior, status in most polyandrous communities.

A third line of argumentation regarding female status and polyandry revolves around the practice of female infanticide. Female infanticide has often been assumed to be the main reason for the pronounced gender imbalance found in societies practising polyandry. The association between these various factors goes all the way back to early evolutionists like McLennan, who believed that female infanticide was the main reason for the scarcity of women in some societies, which in turn forced men to develop polyandrous practices. For example, Tibetan polyandry has typically been explained as an outcome of a shortage of women generated by female infanticide. Similarly in India, where a shortage of women is a demographic characteristic of the whole population; it is especially prevalent in the northern and north-western parts of the country. The significant gender imbalance in favour of men found in parts of India often coincides with precisely those regions in which polyandry is practised. Based on these facts, many researchers have argued that female infanticide is responsible for the significant surplus of males, and hence by implication polyandrous marriage, in areas like Jaunsar Bawar (see Chapter 6). However, there is no simple causal link between shortage of women and polyandry, as pronounced gender imbalance is likely to maintain, rather than necessarily cause, polyandrous practices. Furthermore, female infanticide has also been widely practised among the people of the Punjab, Uttar Pradesh and Rajputana, but they do not practise polyandry (Pakrasi 1987). Many researchers therefore disagree with these causal connections now.

Female infanticide has indeed been, and may still be, practised in those societies that have a surplus of males. There is no simple causality between female infanticide and polyandry, however, for such causality would not explain why polygyny is frequently practised in those societies that have a surplus of males. Instead, it may be that the shortage of females creates a situation where the possession of several women becomes a sign of very high status, thus further increasing polygynous tendencies. It reflects the fact that within a society, it is usually the high-ranking males who practise polygyny, and this may sometimes force low-ranking males to practise polyandry as their only chance of getting a wife and children. This was the case in some Inuit populations, for example (see Chapter 3). In fact, the shortage of women may have arisen precisely because polyandrous practices reduced the need for adult women, leading to such practices as female infanticide, which lower the number of girls reaching sexual maturity. It is, according to Peter (1963: 555), the problem of the chicken and the egg: which practice came first?

Nayar Polyandry in India

The ambiguous status relations in polyandry are perfectly illustrated among the Nayar of Kerala in south-west India. As an ethnographic example, the Nayar appear to fulfil the early evolutionists' vision of classic polyandrous societies entailing matrilineal kinship and high status for women.

The Nayar consist of several distinct populations belonging to certain castes and specialized occupational groups. Today, very little polyandry is practised in the area as a whole, but in the past some Nayar populations could be classified as polyandrous. Traditionally, Nayar polyandry was non-fraternal and women were involved in simultaneous sexual relations with several unrelated men. The sexual partners did not live together but lived with members of their respective matrilineal lineages. A Nayar woman had a ritual husband, whom she married in a group marriage ceremony before entering puberty, and with whom she might or might not have sexual relations. Upon reaching puberty, she could start having various recognized lovers who lacked any ritual status towards her, thus excluding them from any legal rights over her children. A Nayar woman was not formally married to any of her subsequent 'husbands' or lovers, but the partners formed relations of affinity between the linked lineages. Certain elements of 'marriage' were nonetheless involved in the Nayar system, such as the notion of affinity, and the fact that a woman was required to undergo ritual purification at her ritual husband's death (Leach 1955). The literature on the Nayar is often contradictory, because different Nayar populations in the various regions had different forms of marriage. Gough (1961) hence divided the Nayar into regional groupings. The Nayars in North Kerala were traditionally monogamous or polygynous, but never polyandrous. Premarital sexual relations were common, but were not considered marriage and did not confer any rights and obligations on the partners. The Nayars of central Kerala lived in matrilineal households, and allowed polygamous marriages for both men and women. They practised the 'classic' Nayar system of visiting husbands, where several neighbourhood men visited women living in their own household. The men were traditionally soldiers, who left the matrilineally owned estates to be cultivated by serfs and tenants. Fraternal polyandry was and is traditionally forbidden in central Kerala, and is only practised among low caste people.

A Nayar woman's children automatically became members of the woman's own lineage, if they had been conceived under socially acceptable circumstances, which did not involve any prohibited relations between its parents. A child was thus given the full birth right status of its society or caste independently of its particular paternity (except in cases of a woman's known indiscretion with a lower caste man). A Nayar child called all its mothers' lovers by a similar term meaning lord or leader, though this did not imply any legal or biological paternity. According to Leach (1955), this implies that the notion of fatherhood is lacking among Nayars. In contrast, Raha (1987) suggests that the notion of fatherhood is not lacking, and that a Nayar woman's early ritual marriage did serve to establish the legitimacy of a woman's children by establishing a relation between the mother and one or more possible fathers. Furthermore, among the Nayars of Central Kerala, each 'husband' presented his wife with a marriage cloth in the presence of her family before he began having relations with her. This ritualized 'joining together' represented a form of marriage that legitimized the woman's relations to the men and the resulting children. When the wife gave birth to a child, the husband or husbands who were visiting her at the time were required to present gifts to the midwife in attendance as an acknowledgment of their potential paternity. It also confirmed the child's status as a legitimate member of his mother's lineage and caste. Hence, traditional Nayar plural unions can be considered non-fraternal polyandrous marriages rather than forms of cicisbeism because of the importance of a woman's male partners in conferring legitimacy on her children (Gough 1965). Even within this polyandrous and matrilineal system there were patrilineal tendencies, however. Some men got particularly attached to certain wives and children, and in the later years of a marriage, husbands might try to provide a separate house for their favourite wife and children. Gough (1961) suggests powerful men especially might develop exclusive marital relations with their wives, partly to ensure their paternity of sons born to the wife. This was a threat to the traditional Nayar system, however, as it might encourage men to transfer their property to their own children (i.e. patrilineally) rather than to their matrilineal heirs.

Do women in matrilineal polyandrous societies like those of the Nayar have a high or equal social status to men? Traditionally, Nayar women appear to have had a high status through their rights to own and inherit property, their few obligations apart from sexual privileges towards any of their husbands, none of whom had any legal rights over them, their matrilocal residence patterns as well as their personal liberty as individuals and in family and social life. Simultaneously, their status was lower than men's with respect to decision-making. It was traditionally the maternal uncle who had the most influence and authority in his sisters' households, a pattern of male dominance seen in virtually all societies, as mentioned. Even in classic polyandrous and matrilineal societies like those of the Nayar there were patrilineal tendencies working against the matrilineal foundations of society. This structural dichotomy became more pronounced during colonial times, where the British monogamous and patriarchal administration discouraged traditional Nayar ways. Nayar men began to feel ashamed about 'creeping in' to their wives and started to become monogamous; women now had to live in their husbands' households. Matrilocal residence and non-fraternal polyandry was gradually abandoned, though some families began to permit *de facto* polyandrous relations by giving younger brothers sexual access to an elder brother's wife. As Western and pan-Indian values spread, monogamous marriages became the rule everywhere, though among Travancore Nayar some fraternal wife-sharing remains, as do traces of the 'classic' Nayar system of visiting husbands. The traditional matrilineal kinship and property system has been completely undermined by the reformation of family law, the legalization of joint family property partitions and the weakening of traditional property relations. The new property relations and the growth in independent earnings have created increased economic differentiation between brothers, and men now ignore their matrilineal kin and transfer all their resources and property to their own wives and children. The adoption of monogamy and a conjugal family form, where men assume the legal rights for their wife and children, has also significantly decreased women's status and curtailed their liberties. Nayar women now rank lower than men in all aspects of life (Levine 1987a; Nandi 1987; Renjini 1996).

Nayar polyandry, then, was traditionally practised in an environment where women had high status, enabling the practice, but the practice did not necessarily confer high status on them. Neither did the matrilineal social system, tracing descent and inheritance through women, give women power in and of itself, if the power to make familial and political decisions remains in the hands of their brothers and uncles. Nayar women's status and power were at best ambiguous, high in certain regards, low in others, giving no clear answer to whether polygamy presupposes high or low status and power for women.

–8–

Polygamy and Modernity

Polygamy in Pre-modern Africa

A discussion of polygamy and modernity can probably find no better point of departure than contemporary Africa. African polygamy contains all facets of the conflicts inherent in modern polygamy, such as tradition versus modernity, religion versus culture, form versus content, young versus old, women versus men, West versus non-West. Polygamy in contemporary Africa is variously described as increasing or decreasing as a result of modernity, often in the same areas. It is hence a challenging context for examining polygamy and modernity.

Colonialism

When European countries – and Christian missions – colonized Africa, polygyny soon became a thorny issue. Colonists generally held the view that Africans were 'sub-human' and that they were to be made 'human' by gradually being made to follow a European way of life. This involved among its important elements giving up polygamy. For example, traditional leaders unwilling to give up such customs as polygamy, considered incompatible with the Belgians' 'civilizing mission' in the Congo, were gradually replaced by individuals who were Christians and monogamists (Wolfe 1959: 176). For many Europeans, polygamy represented a social evil, based on economic serfdom of women, children or slaves (Crosby 1937). Polygamy was seen as hindering the economic and intellectual advancement of the country, and colonial governments in Africa typically wrote its gradual abandonment into their charters. Their main problem was how to integrate polygyny into a marriage and family law code that was based on Western monogamous marriage and had no foundations in an African context. Colonial governments typically enacted legislation to enable Africans to convert their marriage into a monogamous Western type of marriage; after conversion, the colonial family law would govern people. No provisions were made for the conversion of monogamous marriage into the customary potentially polygynous one, because it was unthinkable that anyone might wish to do so (Kuria 1987: 289). In the Union of South Africa, for example, a basic distinction was drawn between 'marriages' and 'customary unions', and this meant that the courts refused to recognize a union that allowed polygamy as a marriage, even if it was recognized by the law of another country (Phillips 1953: 178).

Polygyny was officially discouraged in all of colonial Africa, but the discouragement was rarely reinforced by any sanctions or laws against polygynists. European legal principles and procedures never displaced customary law in matters of marriage, though the two sets of laws were often modified as legislators and traditional leaders attempted to adapt them to each other. Similarly, when a conflict occurred between Muslim law and African customary law, customary law usually prevailed. Muslim law was often incorporated into customary law, however, and this amalgamation made up the legal system among the population concerned. In most countries, monogamy was sanctioned by civil law, and polygyny was forbidden to men married under civil law. African customary law and public opinion accepted polygynous marriages, however, and so polygamy was sanctioned by 'native law and custom' (Bascom and Herskovits 1959; Phillips 1953: 235–7). This duality meant that colonial governments generally did not pass any laws that directly prohibited polygyny.

The colonial governments in Africa instead implemented various policies interfering with traditional social structures. Among their favourite weapons was the imposition of head taxes. Taxes were considered to work on two levels: they generated income and they would in the long run obliterate polygyny by creating an economic burden. In South Africa, for example, a man who had more than one wife had to pay an additional tax for each wife. The additional wealth generated by an additional wife was not usually readily convertible into cash, however. The tax payable upon them hence tended to make extra wives an economic liability and rendered it impossible for men to keep their usual three or four wives (Mair 1953: 25). In colonial Congo, a similar tax was passed on all wives above the first, but this was always paid by the women themselves, not the polygynous husband, and often not paid at all. Instead, it had the unintended effect of rendering many more or less stable concubine relations legal in the eyes of the people who paid this tax, giving them a legitimate right to be bigamists. A law giving tax relief to all monogamous men who had a least four minor children also had the unintended effect of encouraging *de facto* polygyny, since men always wanted to have many small children and hence needed to have several young wives to produce them (van Wing 1947: 97). Furthermore, the head taxes were to be paid in European currencies, obtainable only through employment, compelling men to seek wage labour away from home for periods extending months to years. Such circumstances encouraged some men to have a wife in their rural residence as well as one in their urban residence. The overall result of the taxes was thus increases in polygynous marriages (Gwako 1998: 336–7).

Taxation did not have the intended long-term effect of phasing out polygyny, but rather encouraged polygyny in some cases and the transmutation of polygyny in others. One of the taxation schemes' most long-term effects is that it remains difficult to assess the true number of polygynous households in Africa. There is a widespread obstruction of surveys, for if a head of a household were to list all the actual members of his family, he would be taxed accordingly. Therefore, in order to avoid high taxes, many polygamous husbands do not disclose how many wives and children they have (Kosack 1999: 562). The lack of reliable data has been a constant problem in research on African polygamy. For example, colonial administrators in French Togoland thought that the incidence of polygyny in the country was extremely high, much higher than subsequent quantitative data suggested it was. Such overestimation of polygyny levels is common in the literature on Africa. Problems arise because most of the data is synchronic, with few re-studies of the same population. Data collected for different generations are difficult to use, since younger age groups taken alone may not have the same incidence as the total adult male population in societies where men marry later in life. Lacking reliable quantitative data, statements in the ethnographic literature about the increase or decrease of polygyny among populations in sub-Saharan Africa are thus not always statistically sound, but may rather represent trends (Dorjahn 1959: 98–101). Furthermore, as Solway points out, 'since polygyny is an institution considered by many Westerners as uncivilized, it is undoubtedly underreported by local people and perhaps overreported by observers wishing to emphasize the exotic and sensational' (1990: 46).

Christianity

Hand in hand with the colonial governments' disdain for polygyny went the Christian missionaries' crusade against polygyny (see Chapter 2). The mission churches regarded marriage as central to Christianity, and 'proper' domestic behaviour became an outward sign of inward religious faith. Where local marital arrangements included polygyny, the missionaries equated Christianity with monogamy (Mann 1994: 169). The Catholic Church in particular has been waging war against polygyny throughout its missionary history. 'It is only by the law of the Gospel, incorporated in social life, that the Black woman will be delivered from the shame and slavery of polygamy and attain to the liberty of the children of God and to the high dignity of the Christian wife and mother' (van Wing 1947: 102). To many Africans, Christian opposition to polygamy appeared contradictory: it was common practice in the Old Testament, and there was no specific prohibition against it in the New Testament. This was the same argument early Mormons in the USA used to legitimize their polygyny, incidentally (see Chapter 5). In an attempt to reconcile the pull of polygyny with the push of Christianity, a new class of elite African men emerging in the early twentieth century therefore began to reject the association between monogamy and Christianity. This reconsideration of Christian domestic ideology coincided with the creation of African churches. The churches were founded for political and constitutional reasons, not to legitimize polygyny, but they were open to polygynous members. The African churches introduced a type of 'native Christian marriage', sometimes called 'parlour marriage' because the ceremony took place in people's homes, in which the union received Christian blessings but was not registered under the marriage ordinance, and did not carry the expectations of monogamy and a Victorian conjugal relationship. These African churches gave men the possibility of taking multiple wives while remaining good Christians (Mann 1994: 181). The majority of African men, however, had to contend with Christian churches that were vehemently against polygyny.

Christian teachings had a strong impact on African social structure. It condemned beliefs in ancestral spirits and magic, and practices that expressed these beliefs; it also condemned polygyny and initiation, and often marriage payment as well, refusing to accept a marriage as valid where bridewealth had been paid (Mair 1953: 19). The missionaries' denial of the power of the ancestors had deleterious effects on the solidarity and collective responsibility of clans and lineages in which Africans typically found security. This has in modern times resulted in a decrease in the authority of, and respect for, elders. Christian doctrine stresses patrilineal descent, conflicting with the systems of matrilineal descent found in many African societies and hence leading to their gradual breakdown. Furthermore, Christian worship entails living a sedentary life near other people and a church, recognizing a religious leader with authority, and abandoning polygyny and circumcision. To many Africans, these implications are undesirable, if not impossible to live up to. The missionaries face great difficulties when they demand that a young man must choose between circumcision and baptism in a culture where an uncircumcised man is not considered a man, for example (Schneider 1959: 160). For people already in polygynous marriages, conversion is equally difficult. Co-wives cannot be baptized as long as their husbands are alive and cohabits with them, for example. Many Africans were, and are today, reluctant to conduct marriage ceremonies in Christian churches because of the many adjustments to their traditional way of life necessary to be baptized. By marrying according to customary procedures, the greater costs of the church ceremony and the restriction it imposed upon subsequent polygynous marriage were also avoided. Since marriage by customary procedures had the same legal status as marriage by Christian rites, there was no legal device whereby the missions could implement their ban on polygyny (Colson 1958: 120; Lystad 1959: 192).

The other main world religion that affected polygynous practices in pre-modern Africa, and still does today, was Islam. Islam spread from the Middle East into Africa from the seventh century onwards, following the network of trade routes; Islam established itself primarily in trade-oriented urban areas (Spencer 1998: 253). Islam and Christianity had contrasting approaches to the practice of polygamy, however. Islamic norms regarding polygamy are often very similar those of African communities, and where they clash solutions can easily be found. For example, a man may not have more than four wives under Muslim law, so if he already has this number, he must dismiss one of his wives before marrying a new one. This usually took the form of men 'pensioning off' their older wives in order to marry younger women. Wealthy Nupe men in Nigeria, for example, continue to marry additional women all their adult lives, and evade the Muslim limitation of four wives by formally divorcing their older wives, while allowing them to live on in the household (Mair 1953: 137; Smith 1953: 284 n.13). In contrast, Christian missionaries were completely opposed to polygamous marriage. They were totally committed to the Western nuclear family model with all its moral implications, and left no room for compromise. These different approaches underscore the two religions' ongoing competition for African converts. Many Christian churches have been forced to accept polygyny among their members, because if they demand strict monogamy from their members, they risk losing them to the African native churches – or to Islam. Generally, Christianity's effect on polygynous practices in Africa has been ambiguous, and in contemporary churches, there is typically either a lax interpretation, or a total disregard, of official doctrine because of its impracticality. In contrast, native syncretic churches and Islam accept polygyny, and recruit many converts. The incidence of polygyny may as a result vary substantially by religious denomination (Burnham 1987: 47; Lesthaeghe, Kaufmann and Meekers 1989: 243).

Vehicles of Westernization

The practice of polygamy was widespread up into the early colonial period at the turn of the twentieth century, but it was never as common as popularly imagined. The trend away from polygamous unions evidenced since 1900 is generally seen as depending primarily on the extent to which the 'vehicles of Westernization' – industrialization, urbanization, education and Christianity (cf. McDonald 1985) – have penetrated African societies as a direct result of European colonialism.

Industrialization

Industrialization of the kin-based agricultural or pastoral societies making up most of Africa meant the introduction of wage labour and a cash economy, a process that was started under colonial rule. For polygynous families it quickly became reality in the form of a tax on plural wives to be paid in cash rather than goods or services. African economic development has thus directly undermined part of the economic foundations of polygamy by demanding wealth in cash rather than in people or produce. It used to be that the more wives a man had, the more he could produce, since wives represented labour at their husband's disposal. For many young men today, many wives and children will obstruct their economic mobility to migrate or produce cash crops for sale, as many children and wives mean many mouths to feed, which would reduce the surplus of food for sale. Many men are now able to farm with wage labour and for them a polygynous household would be an economic liability. The increased use of ploughs and machinery has similarly diminished the need for female labour, and agricultural activities no longer require large labour inputs as the size of landholdings has decreased. Most men now do not have enough land to give fields to several wives, and some women have challenged men for ownership of land. These new productive relations have reduced the need for extra wives and children, one of the prime motives for polygyny. Another factor leading to a decline in polygyny in many rural areas is that cattle – the traditional form of bridewealth payment – can now be used more profitably as a source of cash income than for obtaining wives (Lystad 1959: 220–1; Kosack 1999: 561; Mair 1953: 26, 69; Price 1996: 427).

A further effect of industrialization on polygamy is indeed that the economics of obtaining a wife has changed substantially. As marriage payments began to be demanded in cash rather than cattle (or some other goods), men who could not come up with the cash could not marry any or additional wives. Bridewealth payment at marriage has remained common in most African societies, but in both semi-urban and urban communities there has been a drastic inflation in the amount of bridewealth demanded. It may vary according to the amount of formal education a girl has, for example, for a father is considered entitled to a return of the investment he has made in his daughter's schooling. Payment has become increasingly difficult for men, and few men can now afford to marry several wives. Bridewealth is directly linked to polygyny in Africa, such that increases in bridewealth sizes generally leads to falling polygyny levels. From an economic perspective, polygyny's survival rests on its wealth-generating properties, which make it an economically viable production system. The high cost of marriage, and the costs involved in supporting a wife and children, now act as deterrents to polygynous marriage. There are still individuals who prefer to expend their wealth in building up a large household rather than in acquiring material goods, however. This appears to be true mainly in West Africa, where cash incomes are obtained by cultivation, and women's work therefore contributes to cash income as well as subsistence. For example, among the maize-producing Tonga in Zambia, additional wives have always been economic assets because of the cost and difficulty in obtaining wage labour. Plural marriages will probably continue as long as they have an economic basis in areas where subsistence cultivation has not been replaced by wage labour. But as population expands and mortality declines in West Africa, systems of wealth-increasing polygyny are likely to be undermined with the loss of new lands for expansion (Colson 1958: 123; Goody 1973b: 4; Mair 1953: 153; White 1988: 557).

The disruptive influence of industrialization, migration and urbanization on traditional social systems has resulted in, among other things, a new and freer choice of partner, a general effect of the 'vehicles of westernization' (Lesthaeghe et al. 1989: 333). Partner selection in modern urban Africa has been greatly influenced by Christian missionaries, who insist that Christian marriage unites two individuals, not two kin groups, and stress that it should be based on Western ideals of love and companionship. This personalization of marriage is a potential threat for polygynous marriages, as polygyny tends to make the bond between man and wife less intimate than in monogamous marriages. In polygynous societies, women and men tend to experience married life differently: most men, even if they later become polygynists, will go through long periods of first bachelorhood and then monogamy, whereas many women will enter a polygynous marriage at puberty and never experience unmarried life or life in a monogamous marriage. For women, marital relations will typically last longer and be less intense than for men in polygyny (Krige and Krige 1943: 71; Mann 1994: 169; Ware 1983: 15–17). Love, therefore, tends to lead to (a preference for) monogamy. In contrast, in 'polygynous societies, "love", in the sense of a preference of one above another, is often a dangerous thing. Favouritism leads to jealousy' (Goody 1973b: 38). Such concerns are typically voiced by women faced with involuntary polygyny, such as early Mormon women (see Chapter 5) or contemporary Malay women (see Chapter 4).

Many urban Africans hence find themselves at a crossroads between traditional marriage based on lineage decisions and new marriage forms based on personal decisions. Among urban educated Africans, marriage may no longer involve corporate lineages, kin-group selection of spouses and distant formality, but rather elementary families, personal choice of spouses, and love and companionship as the basis for marriage. Modern urban marriages, which are officially recorded, do usually contain some elements of customary marriage, such as transfer of bridewealth. Polygynous marriage has similarly become much more individualized, focusing on personal choice and strong relationships between people, thereby giving kin and community less control over individuals. The change in partner selection has been especially dramatic for young women with independent incomes, who now have considerable independence from their families to select a partner. They also find it easier to resist polygyny and to divorce or separate if their unions prove unsatisfactory. The freedom of women to choose a partner is often curtailed by their close kin, however, even in urban areas. Especially in areas where competition for housing and jobs is between main ethnic groups, there might be strict control over women's marriages and few inter-ethnic marriages (Bledsoe and Gage 1994: 148; Gwako 1998: 344; Locoh 1994: 215, 225; Spencer 1998: 83).

Urbanization

The increasing urbanization of Africa, which develops in tandem with industrialization, has generally meant a reduction in polygamous marriages. First, there are economic reasons, as mentioned: in urban areas the economic function of many wives has mostly disappeared, while the wages a man earns might not even be enough to pay for one family, let alone several. The economic incentives for polygamy, as well as men's ability to support large families, are decreasing with the ever-increasing cash requirements for a family's access to shelter, education, clothing, health services and intermittent purchases of food as a result of decreasing local food production. Rising expectations of living standards, and the expenses associated with fulfilling urban women's increasing demands for jewellery, nice clothing, etc. make it difficult for urban men to have more than one wife. Polygynous practices wane with the worsening economic situation, especially in urban areas, where the costs of raising children and keeping extra wives has risen sharply.

Second, urban housing conditions make polygyny impossible, as there is typically no room in the overcrowded cities for the traditional polygamous households, which demand a separate residence for each wife. Houses in towns are usually built by public authorities to accommodate one couple and their minor children, as municipal authorities typically do not recognize more than one marriage as legal, even if all have been contracted under customary law. If a man brings a second wife into his house in town, this is usually done without contracting a marriage. His first wife may then complain to the authorities and if he will not give up his second wife he may be evicted (Mair 1953: 29). Some of those rural migrants who contract a second marriage in town therefore choose not to reveal that they are already married to another wife in their rural hometown. As such, urban polygyny contributes to a nuclearization of the African family through the emergence of separate one-family households. Urban dwellers are thus generating new patterns of marital residence in the form of several separate households in order to cope with the economic as well as ideological pressures of urban ways of life; in so doing, they regain some of the flexibility that rural polygyny offered (Bledsoe and Pison 1994: 7; Locoh 1994: 215). The adaptation of traditional polygynous structures to modern urban conditions is seen among migrant communities in towns along the coast of Ghana, where young 'maidservants' are incorporated into Bulsa households through the *doglientiri* system, mentioned above. Women who bring young female relatives to their urban households are not rearing the girls as companions and future co-wives, as they would have in rural settings, but rather keep them as unpaid servants, a necessity in an urban setting where all food has to be bought, and housing is a constant problem (Meier 1999: 103–4).

Third, urbanization generally implies a weakening of lineage control over its individual members. As urban migrants gain economic independence as a result of integration into the capitalist economy, the freedom of young lineage members is strengthened as the control of their elders and their lineage is weakened. Urbanization and the establishment of urban-based political structures has brought about a decreased emphasis upon both regional group identity and the power of the traditional and inherited rural leadership; the need for making unions based upon political expediency has lessened considerably. Economic development has thus helped create an inversion of traditional values, as the development of new urban areas is accompanied by the polarization of wealth. Today, there is an individualistic disregard for traditional ideals of equality between peers of the same age set as well as respect for age. There is also an emphasis on wealth itself as a means towards influence, patronage and more wealth. This overturns the traditional age stratification system, which has been in operation in most African societies. In rural areas, such structures may remain more intact, though rural peoples are also increasingly integrated into the wider national and international economy. Modern urban living allows young men to quickly make money, marry and perhaps become polygynous at a much younger age than was possible before. This undermines the authority of elders, which was linked to their control over younger men's access to cattle and other goods for marriage payments through bridewealth. It is a self-reinforcing process, as many young men are forced to become migrant labourers or urban workers, precisely because no marriage cattle are available for them among their kin. An imbalance in social control is thus created by young lineage members acquiring new skills and abilities which make them able to acquire the trappings of elderhood much sooner and independently of their lineage (Clignet 1987: 201–2; Goody 1973b: 5–8; Lesthaeghe et al. 1989: 241; Spencer 1998: 264).

Polygynous practices can therefore also increase as a result of urbanization. Urbanization of Africa gathered pace during the colonial period, where head taxes were to be paid in European currencies, as mentioned. As European currencies were obtainable only through employment, men were compelled to seek wage labour away from home for long periods, extending from months to years. The newly arrived and generally poor urban migrants typically did not practise polygyny, nor would they have as young men had they remained at their rural home. Today, the many young rural men who migrate to cities to find work might similarly stay away for prolonged periods to make money. This means that some men living and working in the city may prefer to have two wives and two families, one in the city and the other in their ancestral rural land. This is especially so where various ethnic groups compete for housing and jobs in urban areas, such that maintaining strong rural links and having a rural wife becomes advantageous. The result is two separate 'nuclear' family households, one urban, one rural, replacing traditional joint polygynous ones. In Senegal, for example, people jokingly distinguish between *une femme de cour* (the wife running the rural homestead) and *une femme de coeur* (a 'love wife', i.e. of the town). Polygyny thus appears to increase among many urban dwellers after they become securely established. Rising incomes may increase the frequency of polygyny, at least in the short run, as more men are able to afford bridewealth for, and/or support of, two or more wives. The result is that with time and success, established city dwellers return to polygyny or 'outside wives' (see below) (Bledsoe 1980; Clignet 1987; Gwako 1998; Lesthaeghe et al. 1989; Obi 1970; Spencer 1998).

Education

The introduction of education to still more African peoples is generally considered to have a depressing effect on polygyny. The effect of education on polygamy is twofold: first, as education is expensive, parents eager to educate their children may have to limit their number in order to afford educating them. The easiest way to do that is to marry fewer wives and thus have fewer children, as begetting numerous offspring was a prime motive for polygyny. The cost of educating children, though it may be repaid in assistance from them when they are earning good salaries, is a burden which had no counterpart in pre-colonial days (Mair 1953: 69). Generally, polygyny has remained an ideal in those areas where it is still an economic asset rather than a liability, but dwindling in those areas where the education of children and other modern expenses have altered its economic advantages. This encourages alternative ways of investing in future security. Today, parents no longer see agricultural production by their children as a pension security; rather they see an education as more important in achieving this aim. Particularly in urban Africa, people whose standard of living has been raised to resemble those of Europeans, and who are eager to give their children an European-type education, will often voice strong opposition to polygyny. Their opposition may also stem from the fact that their salaries are usually not high enough to support a polygynous family comfortably, rather than because they believe in monogamy as a principle (Bascom and Herskovits 1959: 6; Lystad 1959: 197; Spencer 1998: 53).

Second, the education of girls in particular has had a profound effect on polygamy patterns. When the missionaries first introduced Christian schools to the coastal areas of West Africa, for example, the classes contained equal numbers of male and female students. However, a reaction against the education of girls soon set in, in part because the demand for educated Africans to work in the colonial system was restricted to educated males. More importantly, female education had extremely disruptive effects upon the marriage market. Not only did bridewealth payments increase, as mentioned, but educated girls learnt to regard marriage as a matter of individual choice. Their insistence upon their individual rights constituted an attack upon the social system as a whole, if marriages could no longer be used by elders to regulate social and political alliances (Ware 1983: 10–11). Western education teaches women new lifestyles, opens up new economic opportunities, creates new wants, sets new standards. When a population becomes literate, often as a result of Christian mission activities, it may be more open to Western thinking. The spread of the Western family model, with its ideal of conjugal closeness, is reinforcing the 'privatization' of marriage away from community and lineage responsibilities. It is thereby changing the social and economic relations in families, as well as between generations and genders (Lesthaeghe 1989: 6–8). In contemporary Kenya, for example, education has increased women's economic independence by enhancing their chances of participating in the formal labour market, and has resulted in their postponement of marriage and reluctance to enter polygynous marriage (Gwako 1998: 339–40).

Female education has therefore made polygyny a highly brittle institution, because educated women are increasingly unwilling to enter polygynous households, which they see as incompatible with their aspirations. Many women in urban areas make their own money, and they might be less inclined to share a man with another woman. They particularly resent becoming junior wives to women with less education. Highly educated women may not want to marry at all, while others find it increasingly difficult to find an unmarried educated man to meet their new aspirations. To protect themselves, highly educated urbanites usually insist on a Christian or civil ceremony, which precludes polygyny (Bledsoe and Gage 1994: 149, 159). Urban women's ability to withstand some of what they consider the negative aspects of polygyny stands in sharp contrast to many rural women's inability to do so. Migrant husbands, who as mentioned may have an urban and a rural wife, typically have wage incomes that are inadequate to maintain two families. Their rural wives' work is therefore essential to the survival of the group. But the rural wives left behind often know nothing of their husbands' whereabouts or whether they have another wife in the city, as they typically receive no news or money from them. When the men do come home, they have a right to be fed and sleep with their wives, even if they contribute nothing to the income of the household or refuse to help with the farm work. Such visits often leave the wives pregnant (or possibly infected with a sexually transmitted disease such as HIV/AIDS acquired by the husband in town), giving them an even greater burden to bear without any help from their husbands. Urban polygynous wives may not fare much better, and often amount to little more than domestic helpers for their husbands (Gwako 1998: 336–43; Kosack 1999: 561–2).

Christianization

It was long thought that the universal reason for the decline of polygamy in Africa was the movement towards Christianity. In Igbo society, for example, women now are more reluctant to enter polygamous families and have large families because they feel that it takes more time, more money, more anxiety to bring children up today than in the past. It is not enough to bring children into the world; one must also be able to educate them. Such views underscore the impact of the Christian religion and through it contact with Western civilization, with its emphasis on higher education and a higher standard of living (Obi 1970). On that level, Christianity with its emphasis on monogamy has significantly depressed the practice of polygyny. The spread of Christianity, and through it Western culture, undermines the normative basis of polygyny in African societies by removing some of the norms, beliefs, values and taboos associated with polygynous marriage. The penetration of Christianity has far from wiped out polygyny in Africa, however. Young men more interested in making and spending money than becoming good Christians may be less willing to make such sacrifices as being monogamous. Their concession to Christian teachings is not to make their polygyny official or public. So while official polygyny may be declining, other forms of relationships that closely resemble polygyny are increasing (Gwako 1998: 339–42; van Wing 1947: 93–4).

Colonialism and the 'vehicles of Westernization' in Africa have thus had a depressing effect on polygyny. Westernization, through such associated socio-economic changes as the growth of a wage economy, the emergence or restructuring of class stratification, and the spread of education, nearly always alters prevailing patterns of household formation in systems with kinship-based modes of production. Typically, Western ideals of nuclear residence patterns and conjugal marriage are spread through the mass media, school textbooks, and Christian doctrine and teaching. As diametrically opposed to the Western conjugal family type, polygyny will often meet the most persistent opposition from Westernizing forces. Studies of Kikuyu women in Kenya show that most of the younger women reject the idea of polygynous marriage and instead attempt to arrange their marriages based on their understanding of Western Christian practice. Studies of Kikuyu men similarly showed a drop in the number of men in polygynous marriages because of attitude changes as a result of education and Christian teachings. Reduced polygyny among men was also attributed to their reduced opportunity to acquire several wives as a result of the increased expectations and cost of a higher standard of living, as well as the increased possibility of the husband acquiring a mistress, which carries a lower cost than a second wife (Adams and Mburugu 1994; Hetherington 2001). As a result, marriage age in Kenya is now much more fluid and marriage itself much less certain. High levels of polygyny are made possible by a large age gap between husbands and wives, as mentioned, resulting from early marriage for women, late marriage for men and rapid remarriage for widows and divorcees. Westernization means that African women now marry at later ages, but so do most men, meaning that the relative age gap has not changed significantly. Disregarding other factors, this means that polygyny levels can remain about the same (Lesthaeghe 1989: 8–9).

The evolution of the polygyny and age difference indicators thus provide no real support for the hypothesis that Westernization automatically leads to falling polygyny levels. While some of the institutionalized foundations for polygyny are disappearing in contemporary Africa, polygyny can still fulfil important functions and so persists, though perhaps in different forms than before. Polygyny still allows women to gain support, solidarity with co-wives, help with childcare, and relief from sexual duties, while allowing men to accrue power and prestige. Some African countries have made polygyny illegal, usually as a result of pressure from missionaries and policy-makers, but legal abolition has not deterred polygynists. Neither has urbanization and industrialization, since rural populations moving into towns to work tend to bring with them or recreate a wide range of marital arrangements, including polygyny, adapting them to the new urban conditions. Polygyny thus appears to persist in

Africa despite growing economic, legal and religious pressures (Bledsoe and Pison 1994: 11; Handwerker 1982: 259–60; Lesthaeghe et al. 1989: 240–3).

Policy-makers and scholars often view polygyny as an anomaly in urban areas, where plural wives may drain rather than augment household resources. While men's pursuits of power and prestige through polygamy can take many forms in contemporary Africa, economic considerations are often paramount in their decision to take a second wife. Men may make several types of economic calculations before marrying a second wife, such as a simple profit and loss accounting of the woman's productive activities. However, polygamy may be valued for precisely the opposite reasons: if taking multiple wives represents a substantial financial drain on a man's resources, polygamy may serve to symbolize high status. In fact, urban residence, waged employment and high educational level all tend to correlate with higher rates of polygamy: men with 'many powers' are liable to take many wives as symbols of their high status. Paradoxically, therefore, it is the modern, urban, educated, Western-oriented elite which may have the highest number of second wives, simply because they can afford it! The economic situation in contemporary Africa has encouraged the emergence of new forms of polygyny, however, which do not require the same sort of economic or familial commitment as traditional polygyny. A cultural tradition which does not demand an exclusive sexual partnership of one man with one woman has encouraged the spread of concubinage, or 'outside wives', as a means of securing the benefits of polygyny without the economic burden (Bledsoe and Gage 1994: 148; Burnham 1987: 47; Mair 1953: 25).

Polygamy in Modern Africa

Reinvention of Tradition

Sub-Saharan Africa is today the only major world region where polygyny is still widely practised, despite the many legal and religious codes that colonial and modern states have invoked to control or eliminate it. In most urban areas of Africa, the outward form of marriage has shifted toward monogamy, especially among educated elites; yielding to social and legal pressures, many urban men take only one legal partner at a time. Many of the new marriage forms that outwardly resemble monogamy actually follow patterns of *de facto* polygyny, however. In urban Africa, polygyny is being transformed and replaced by other forms of union formation such as 'serial polygyny', 'informal unions', 'sugar daddy relationships', 'polyandrous motherhood' or 'outside marriage'. In outside marriage, men marry one woman by statutory law and also form extra-legal domestic and sexual unions with other women. Because the logic of polygyny thrives in new forms in urban areas, polygyny levels and their ethnic and geographical patterning have essentially remained intact in Africa. To many researchers, such 'outside marriages' represent modern forms of polygyny with implications for nuptiality and fertility, acting as important agents of change in African domestic life. The phenomenon is not new, but dates to the advent of missionary and colonial contact. Nonetheless, these 'outside wives' have mostly been lost between marriage categories, classified as being in consensual unions or single. At issue, of course, is whether unions falling under such labels as 'outside marriage' are really modern manifestations of polygyny. They might be if the secondary wives or mistresses and their children are accorded full rights in relation to, for example, maintenance and inheritance. From a demographer's point of view, these women are effectively married in that they are in a regular sexual union and usually have children, and they are demographically significant as an alternative mode of reproduction in societies undergoing socio-economic change. From an anthropological point of view, however, these women are not married. As marriage legitimizes and institutes social inclusion of sexuality and fertility, the external and often secret 'outside wives' are in fact more like concubines than wives in polygynous unions (Bledsoe 1995: 135; Lesthaeghe et al. 1989: 244; Mann 1994: 167; Parkin and Nyamwaya 1987: 12).

An 'outside wife' can be defined as a woman with whom a man has regular sexual relations for a long period, who is financially maintained by the man throughout the relationship and who has children whose paternity is acknowledged by the man. An 'outside wife' has limited social recognition and status because her husband typically refuses to declare her publicly as his wife. She also has much less social and politico-jural recognition than an 'inside wife' because no bridewealth has been paid and no marriage rites publicly performed according to church or statutory law. If a man who originally married under statutory law or in a church wedding decides to marry an additional wife through customary law, his new wife would not be an 'outside wife', even though this second marriage is illegal in countries which do not allow polygyny for men married under statutory law. If the marriage is publicly contracted with families and friends participating, the second wife may acquire the same status as the first wife married in a church wedding. The 'inside' wife may not acknowledge her as a properly married co-wife, but society probably does, because she was married to the man, albeit through a traditional and not legally binding ceremony. An 'inside' wife is typically an elite woman who has been married in a church wedding or through statutory law (usually both). In Nigerian local parlance she is therefore sometimes referred to, especially by outside wives, as a 'ring' wife. She usually lives with her husband and their children in an 'official' residence, and expects financial support for herself and her children regardless of her own economic standing. An inside wife will typically subscribe to the Christian ideology of monogamous marriage, at least as an ideal, and adhere to Western concepts of love, affection, companionship and fidelity (Karanja 1987: 251–3).

In contrast to traditional polygyny, a unilateral resource flow from 'husband' to 'wife' is one of the major and crucial criteria of 'outside marriage'. The flow of resources is one-sided because only well-to-do men can afford to have outside wives, who are almost always inferior economically to their 'husbands'. It would in most cases be nonsensical to call a woman an 'outside wife' if she was not financially maintained by her 'husband', as the prime consideration for becoming an 'outside wife' is usually economic. 'Outside marriage' relationships are therefore mostly of a patron–client nature, where the men engage in reciprocal relationships with the women, obtaining sexual services in return for rents, property and often child support. Economic considerations encourage the majority of African women to consider some kind of marriage better than no marriage at all (Karanja 1994: 194–202; Obbo 1987: 264). Economic considerations are similarly at the heart of 'inside wives' rejection of polygyny. Most elite women adhere to Christian teachings on marriage, which besides demanding monogamy may also encourages a wife's retreat from the workplace to the home. This ideology stems from the Victorian domestic culture that missionaries brought with them to Africa. Many elite women have thus sacrificed the economic autonomy that women usually enjoyed in local culture, and now depend on their husbands for their social and economic well-being. Furthermore, colonialism curtailed women's access to resources and opportunities, making elite women unable to compete with elite men economically. Well-educated women today are often still forced to secure their status through Christian marriages to elite men. African women nonetheless consider Christian marriages advantageous, for example by freeing them and their offspring from the threat of competition and conflict often associated with polygyny, and securing their inheritance (Mann 1994: 171–2).

In Africa's urban industrialized areas, 'official' or public polygyny has thus become relatively rare, especially as statutory and Christian marriage generally impose the legal obligation of monogamy. Men are also drawn to Christian marriage as a mark of elite status and as a means of forming alliances with elite families. Lagos elite men in colonial times, for example, did not marry polygynously despite few legal or institutional obstacles, because Lagos elite society disapproved of such 'backward' behaviour. As the Lagos elite grew, however, many of those who would have practised polygyny traditionally, but who now considered themselves too modern to go 'native', instead began to acquire 'girlfriends'. Maintaining a girlfriend became a status symbol, since only the rich and successful could afford to do so. Such 'outside marriages' were based on traditional norms that linked a man's power and prestige to his marital status: the more wives he had, the higher his position in the power structure. A successful man from a non-elite family may, like his elite counterpart, take an 'outside wife'; acquiring an 'outside wife' signals to his family and community that he still upholds the principles of his traditional culture. At the same time, it may signal to the man's peers, and even to his monogamous wife, that he has become successful – and modern. People in urban areas are thus increasingly turning to a more private form of polygyny, which is considered more in tune with their perceptions of modernity, not least by allowing men to appear monogamous in public. The great increase in the number of outside unions is fuelled by a growing acceptance of polygyny that has not been coupled with a decline in the perceived value of Christian marriage. Because 'outside marriages' are now so common and more widely accepted, more men may now be willing to recognize and take responsibility for their outside children and the mothers (Karanja 1987, 1994; Mann 1985, 1994).

Modernization and Westernization of Africa has meant that public polygyny, as practised in African 'traditional' societies, has been replaced to a large extent by private polygyny in urban areas. Those who practise private polygyny disapprove of public polygyny, which they perceive of as a 'lesser' form of marriage, and regard those practising it as 'backward'. The practice of keeping 'outside wives' instead of legal polygynous wives may represent African elite men's attempt to embody Western ideals of a modern man. While recognizing Christian monogamous marriage as a path to elite status, they may secretly strive towards the African ideal of polygyny. Men adhering to the monogamous mores of urban life might thus condemn a man for having an 'outside wife', but may secretly admire and envy him, or indeed have an 'outside wife' of their own. Elite women, typically the 'inside wives', do not generally accept polygyny, and disapprove of both private and public forms, which from their perspective are often indistinguishable. Men thus have good reason to keep their private polygyny hidden and ambiguous, not only because it is resented by most Christian wives, but also because outside unions are forbidden by the churches and outlawed by the State. The ambiguous nature of private polygyny makes it easier to manipulate, however, allowing both men and women to claim one sort of relationship on one occasion and another relationship on another occasion, to suit their needs. While 'outside wives' may benefit from the arrangements to a certain degree, men's attempt to combine monogamy with polygyny has negatively impacted urban elite ('inside') marriages. Husbands and wives' conflicting conceptions of what modern marriage entails have resulted in continuous tension between women's monogamous ideology and men's polygynous ideals (Karanja 1994: 203–4, 257–9; Mann 1994: 176; Solway 1990).

For many men, the institution of 'outside wives' or private polygyny may represent an African cultural renaissance, since it is based on principles rooted in African traditional cultures. Elite men may find it crucial to 'reinvent' African traditions (cf. Hobsbawm and Ranger 1983) as a way to free themselves from their colonial past, which suppressed traditional customs. They may accuse elite women, who are generally opposed to polygyny, whether private or public, of betraying their African roots (Karanja 1994; cf. Egbuna 1964). As Pitshandenge (1994: 126) notes, legal concessions to various groups allow elites to deviate from the principles of the legal system through a manipulation of the laws to suit their needs. Marriage laws in sub-Saharan Africa remain essentially patriarchal, and a husband is mostly able to decide freely whether to make his marriage monogamous or polygynous. The new forms of polygyny such as 'outside wives' also allow would-be polygynists to confront their changing socio-economic circumstances. This modern reinforcement of polygyny is related to economic development, a factor that is usually considered to depress polygyny levels. Western models of progress assume that polygyny levels will fall as part of the universal progression towards a nuclear and conjugal family following in the wake of development and Christian penetration. But Western-based models tend to ignore that other people in other cultures might have other needs and other ways of expressing them than Westerners do. Among the many concomitants of modernity are changing attitudes and definitions of marriage, but African men's desire to be polygynous appears to remain unchanged. Becoming schooled, Christian and part of a global cultural community through the vehicles of Westernization can also give people strength to remain what they (think they) were. To be polygynous can indeed be to be modern. For men mostly; for many urban African married women, modern 'outside wives' are more likely to represent regression than modernity.

Urban Polygyny in Ghana

Ghana in West Africa is characterized by general polygyny. Officially, there are three different forms of marriage in Ghana today: marriage under various systems of customary law, which is potentially polygynous; marriage according to Islamic law, which is also potentially polygynous; and marriage under the Ordinance, performed either by religious rites in church or by civil rites before a registrar. Ordinance marriage is most closely related to the Western form of marriage in that a man can lawfully marry only one wife, certain property rights are guaranteed to the wife, and marriage can only be terminated by legal divorce in courts (Dinan 1983: 364 n.8). Marriages registered according to provisions of the Marriage Ordinance in Ghana, as elsewhere in Africa, legally preclude polygyny.

> The penalty laid down in the Criminal Code for contracting more than one Ordinance marriage is seven years (section 440). The offence for marrying a second wife under the Ordinance while being married by customary law carries a penalty of five years imprisonment (section 448). The case of contracting a customary marriage to a third party, while being married under the Ordinance, carries a penalty of two years (section 449). (Oppong 1974: 51 n.47)

However, few cases of bigamy ever reach the courts, not least because a man married under the Ordinance is usually incapable of contracting another legally valid marriage. In addition to these three main categories, there are many different forms of recognized unions in Ghana. There are few obstacles in the way of cohabiting and having children with a minimum of formalities or public rites performed, and women's social status is not adversely affected by doing so.

Missionaries and British colonial officials were continually perplexed by the numerous forms of marriage and heterosexual relationships in Ghana, and conflicts regularly arose when they attempted to define marriage and its consequences strictly. This created not only confusion, but also gave Ghanaians the opportunity to manipulate various authorities: the British, the churches and the traditional rulers. Europeans were particularly perplexed by the fact that the most binding family ties were with kin rather than with spouses, such that maternal kin rather than widowed spouses inherited property, for example. This matrilineal principle makes it impractical for husbands and wives to pool their income: most women operate their own separate budget to avoid their husbands' kin making demands on a common budget. There is a strong fear among women that common resources are diverted to their husbands' kin, or indeed other wives or concubines, and that they have to compete with kin and co-wives for those resources. For many contemporary women, this fear acts as a sort of financial disincentive for marriage. Many legal battles over inheritance arise between a widow and children of an Ordinance marriage and the deceased's lineage members.

Resource competition and conflicts over inheritance stem from the general problem in Ghana, as in most of Africa, of how to define marriage in a cultural environment that has numerous forms of unions. Determining whether a woman was a wife or a concubine may revolve around the relationship between the families involved, for example, leaving much room for manipulation and ambiguity. During colonial times, the traditional rulers, chiefs and court officials had considerable experience with case law in the traditional courts, and church elders from the main churches in Ghana – Presbyterians, Methodists and Anglicans – often settled marriage, divorce, seduction and inheritance disputes as well. In contemporary Ghana, women have campaigned for a comprehensive law protecting wives married under customary law, because financial considerations have made more and more men claim that a woman who would be considered their wife under traditional law is only their concubine and does not deserve support once she no longer 'serves' them. The Ghanaian government has thus, through several legislative moves, been forced to raise such questions as 'who is a wife?', 'what are a legal wife's rights?' and 'what are the rights of children?' (Dinan 1983: 351; Pitshandenge 1994: 117; Vellenga 1983: 145–50).

Protecting their rights to maintenance and inheritance are paramount for women in Ghana not just because the distribution of property within the lineage rather than between marital partners is still strong, but also because of the persistence of polygyny. In a study of urban schoolteachers, nearly all claimed allegiance to Christianity and were monogamously married according to customary rites. Fewer than one in ten marriages had been formalized in church or under the Marriage Ordinance, which legally precludes polygyny. The minority of couples who married under provisions of the Marriage Ordinance were usually educated and salaried people, as registered marriages are thought to enhance the prestige of the partners and their families (Oppong 1974: 31; 1987: 169). Generally in Ghana, education, urban living and Christianity are positively related to monogamy, such that more urban, educated Christian women than rural, uneducated non-Christian women are found in monogamous marriages. Followers of Islam and traditional religions have higher levels of polygynous marriages (Klomegah 1997). In contemporary urban Ghana, as in most other urban areas of Africa, traditional polygyny is being replaced by modern versions adapted to urban living conditions. Many husbands married under the Ordinance, as is common among the urban elites, are thus part of other 'conjugal' relations producing children whose paternity is acknowledged. The offspring of such 'outside marriages' may be completely legitimate in the legal sense that they have the right to inherit a share of their father's property at his death, whatever degree of public recognition given to their mother (Oppong 1974: 45, 72).

The transformation of polygyny into new urban forms is illustrated by the virtual disappearance of the levirate or widow inheritance. Formerly a man's heir inherited his widow with his property, and this meant that he took over the deceased's responsibility and care for his wife and children. The combination of Christian objections to polygyny and pressing financial considerations has undermined this traditional way of securing the socio-economic welfare of widows and orphans. Widows with children to care for are now mostly left to their own devices. Even in those societies where it is still considered correct for a husband's family to offer another man to a widow, however, many women may now refuse to become inherited (Bleek 1987: 146; cf. Mair 1953: 99 and Whyte 1980: 144).

For many men, then, the status quo is fairly satisfactory, they can engage in multiple sexual relationships without the financial outlay of former times, as well as avoiding the economic burden of inherited widows. They can, in effect, live a polygynous lifestyle without any long-term commitments. For most women, the status quo is not satisfactory, because they have to provide the same 'services' to men as before, but do not get the same socio-economic security in return which they used to. In Ghana men are allowed, and even expected, to be involved with more than one woman, and can only be accused of adultery if they are involved with a married woman. Adultery for women, however, is defined very broadly, and for a married woman all men are taboo (Oppong 1974: 137, 141). There is thus a built-in potential for conflict in the unequal opportunities for husbands and wives in Ghana to contract additional sexual partners, either within or outside marriage. Only men are able to take a second partner in marriage or engage in extramarital liaisons more or less openly. This sexual inequality is expressed in the popular Ghanaian 'highlife' songs, which proclaim the superiority of men. In highlife songs, polygynous marriages are portrayed as rife with rivalry and jealousy, and co-wives – called *kora* (rival) – are presented as competing for the sensible, but troubled husband's favour (Asante-Darko and van der Geest 1983: 246–8).

The superiority attached to the masculine role in Ghanaian society is expressed in men's ability to attract and maintain attractive 'girlfriends'. In the capital Accra, as in the rest of urban Ghana, people increasingly reject official polygynous unions. This move away from polygyny is more an economic adaptation to urban conditions than a normative commitment to monogamy as such, a process seen in all of urban Africa. Contemporary monogamous Ghanaian men instead engage in an informal, private form of polygyny in an institutionalized system of 'girlfriend' relationships. The resultant 'sugar daddy' and 'gold-digger' relationships are viewed as straightforward exchanges of services: sugar daddies (established married men) need the services the women can offer, and the gold-diggers (young single women) need the resources the men can provide. The system allows women to maintain the traditional pattern of men assuming responsibility for their main financial outlays (rent, food, clothing, etc.) in return for their sexual services. The major difference from traditional forms of polygynous unions is that the relationships are not socially or legally recognized as marriages. The urban environment thus allows young single women to maximize the economic potential of their sexuality by cultivating male patrons. Engaging in 'girlfriend' relations with married men can, for example, pay occupational dividends for women, as men continue to play crucial roles in women's occupational lives, enabling them to advance their careers and giving them upward mobility (Dinan 1983: 351–6). Though some women clearly benefit from these 'outside marriages', they tend to be very insecure long-term and may leave women destitute if the cash-paying boyfriends lose interest in them. For the monogamously married 'inside' wife, they create tension in the marriage by violating the monogamous foundation of her marriage. The new forms of urban African polygyny thus appear ultimately to be to men's advantage, with little to offer women in the long term. Modernity and its effect on polygamy has seemingly brought some women some cheer, but has probably taken most African women one step forward into the new modern world, and two steps back into the old.

Polygamy in Contemporary Societies[1]

Polygamy in Monogamous Societies

Eastern Ways, Western Frays

Globalization and economic development, emigration and immigration, political struggle for civil and human rights, nationalism and separatism, civil wars and international conflicts, ethnic cleansing and refugees, all such circumstances creating large movements of people and of cultures impact the practice of polygamy in the contemporary world. The world is in flux like never before, people travel voluntarily or under duress across the globe in increasing numbers, and no cultures are immune from outside influences or indeed from increasingly self-confident internal forces for change. And so polygamy is in flux with the world. In countries where colonialism, revolution or legislation may have banned age-old polygamous practices, rapid industrialization and economic growth may have brought it back. This is happening in China, for example, where the communist regime seemingly turns a blind eye to the reappearance of the age-old 'anti-social and unequal' practice of concubinage in the wake of a burgeoning economy. As in pre-revolutionary days, it serves important prestige purposes for the newly powerful classes in Chinese society (Lang and Smart 2002). In countries where people do not practise polygamy, new immigrants may bring the practice with them, and demand legal recognition of their practices. For example, the monogamous Christian majority in Germany is forced to tackle such issues as Turkish women's rights under polygamy, because Turkish immigrants to Germany may practise it. The government may ban the practice, but will it enforce the ban if it results in disrupted families? Does the rule of law always take precedence over the rights of individuals to follow their beliefs? Christian German citizens may feel that it is an affront to moral, religious and legal principles that polygamy is tacitly allowed in their country, and so the government must act.

All over the world, polygamy is becoming part of the contemporary rights debate, which is both about the right to practise individual lifestyles, as well as a person's civil and human rights. It may be the right of a Mormon or Muslim to practise what he believes is his prophet-ordained commandment to be polygynous in the USA, or the right of a Himalayan tribesman to practise polyandry in the face of Hindu and monogamous Indian domination. For some, legal recognition becomes paramount, for others, practising polygamy in obscurity seems preferable, but common to all is the emergence of polygamy as a social force in both East and West, North and South, even for those people who would never dream of engaging in it.

The Hmong, a mountain tribe in Laos that was recruited by the CIA in the 1960s to fight a guerrilla war against the communists during the Vietnam War, have come in great numbers to the USA as refugees. There they might have lived a quiet life were it not for the fact that they practise polygamy. They thus join the fray with Mormons and Muslims who also illegally practise polygamy in the USA. Hmong men traditionally practised polygyny as part of their clan-based kinship system, which requires and values large families. In the USA, there are several thousand Hmong living in polygamous families. Hmong women are less than satisfied with the persistence of polygamy in their communities, however. Women have low status in the patriarchal Hmong culture, and it is not unusual for girls to be married in their early teens. To many American women, polygamy has become synonymous with child abuse and slavery, in which young girls are sold to older men. Bigamy is a felony in Minnesota, which has the largest Hmong population in the USA, and grounds for denial of US citizenship. Besides being illegal, polygamy clashes with the traditional American view of what constitutes a family unit. This clash has become all the more relevant now when the definition of marriage is central to the national debate on same-sex marriages (see below). To many Americans, polygamy is culturally irreconcilable with American values. In 2004 the American public, which in the nineteenth century fought a long moral and legal battle with the Mormons to prevent them from practising polygamy (see Chapter 5), was therefore up in arms over a suggested mass transfer of Hmong refugees to Minnesota. When talks began over the fate of more than 14,000 Hmong living in camps in Thailand, polygamy became a stumbling block in the negotiations. Men would only be allowed to bring one wife to the USA, but, as many Hmong have several wives, the authorities would be forced to separate family members. In practice, however, they could all move to the USA and stay together as a family group, though for some second wives it involved a forcible divorce from their husband in order to enter the USA.

On paper then, polygamy hinders Hmong entry into the USA, but in reality the USA, like other Western countries with large immigrant populations, has had to accept *de facto* polygamy among immigrants who brought polygamous families with them. The same scenarios are being played out in all countries where immigrants bring polygamy based on religious or cultural traditions with them into primarily Christian Western societies, which do not allow polygamy or bigamy. In Western European countries such as France and Germany, the growing immigrant populations practise polygamy more or less openly, even though it violates these countries' laws. In France alone, an estimated 140,000 people are living in polygamous families. This is mostly a consequence of French immigration policies in the late 1960s and early 1970s, which encouraged men from West Africa to come and work in France. Many of them came from (Islamic) polygamous cultures, and brought their families with them. For years polygamy was tolerated, but in 1993 the politician Charles Pasqua pushed through a law banning the practice. Initially the law was not enforced, and polygynous wives were still allowed to join their husbands in France because they had 'French' children, meaning children of residents of France. In recent years, the French government has been cracking down on what they regard as an affront to women's rights. Under new legislation polygamous families must split up or lose their livelihoods – men who refuse to 'de-cohabit' lose their work permits. It means uncertainty and financial hardships for almost all the families involved. The consequences can be catastrophic, especially for second or higher order wives and their children, leaving them with no place to live and little financial support. It also means breaking up families with the ensuing psychological (and material) costs.

As long as Western governments uphold the ban on polygamy, it will remain a pressing problem for immigrants who can lose their residency or work permit, or indeed be barred from entering a Western country because of their practices. To the immigrant, the ban on polygamy may appear to be part of a government-generated complex making immigration and integration very difficult or even obstructive. Malian women migrating to France, for example, are confronted not only by restrictive immigration policies, including the ban on polygamy, but also by public disapproval of their often high fertility. Some Malian women in polygynous families therefore engage in 'pregnancy rivalries' with their co- wives, in order to maximize their fecundity and thus retain immigrant status by giving birth to larger numbers of children than French women (Sargent and Cordell 2003). As such, polygamy becomes a political statement, both for the immigrants and for the host country. To the French government, banning polygamy was a question of equal rights between men and women, based on the common Western assumption that polygamy entails subjugation of women. Some French politicians have also suggested that polygamy causes maladjustment in immigrant youths, such as those participating in the violent night riots in the suburbs of Paris in late 2005. The push to enforce the ban on polygamy has now escalated into a conflict between two sets of rights, the rights of women as defined by the French majority and the rights of ethnic minorities to practise their culture and religion.

As in the Hmong case in the United States, many Westerners see the minority's right to practise polygamy in a majority monogamous society as a clash between irreconcilable cultural and religious differences. However, France's attempt to strengthen women's rights by banning polygamy cannot automatically be seen as a result of its Western Christian orientation, but rather as a consequence of what France would call its defence of universal human, civil and women's rights. France can refer to legal precedents in the Muslim world: in Morocco, modernizing forces now spearheaded by a reform-minded king have made access to polygamy difficult for Muslims. As in Western countries, the attempt is to give civil law precedence over religious law. In Tunisia, a groundbreaking 1956 decision bans marriages with multiple wives and allows only monogamous unions. The rights of women versus the right to practise the tenets of one's religion or culture even if it clashes with the rule of law takes place within both Western countries and the immigrants' home countries. In the debates about Turkey joining the EU, for example, there is concern over women's rights in Turkey. Human rights groups have repeatedly highlighted abuses of women, particularly in Turkey's underdeveloped south-eastern region, which is known for its conservative traditions. Although polygamy is illegal in Turkey, it continues to be commonplace in the region. Such traditions are now being challenged as Turkey seeks to join the EU.

A main polygamous battlefield is thus in the West, where local and national governments have to deal with the *de facto* polygamy being practised in clear violations of their laws and cultural and religious sensibilities. As such, the Western conflicts mirror the many local battles being fought all over the polygamous world as a response to the push and pull of development and globalization. For many contemporary practitioners, polygamy becomes a way of expressing allegiance to their version of their traditional culture, society or religion, which is perceived to be under threat from the encroaching globalized world. Defenders of polygamy are typically confronted by women's rights activists who want to ban polygamy (see below). Such opposing trends are found in numerous societies, in varying forms, as polygamy becomes part of the social and political discourse in contemporary societies.

Redefining Marriage

The practice of polygamy in the West has created a legal battlefield, where monogamous countries have to deal with the *de facto* polygamy being practised by immigrants in clear violations of their laws. Where the immigrants' polygamous lifestyles collide head on with the legal and cultural basis of their host countries, it has led to a politicization of polygamy among the large immigrant populations in the West. Immigrants are of course aware of their precarious legal situation and have become more engaged in seeking legality for their practices. The ongoing debate in the USA and Canada over gay marriage (see below) has led to suggestions that polygamists should also be within their rights to have their choice of family life made legal. This has created public anxiety that legalized homosexual marriages may lead to constitutional changes allowing minority groups who claim polygamy as a religious right to also demand their rights. Similarly in the UK, some Muslims are hoping that the new Human Rights Act will make it possible to legalize polygamy. Detractors, however, argue that if polygamous marriages are recognized under British law, polyandry and other forms of multiple couplings could also become law under the equal rights legislation, undermining the monogamous society that has existed in Britain for centuries. Furthermore, if polygamy were to be legalized it would allow everybody, not only Muslims, to have more than one spouse. British

Muslims might envision the UK following the example of Malaysia, where only Muslims are allowed to be polygamous (see Chapter 4), thus not interfering with the marital structure of the rest of British society. But the legal premises for such segregated legislation are not present, so polygamy is unlikely to be made law in the UK. Similarly, it is highly unlikely that any Western country in the near future would pass such legislation, even in those countries where same-sex unions are legally permitted. The battlefield is set, however, because polygamy is a growing phenomenon all over the Western world.

Polygamists in North America have received indirect support for their battle from a powerful lobby, namely homosexual rights activists. Like Mormon polygamists, they seek to legalize their particular form of marriage, which involves two people of the same sex. The right of homosexual couples to marry is being put forth as a civil rights issue, and polygamists frame their argument in a similar way. The debate over same-sex marriage in the USA turned a major corner in 2003 after the Massachusetts State Supreme Court ruled that denying marriage rights to gay couples violated the state constitution. The ruling states that the right to marry the person of one's choice is a fundamental right, subject to appropriate government restrictions in the interests of public safety and welfare. The Massachusetts ruling, which ordered the state to legalize same-sex marriages, opened up the possibility for constitutional challenges to state and federal anti-bigamy laws. Many polygamists hope that if same-sex marriage becomes legal, polygamy will be next. Many people now appear to believe that same-sex unions in Canada and the United States will act as vanguards for marriages not just of two but several partners. The cause of polygamy is thus increasingly linked in an uneasy alliance to the cause of gay marriage. Uneasy, because the people who practise polygamy often do so from a religious background that condemns homosexuality. So while Mormons and gays may have very little in common in their beliefs and lifestyles, they nonetheless share an interest in broadening the US definition of marriage. The US debate has hence moved to be less about moral objection to homosexuality and more about the definition of marriage.

Now that gay and polygamous marriages have surfaced in the national debate, the question is whether same-sex unions can pave the legal way for polygamy. Proponents of same-sex unions speak of 'a struggle for civil rights', and polygamists argue that civil rights include the right to marry more than one person. Opponents of gay marriage condemn such unions as 'counterfeit marriage' and have termed the legalization process the 'slippery slope': they fear that allowing gay marriage will eventually lead American society toward the total abolition of marriage. Historically in Western Christian culture, marriage has meant the union of one man and one woman, so if the definition of marriage is changed from being between a man and a woman to include a union between two men, who is to say that it should not be redefined further to include a union between one man and two women. And if at some point polygyny is legalized might not female activists demand equal rights for polyandrous unions between one woman and several men? And will insistence on legalized group marriage between several men and several women come next? The Massachusetts court dealt with the polygamy issue by stating that the (homosexual) plaintiffs in the case 'do not attack the binary nature of marriage'. Legally speaking, there is a major difference between gay marriage, which is monogamous marriage, and polygamous marriage, which changes the numbers of spouses, not their characteristics or status, and as such represents an entirely different form of marriage. Anti-polygamy statutes draw the line at the number of spouses, and limiting number of spouses does not violate any constitutional rights of US citizens. As such it is difficult to challenge, and many observers believe such legal challenges are futile. Another difference between promoting same-sex marriage as a civil or human rights issue and polygamy is that polygamy in the West is most often practised in response to what practitioners believe to be a mandate or allowance of their religious belief system. Practitioners make a conscious choice to adhere more to religious principles than to secular laws; this allows them to redefine 'family' in a way that maintains their communal culture and family structure.

Gay and plural marriage both challenge accepted norms of what constitutes family, and force people to ask whether it is acceptable to grant homosexuals and polygamists the same rights as those conferred upon the heterosexual and monogamous majority. Though many Americans do not believe that gay marriage will lead to demands for legalized polygamy, groups who favour polygamy are likely to suggest that polygamy is an acceptable lifestyle choice for an increasingly multicultural nation. Opponents of plural marriage argue that legalizing polygamy would alter the institution of marriage far more than gay marriage could, not least because polygamy is considered by many Americans to involve abuse of women and young girls. They fear that legalizing polygamy would open the floodgates for men wanting to marry their mistresses to legitimize *de facto* marriages, to the detriment of women. Even if people never exercise their option to practise polygamy, the fact that it would be legal would fundamentally influence marital relations between spouses. The knowledge that polygamy is possible and permissible can be a destabilizing factor in marriages, a phenomenon well documented in polygynous societies (e.g. Kosack 1999: 557). As Ware points out, 'in a polygynous society all marriages are potentially polygynous, and women and men learn to structure their relationships on this basis' (1983: 17).

There is massive opposition in the USA not only to polygamous marriage, but to any form of unconventional bonding, such as same-sex marriage. Hence, the fight to legalize polygamy is both being helped and hindered by its alliance with the struggle for gay rights. Being caught up in the anti-gay-marriage struggle led by the Christian right is probably mostly hindering it. Like Mormon pro-polygamists' ill-fated attempt to align themselves with the pro-slavery South before the Civil War (Gordon 1996), it might not merely fail, but might even backfire and make things more difficult. The push to legalize polygamy in the wake of gay marriage laws has thus yet to gather great momentum, not least because of the massive resistance it will continue to meet in the American (and Canadian) public. The primary issue is not the legal benefits granted to multiple spouses but the perception that the State, and by implication the people, will sanction something a majority of Americans regard as morally objectionable. The same issues are at stake over gay marriage. Yet the polygamy rights movement may still gather cultural and political momentum in the future, and American courts may still discover a constitutional right to plural marriage. The battle rages on.

Polygamous Battlefields

Fighting for Polygyny in the USA

Contemporary fundamentalist Mormons in Western United States have launched the best-known legal challenge to legitimize polygamy in the Western World. At issue are the legal implications of polygamy, religious freedom and constitutionalism in the USA. Mormon polygamy is not primarily a matter of status or politics, as among many other contemporary practitioners, but rather a religious statement of allegiance to an idealized nineteenth-century Mormonism, where it was part of church doctrine and practice. Mormon polygamy presents a special case among the polygamous people described in this book. They are not special because they practise plural marriage without the consent of the law and officially engage in an illegal activity, for so too do many immigrants to the West, and indeed people living in societies that used to allow polygamy but have now banned it. The Mormons are special because they are 'home-grown' American Christians and early monogamous pioneers, who practise polygamy in an officially and fervently monogamous society without finding any support or even understanding from the overwhelming majority of the non-Mormon American public. In former polygynous societies where polygamy has now been banned there might be sympathy for illegal practitioners, but not so among fellow Christians in the USA. The general public feel that fundamentalist Mormons violate not only legal but also moral, social, cultural and religious mores in their practices. For contemporary polygamous Mormons, therefore, it is of outmost importance to secure legal legitimacy for their practices, for it is their legal predicament that impinges most directly on their practices.

Mormons have a long history of refusing to accept federal anti-polygamy legislation. After Congress outlawed polygamy in 1862, Mormon Church leaders continued to practise it for thirty years, and after the Manifesto officially banned polygamy in 1890, the Church allowed the contracting of plural marriages for almost fifteen years more. Ineffective federal laws and law enforcement allowed Mormons to violate anti-polygamy legislation for decades. In 1953, there was a raid on the Short Creek fundamentalist community (now grown into the two fundamentalist towns of Hildale, UT and Colorado City, AZ), which was widely criticized for, among other things, its insensitive approach and its exorbitant costs. Its main effect was to strengthen fundamentalist belief in their cause as well as to extinguish non-Mormon desire to prosecute them. For almost fifty years, officials did not initiate any charges against polygamists because it was held by the majority of the American public that no significant harm to the community was being perpetrated, there were too many polygamists to prosecute, it was too expensive, and there were more important legal and criminal matters to attend to (Altman and Ginat 1996: 48–52). As suggested in Chapter 5, however, there have been a number of recent prosecutions against fundamentalists accused of practising or aiding in the practice of polygamy. One of the most (in)famous anti-polygamy cases in recent years was that of Tom Green, who was sentenced to five years in prison for bigamy in Utah in 2001. On a more serious charge, Tom Green was sentenced to life in prison for a child-rape conviction, as he had sex with his first wife Linda Kunz when she was only thirteen years old, and he was thirty-seven. Tom Green's five sister-wives are literally two sets of sisters, who all married him when they were fourteen or fifteen years old. The family, including more than thirty children, lives in a collection of trailers making up an isolated Utah desert community. To avoid engaging in illegal behaviour, Tom Green married and then divorced each of his five wives, but continued to live with them. The State prosecuted him for bigamy nonetheless because they considered him married to his five wives by common law. It was the first high profile bigamy case in Utah in half a century.

Today, the fight against polygamy is not based on moral outrage as it was in the nineteenth century. Contemporary legal action against fundamentalists is focused on specific issues, not on the practice of plural marriage as a crime in and of itself. The specific issue of most concern to the American public is that of under-age girls being forced into polygamy. Critics claim that contemporary polygamy fosters and condones statutory rape. There are also claims that under-age girls are being trafficked across state and international lines, for example between Mexican and American polygamist communities, for purposes of polygamy. This is a federal offence under the Mann Act, which prohibits transportation of women across state boundaries for immoral purposes. Polygamists claim that they are merely abiding by the traditional nineteenth-century Mormon marriage system, in which girls often married at age fourteen. Polygamists can point to their founding Prophet, Joseph Smith, whose youngest plural wife, Helen Mar Kimball, was fourteen when she married him. Tom Green's wives, as mentioned, all married him when they were fourteen or fifteen; some groups do defer sexual relations when a girl is so young. Most people in the USA today find it unacceptable for a girl of fourteen to marry or have sexual relations, however. Their concerns are regularly fed by stories such as that of a sixteen-year-old girl from the Kingston clan (see Chapter 5) who accused her father of forcing her to marry her 32-year-old uncle as his fifteenth wife. As she rebelled, her father whipped her with a belt and dumped her semiconscious in a remote area. The girl contacted the police, and her father was charged with assault and child abuse and her husband charged with incest. The incest charge has not been levied against polygamists before, because the communities are very secretive, and nobody comes forward to file charges against their abusers. The girl's parents are half-brother and sister, and the Kingston clan is suspected of practising incest as a way to find enough spouses to continue their polygamous family structures.

At present, polygamy is not protected by the First Amendment to the US Constitution, which guarantees the free exercise of one's religion. Mormons have nonetheless always attempted to justify polygamy by reference to their constitutional rights to freedom of religion. In Utah in 1874, George Reynolds, secretary to second prophet Brigham Young, was indicted for bigamy. Church leaders appealed the case to the Supreme Court hoping to set a precedent. However, in 1879, the Supreme Court in *Reynolds v. the United States* established that although people could freely 'believe' in certain religious principles, such as plural marriage, religious belief could not be accepted as justification for an act made criminal by the law of the land. *Reynolds vs. the United States* still stands today (Altman and Ginat 1996: 34; van Wagoner 1989: 110–11). The hopes of pro-polygamy activists have been revived, however, by several recent prosecutions and lawsuits against polygamists in Utah, which have raised a number of constitutional questions. First, they argue that the First Amendment's free establishment and exercise clauses relating to religious freedom allow them to practise their religious beliefs freely, including heavenly ordained plural marriage. This argument is usually refuted by stating that the right to religious freedom does not put a person over federal law, which clearly prohibits marriage to more than one spouse. Second, activists refer to the due process 'right to privacy' concepts. In 2004, the United States Supreme Court overturned Texas sodomy laws and established in their ruling that adults have a privacy right that extends to private, consensual sex acts. Mormons believe that they receive unequal treatment under the law, because individuals have a recognized constitutional right to engage in any form of consensual sexual relationship with any number of partners. They find it unequal that a person can live with and have children with any number of partners as long as they do not marry, but as soon as they make a commitment to each other as spouses, they are put in jail. In 2005, a US district judge in Salt Lake City, UT, dismissed a lawsuit by a man and two women to have their union recognized by the State, by ruling that the State 'has an interest in the practice of monogamous marriage'. The trio had based their lawsuit on the 2004 overturn of the Texas sodomy laws, hoping to establish a precedent.

A further legal challenge facing Mormon fundamentalists today stems from one of the central management problems for polygamous communities: the excess of young unmarried men when older men marry two or more wives. In the early days of Mormonism, when the religion grew primarily through new converts, the problem was not so marked, as more women than men appear to have converted. But this picture soon changed, and in the late nineteenth century the gender imbalance on the marriage market created by polygamy started to impact polygamist communities. Sending young Mormon men abroad to do missionary work for several years was one solution to this problem. Another solution was to send young men into mines, industries or railroads, a necessity after all available agricultural land was taken after four decades of settlement in Utah. Opportunities for industry in the region was limited, however, so Mormon families struggled to educate their surplus sons for whom there was no available land or wives, to enable them to find work in the cities. When the young men moved to the cities, however, it often resulted in a separation not only from their families, but from their faith as well (Anderson 1937: 607; Dannin 2002: 224). There is a straight line from the early more or less voluntary expulsions to the modern 'Lost Boys', young Mormon males thrown out of their communities and excommunicated from their Church. In 2004, several of these 'Lost Boys' launched legal action against the FLDS (see Chapter 5) and its leader Warren Jeffs for conspiracy to purge surplus males from the community. The boys claim that they had been forcibly removed from their families, faith and communities to give elder male members less competition for wives and make more young women available to them. The authorities believe that the leaders of the FLDS have expelled as many as 1,000 teenage boys. Many of the boys, some as young as thirteen, were simply dumped outside towns and told that they would never see their families again, nor go to heaven, leaving them traumatized.

FLDS officials and lawyers argue that the expelled boys were teenage delinquents who refused to comply with FLDS rules and dishonoured their moral codes. Investigators acknowledge that the boys may have rebelled against FLDS's very conservative views and ways, but nonetheless emphasize that the boys were most likely expelled because there are too many of them to continue polygamous family patterns. Life in the FLDS compounds is closely controlled by church leaders, who among other things decide which wives to give or take away from the men. This has led to charges that 'obedient disciples are rewarded with teenage brides' and that leaders 'squabble over desirable young girls'. The FLDS, which has about 10,000 members, believes that a man must marry at least three women to go to heaven. If most men were to marry three or more wives, however, there would not be enough marriageable women available in the community. Investigators charge that the FLDS addresses this impasse by selectively expelling those boys deemed unfit to be part of their faith. The FLDS has, for example, reproached the boys' modern and frivolous dress style as evidence of their lack of respect for the group's dress code, which must be modest and conservative for both men and women. According to community leaders, the dress code indicates the degree to which people are willing to uphold the standards of the community. This entails that faithful women are obliged to wear nineteenth-century 'pioneer' style dresses, which are ankle-length, high-necked and long-sleeved, as well as wear intricate nineteenth-century hairdos (Altman and Ginat 1996: 68; van Wagoner 1989: x). As such, fundamentalist Mormon polygamy and its practitioners are just as culturally alien to the American public as Hmong refugees, and therefore receive similar scant understanding.

Fighting against Polygyny in Africa

Development has according to some observers been detrimental to African women and to African gender relations. Colonial policies and their associated notions about the dependent status of women (and men) are seen as having destabilized women's status and rights in sub-Saharan Africa. Christian missionaries similarly built their platform on Victorian domestic arrangements, which implied women's retreat from public life. In West Africa, for example, the self-sufficiency that was part of both men and women's self-concept has been undermined, as have the relatively egalitarian aspects of West African gender relations. Polygyny was also challenged by colonial administrators and Christian missionaries, who considered it detrimental to women and attempted to eliminate it through various laws and decrees. They have been partly successful in their endeavours, often backed up by post-colonial legislation. The result is a situation where the traditional means of achieving status and power for many of Africa's women have been seriously undermined. First, women were made dependent on men in return for responsibility through marriage, then they were denied access to this responsibility, when the urban phenomenon of 'outside wives' emerged in polygyny's place. But as official polygamy has all but disappeared in many parts of urban Africa, so has its positive aspects. Polygyny may offer women advantages in the form of shared workload, cooperation in household tasks and raising children, as well as social companionship. The loneliness and social stigma that unmarried women endure in societies where marriage is universal, may appear to many women far worse that the potential conflicts in a polygynous household. Women appear not to be overtly jealous over their husband's relations with a co-wife, though this does not preclude great emotional difficulties and sexual jealousies between co-wives. Wives appear to be more jealous when their husbands have relations with women outside the household, because these relationships are uncontrollable from the standpoint of the wives. Such jealousies usually diminish or disappear when the 'outside women' are brought into the household as co-wives. This does not happen in modern *de facto* polygyny, however (Kosack 1999: 556–60; Oppong 1983: 205; Ware 1983: 30).

The contemporary situation in urban Africa, where plural unions involve concubines rather than second wives, might hence make women worse off: 'real' polygyny involves official wives sharing resources as well as controls and sanctions in interpersonal relations, whereas concubines are unofficial and may get more (or less) of the husband's attention and resources than his official wife. The move towards Western monogamy that many African women wish for will not improve their matrimonial relations as long as men are unwilling to suppress their polygynous tendencies. Official polygyny may thus seem preferable to *de facto* polygyny or concubinage for some women. To many African feminists, however, polygyny remains a social evil allowing men to subjugate women, and like all social evils, they believe it should be removed in order to improve the lives of both men and women. While many African women would not consider themselves feminists or formulate their views on polygyny quite so strongly, there is growing opposition to polygyny among women. This is reflected in the many anti-polygyny campaigns that seek to inform and educate women about their rights, often by focusing on particular issues of concern to women.

One of the major challenges polygynous wives faces in Africa today is HIV/ AIDS. Women bear the brunt of the AIDS pandemic in Africa, making up over half of those infected as well as having the fastest growing infection rate. The UN has emphasized that international efforts to fight the AIDS pandemic must put women at the centre, because only by giving women the freedom to make their own sexual and other decisions can it be addressed successfully. This involves addressing various traditional practices, such as naming ceremonies, female genital mutilation and polygyny, which are considered to increase women's chances of contracting HIV. There are several ways polygyny can contribute to higher infection levels. Polygynous husbands can be the source of the virus, for example when they migrate for work and have casual relations with women. If they become infected, they may pass on the virus to their wives upon their return. In those societies where wife-sharing with male relatives is practised, the chances of exposure to the virus are augmented. In polygynous societies the levirate or widow inheritance is often practised; when a husband inherits a widow from a brother who died of AIDS, he might become infected as well, and pass it on to his other wives. Wives can be the source of infection in gerontocratic polygynous societies, where older men monopolize young girls as wives. Some of these young women may have lovers among the bachelors of their own age grade. These bachelors may, through lack of a wife, visit prostitutes or have affairs with various married women, become infected and pass on the virus to their polygynously married lovers. Children in polygynous families are also exposed to increased risk of infection, because communal breastfeeding is practised in many tightly knit African communities and in polygynous families, where women rely on each other for childcare.[2]

Many of the wives and sexual partners of polygynous men therefore fear becoming HIV-infected, as they have little control over the sexual behaviour of other members of their household. Simultaneously, through the sharing of a husband, an infected individual can knowingly or unknowingly pass on HIV to all other members of the family. This fear has galvanized women's opposition to polygynous marriages, arguing that polygyny places them at risk of contracting various sexually transmitted diseases. All over Africa, women are beginning to question a man's right to have many wives in light of the HIV/AIDS crisis (Gwako 1998: 342). This is especially so in countries like Swaziland, where up to 40 per cent of the population is infected and polygyny is legal and common. Simultaneously, many men believe that they can better protect themselves and existing wives from possible infection by marrying more wives and thereby keep all sexual relations within marriage. It illustrates the common stalemate between male and female conceptions of marriage in general, and polygyny in particular, in modern Africa: women want to avoid polygyny for fear of being exposed to HIV infection while men want to practise polygyny for the same reason! Nonetheless, the threat of HIV/AIDS, alongside modernizing influences such as women's emancipation, development and globalization, seems to have a depressing effect on (official) polygyny levels in Africa.

HIV/AIDS, economic, social and sexual oppression, and all other concerns African women may have over polygyny have galvanized them into campaigning against polygyny at the national level. Women's rights movements concerned with polygamy have been strongest in the North African Muslim societies. In Morocco, Mernissi (1987) relates how development and decolonization, as well as a strong civil movement, have challenged and effectively abolished polygamy. Women's rights movements in sub-Saharan Africa are now gaining pace as well. It is an uphill battle, because many women's groups organized around other issues are unwilling to join the fight; they might not share the concerns or political stances of anti-polygyny activists, or they might be reluctant to engage in political advocacy because of co-option or harassment. Failing on the female front makes it harder to succeed on the male front in societies where polygyny is culturally entrenched and considered a badge of affluence, power and prestige. In Kenya, for example, attempts to outlaw polygyny have not succeeded in parliament, because legislators are almost always male; at best, they are not convinced that such legislation is needed, at worst, the men simply ignore women's issues (Gwako 1998: 34; cf. Maillu 1988). Uganda's parliament has similarly debated limiting men's access to polygamy, as part of a Domestic Relations Bill aimed at regulating family relations and protecting women's rights. The country's Muslim population has reacted angrily to the proposal, which they see as an attempt to rewrite the Koran; they consider polygyny their religious right. The government is nonetheless keen to reform the country's marriage laws, most of which were formulated a century ago. Many legislators believe that polygyny blocks socio-economic development, and they have also called for the end of such traditional practices as widow inheritance and bridewealth payments. In the Cote d'Ivoire, polygyny was legally abolished in 1964, but this has not prevented some groups from having the highest levels of polygyny in Africa. However, local women's rights groups campaign not against traditional rural polygyny, which often serves important purposes, but against the modern urban forms of plural unions involving multiple mistresses rather than wives. Activists argue that such unions undermine the lives of African women by removing men's responsibilities towards them and their children, and instead perpetuate men's sexual privileges.[3]

African women's fight to abolish polygyny is thus increasingly turning to legislative attempts to ban the practice. These attempts are primarily focused on the national scene, but also include the international level, where various United Nations conventions, declarations and charters are enrolled as ammunition in the fight. Activists argue that polygyny violates the Universal Declaration of Human Rights from 1948, the 1979 Convention on the Elimination of all Forms of Discrimination Against Women (CEDAW) as well as the 1993 UN Declaration on the Elimination of Violence against Women. African countries that have ratified those declarations should therefore use them to prohibit polygyny. Those African countries not adhering to these declarations may use the African Charter on Human and Peoples Rights, which the Organization of African Unity ratified in 1981, for similar purposes. The call for the UN to step in to protect African women from the subjugation of polygyny is not new. Over half a century ago, a nun working in colonial Africa wrote a symbolic story lamenting local women's trials and tribulations in marriage as she had observed them. Her aim was to bolster the Christian missionaries' attempt to eradicate polygyny as antithetical to Christian marriage and to women's dignity (see Chapter 7). Her story focused on the Fon of Bikom, a leader in the Bamenda Province of the then British Cameroons, reputed to have 600 wives. Women's organizations picked up the story and charged that the Fon's polygynous arrangements and forced marriages in a mandated territory were a violation of the UN charter on Human Rights, and they demanded that the UN stepped in. After visiting the Fon, the UN commission declined to help, noting that the Fon's private life was outside their jurisdiction. The Fon could enjoy life with his about 100 (rather than 600) wives again. As it happened, the UN would probably have been less effective than 'the forces that everywhere are giving women the courage to follow their hearts' desire': though the Fon's any whim was law, fifty-four of his wives ran away (Reyher 1953: 15–19).

Whether polygyny will continue to be a dominant marriage form in Africa in the future will thus depend on women's willingness to live in a polygynous marriage. If most women refuse to become part of polygynous unions, no legislative ban will be needed to eradicate the practice. In many parts of West Africa, for example, young women are very influenced by Christian ideas of conjugal marriage, and so reject polygyny on principle. They typically choose to marry Christian men who are religiously bound to be monogamous, but as they soon find out, Christianity does not prevent those men who want another wife from entering polygynous unions. Traditionally, becoming a polygynous wife of a wealthy and powerful man would secure a woman a higher standard of living, as well as assistance for her family, but the contemporary forms of urban polygyny bestow almost none of the benefits on women that polygyny had in rural areas. A modern urban woman will probably only accept a polygynous marriage if it has specific advantages for her (Kosack 1999). The advantages would have to outweigh all the negative aspects now associated with polygyny by African women. Women may be discouraged by female friends' or kin's experiences, they may fear the quarrelling, jealousy and emotional tensions involved in sharing a husband with several women, as well as the high chance of divorce in polygynous marriage. The success of a polygynous marriage has always depended more on the relationship between the co-wives than between a wife and her husband. A particular husband–wife relationship might be very good, but the marriage will fail if the wife is unable to accept or function with her co-wives. Tensions and conflicts between co-wives are also considered to lead to accusations of witchcraft, which act as another deterrent for modern women. Women may also be concerned about the often limited resources, especially in urban environments, and thus reject polygyny for fear of reducing their own standard of living. In contemporary Kenya, co-wife inheritance and burial disputes also appear to discourage women. The disputes arise because the various forms of (*de facto*) polygyny practised make it difficult to establish who exactly is a wife or a widow under any of Kenya's approved legal systems, i.e. state, religious or customary law (Gwako 1998: 341–4). Women in most of sub-Saharan Africa experience similar problems.

Future Foundations of Polygamy

'Me Culture' and Lifestyle Choices

What are the future foundations of polygamy? At issue is polygamy's survival as an institution in a world where monogamy is dominant. In the West at least, there is today a smorgasbord of bonding forms to choose from – consensual union, open relationship, registered partnership, monogamous heterosexual marriage, monogamous homosexual marriage, open marriage, common law marriage, plural marriage, informal marriage, group marriage, polyamorous union or indeed celibacy – why should the individual feel limited? If people want to engage in polygamy, is it reasonable that the State restricts their choices for their own good when the spouses are presumably consenting adults? Anti-polygamy campaigners clearly believe in limiting polygamists' rights; they argue that polygamy in the West, such as that practised by Mormons or Muslims, may involve the forcible marriage of young or even under-age girls to older men against their will. Plural marriage may prove far harder to legalize than same-sex marriage in part because people who have been personally hurt by polygamy will be there to speak out against it. Practitioners, in contrast, feel that they are simply following their own moral compass and do not feel that they violate any moral laws. They might violate legal codes perhaps, but then they follow the higher order heavenly laws. They hurt no one in the process, so why the antipathy? To more and more people in the Western world who are members of religions that allow (or used to allow) polygamy, becoming member of a plural family represents an individual choice, a lifestyle choice in accordance with the modern ego-centred 'me culture' which places an individual's needs before everything else. There is a feeling that if a person wants something, and they see it as right for them, then it becomes their right. The increasing infertility among Western women, for example, has resulted in having children being seen as a 'human right' which couples expect the State to help them achieve, legally and economically. Human egg sale, fertility treatment to singles and homosexuals, surrogate motherhood, all such controversial issues are fuelled by the 'me culture's' ego-driven demands. Polygamy joins the fray as a choice which some argue should be available to anyone.

In this vein, polygamy has become 'a choice for the black family' in the USA. For many African Americans, maintaining a functional family life is a major challenge. A sizeable proportion of black men in socially and economically depressed urban areas are (considered) unavailable in the marriage market because of such problems as criminal activities, drugs or chronic unemployment. Poverty, discrimination, women's control of benefit resources and strong kin networks also threaten marital or relationship stability (Stack 1975). Lack of opportunities for marriage, and the widespread absence of husbands/fathers in black households lock many women and their children in a cycle of poverty, with African American women comprising a large part of the continually poor in America. The difficulties in finding 'suitable' men with whom to form exclusive relationships have led some African American women to consider alternatives to monogamy. One of them is 'man-sharing', the practice of two or more women socially and sexually involved with the same man, a phenomenon associated with African American urban life for many years (Chapman 1986). Man-sharing constitutes a form of *de facto* polygyny, and is similar to various *de facto* practices found in modern urban Africa (see Chapter 8). As their African counterparts, these practices partly grow out of the challenging circumstances, such as economic deprivation and crowded housing, in which many urban African Americans find themselves. Man-sharing has therefore been called a form of 'crisis polygyny', a response to the crisis in black families (Kilbride 1994: 93).

Some African American activists are indeed campaigning for greater tolerance and legalization of polygamous practices among black families. They believe such practices would foster greater social and legal responsibility in black men for their women and children, as well as provide black women with cooperative networks, which increase their social and economic resources. For some activists, polygamy offers a solution to the crisis in black families because they consider it based on the 'natural' polygamous tendencies among black males (Dannin 2002; Kilbride 1994; cf. Stack 1975). Members of the Rastafarian movement, for example, believe man-sharing can be beneficial to all deprived black women. They urge them to pool their resources and return to their ancient 'Afrikan' tradition, where economy is shared, work is shared, motherhood is shared and husband is shared.[4] Rastafarians are, like fundamentalist Mormons, harking back to their mythological past, in this case pre-slavery Africa, where polygamy was part of kinship structures. Practising it today becomes a symbol of tradition and continuity with one's (imagined) roots. Plural (and gay) marriages among African Americans challenge yet again the hegemony of heterosexual monogamy in the USA. Although Mormon polygamists tend to grab the headlines, there is a growing practice of polygyny among African Americans, especially among adherents to Islam. There is an estimated 4 to 5 million Muslims in the USA, and African Americans comprise the largest ethnic group with about 40 per cent of adherents. Their numbers are increasing rapidly, though precise figures are difficult to come by (Dannin 2002: 11).

Members of African American Muslim communities who practise polygyny tend do so because they believe they are following the tenets of Islam: since marriage and family are considered integral to their religious practices, polygyny allows them to practise their religion authentically. American women are, however, usually unprepared for the more rigid Arab-Muslim marriage system, which is based on a patriarchal family structure. Muslim marriage has therefore been a source of confusion in the USA, because people have difficulties making it function according to their visions of such marriages. Nonetheless, for some people polygyny represents a viable alternative to monogamous marriage, or lack thereof. It is perceived as an 'honourable' family structure which addresses some of the many challenges facing African American communities, such as chronic un- or underemployment, poverty, high divorce rates and increasing numbers of single parents. Polygynous practices can also be ideologically important as revivals of (imagined) traditional ways or as statements of religious identity. Plural marriage continues to be a divisive issue among African American Muslims, however, and the practice has yet to gather widespread support in their communities. Being Muslim does not automatically entail being polygynous; in fact the vast majority of the world's Muslims are monogamous, including those living in the USA. For many, the fact that polygyny is illegal in the USA outweighs any Islamic prescription to practise it. Polygyny is also unacceptable on a personal level for many African American Muslim women. To most African American Muslims, polygyny is incompatible with modern society, a view shared by people even in societies that condone polygamy (Dannin 2002; Rouse 2004). What makes polygyny interesting for some African American Muslims is that it becomes a potent religious and political statement of defiance within a society and a majority culture which they may feel discriminate against them and lack respect for who they are. It is a lifestyle choice that can address both real pragmatic issues in the black communities, as well as give practitioners pride in belonging to a moral minority following a higher law.

Old Ways, New Forms

So what is the future for polygamy? In the West, many people view polygamy as a backward traditional institution that oppresses women. '[T]his Mohammedan barbarism revolting to the civilized world' (Gordon 1996: 835), as nineteenth-century anti-polygamy activists called it. In the East, many Muslims herald it as 'true' Muslim marriage, and their brethren in the West have appropriated Western 'me culture' to demand the legal right to practise polygamy in majority Christian monogamous societies. Elsewhere, governments formulate policies and pass laws to protect women's rights that are in direct conflict with polygamous practices, and activists argue for a UN charter that would outlaw polygamy. In the USA, parts of the population are increasingly intolerant of alternative lifestyles, as lived by American Mormon fundamentalists or African American Muslims, whereas other parts of the population see polygamy as one of a number of lifestyle choices of the twenty-first century. In today's world, polygamy is no longer only a form of marriage or a way of arranging one's family life. For many practitioners, polygamy has also become a statement of religious or political belief. On some level, it has always been a statement of beliefs, in that practitioners were following cultural or religious norms that most people in their societies strived towards, but few were able to achieve. Polygamy, as has been described throughout the book, was always the reality of few and the ideal of many. The practice of polygamy in a given society used to be regulated by a variety of traditional factors such as wealth, prestige and power, or religious, cultural or social prescriptions. Any of these factors put a natural barrier on the amount of practitioners, as few would be able or willing to satisfy all of the norms required. Today, traditional norms are everywhere under challenge from globalization. Hence, the practice of polygamy has become politicized in an increasingly globalized world which presents every individual with an increasing amount of choices from the food they eat to the people they marry.

Polygamy it is not a monolithic mould that people fill, but takes shape from the way people practise it. Like all societal institutions, it can be manipulated to fit the needs and purposes of its practitioners. This is clearly illustrated by the various and evolving forms of polygynous arrangements in urban Africa (see Chapter 8). The flexibility of the polygamous principle is also illustrated by its use in political strategies. In contemporary societies, polygamy rarely serves the political functions it used to serve in many traditional societies (see Chapter 3), but that does not prevent polygamy from having political potential. This is illustrated by people's political use of polyandry as a tribal marker in India, where their way of life is under threat, described below. The impact of modernity is perhaps greatest on polyandrous systems, because the groups practising it are generally minorities surrounded by monogamous or polygynous peoples who often have strongly patriarchal societies and vehemently oppose polyandry. This makes polyandry particularly vulnerable to disruption and disappearance. Peter (1963: 570) calls it a 'recessive cultural trait', arguing that polyandry is fragile because it appeared as a product of very special economic and social circumstances and can thus be easily destroyed when in contact with non-polyandrous societies. As modernity starts to steer people towards monogamous conjugal life, the me-culture's preference for one exclusive spouse is killing off polyandry (e.g. Goswami 1987). Polyandry's only hope for the future, according to some observers, is when it becomes a religious, political or nationalistic symbol, which may then be practised for quite different reasons than it may originally have been.

Since India's independence from British rule, the ethnic status of the polyandrous people living in the Jaunsar Bawar region of the Indian Himalayas (see Chapter 6) has been subject to various changes, which have acted as a counter lever to the forces threatening the foundations of polyandry. From being a partially excluded area in 1935, the inhabitants of Jaunsar Bawar were given the status of scheduled tribe in 1967, despite having both caste and stratification systems. The Jaunsari tribe may still be rescheduled, but the 'protective discrimination' following from tribal status has allowed polyandry in Jaunsar Bawar to become a political symbol through which people can legitimize their claims of tribal status. Other polyandrous societies in the region have become completely integrated administratively into the state of Uttar Pradesh, and here polyandry is now considered so shameful that its previous practice is often denied (Bhatt and Jain 1987: 407). Polyandrous practices are typically strong when isolated from alien cultural influences, but become vulnerable when this isolation is broken. Ridicule and taunts of backwardness from people who look down upon such practices are very effective in this regard. In areas where polyandrous peoples are surrounded by non-polyandrous ones, polyandrous practices will typically quickly become hidden and denied, or completely disappear. In Jaunsar Bawar, however, tribal status has meant that the region has been protected from full integration into the larger state. The polyandrous practices have been saved by a form of local nationalism which proclaims polyandry to be part of the Jaunsaries' identity as a people and which must therefore be protected. Polyandry can hence become a political weapon for people who are faced with an encroaching dominant culture threatening to annihilate the very foundations of their society. Polyandry allows people to claim separateness from those not practising polyandry, and this contributes to polygamy's survival as a social institution (Peter 1963: 550–1).

For polygamy as an institution, then, globalization translates into opposing trends. Among factors supposedly working against polygamy in the non-Western world, where the vast majority of polygynous societies are found, is the notion that modernity will make the 'traditional' practice of polygamy disappear. It seemingly goes against modern ideas of nuclear families, as espoused in most state development and population policies, and particularly in urban areas people feel that being monogamous projects a more modern image. One contemporary trend is thus that some people who would traditionally have practised polygamy might feel more at liberty not to do so any more in a setting where traditional expectations and control mechanisms are disabled. Furthermore, as women become more emancipated, better educated and increasingly socially and economically independent from their families, polygamy is seen by many as a form of 'development reversal', a wrong direction to take with respect to gender relations. Economic development means that women can create livelihoods for themselves, and as women become more self-assertive in traditional polygamous societies they may refuse to become plural wives or have plural husbands. The evolution of societies as it impinges on polygamy is not all about economic progress and women's emancipation, however. An opposing trend is that some people now practise polygamy that would not necessarily have done so previously. In Kerala in South India, for example, fraternal polyandry is being revived among lower castes and outcastes as a way to allow poor men to maintain a wife and children (Johnson and Zhang 1991). People may also feel free to practise polygyny without having the wealth or social background normally required to do so, or they may practise it because it has become politicized as a religious or cultural symbol. This is the case in contemporary Malaysia (see Chapter 4). Especially in societies undergoing rapid social changes, polygamy may give people a way of expressing allegiance to their version of their traditional culture and society, as well as their religion.

Polygamy is, in other words, a very flexible matrimonial system, and as long as circumstances warrant it and it can serve useful purposes it is unlikely to disappear. It may change and mutate in individual societies and (sub)cultures, but it will survive as long as it can address pragmatic concerns. Today, polygamy can also serve as a symbol of allegiance to a cause, such as political Islam, making it a very powerful institution in the modern interdependent world. The modern redefinition of what polygamy entails brings this discussion back to its starting point. In the introduction it was argued that polygamy is difficult to define, because it rests on the definition of marriage, which is itself difficult to define. A review of polygamy cross-culturally has not answered the question about how to define marriage, because on some level it is indefinable. This in turn means that on some level so is polygamy. In particular, the acceptance of *de facto* polygamy as a form of polygamy may nullify the concept: with such a broad definition there will for ever be polygamy, because there will always be men or women who have simultaneous relations to several partners, while being legally married to only one spouse – or to none at all. Some may argue that there will forever be polygyny because it satisfies some basic need in some men to display some combination of virility and wealth, power and prestige. Others argue that polygyny will eventually die out because such displays will no longer be necessary or acceptable in a world where women are empowered sexually, politically and economically. While no one can predict the future, it is unlikely that a system as flexible as polygamy will disappear all together. The growth of prestige polygamy and political polygamy, lifestyle polygamy and faith polygamy, and all other modern variations on the polygamous theme, testify to polygamy's staying power and adaptability. They are old ways in new forms that help people address the new realities of an increasingly globalized world, where individuals are confronted with ever more choices and demands to stand apart and be self-sufficient. For those longing to be part of a collective in an increasingly lonely world, plural marriage may be just the thing. For those insisting on their human right to make individual choices regarding lifestyle, it may as well. For those who find polygamy objectionable, the passing and enforcement of anti-polygamy laws is of prime importance. For women's rights activists who see in polygamy the subjugation of women, it is as well. It suggests that, as each society and (sub)culture in which polygamy is practised is following its own trajectory, the future of polygamy appears as diverse as the institution itself.

Notes

Chapter 1 Forms of Polygyny

1. Source: BBC.co.uk.
2. Persons related to an individual through a marriage link.

Chapter 2 Foundations of Polygamy

1. Descent reckoned through women.
2. Bridewealth (or brideprice) is the transfer of goods or payment from the groom's group to the bride's group to compensate it for the loss of the woman, and her productive and reproductive capacities.
3. Where no other references are cited, this section leans on White (1988).
4. The notion that women may not engage in sexual relations with their husband as long as they are nursing a child.
5. Leviticus 18:18 forbids a husband from creating rivalry between sisters by engaging in sororal polygamy but does not explicitly rule out consensual sororal polygamy. Indeed, Jacob/Israel, the eponymous founder of the twelve tribes of Israel was married to sisters, Leah and Rachel.

Chapter 3 Theories of Polygamy

1. See Bretschneider (1995) for a discussion of various economic explanations of polygamy.

Chapter 4 Muslim Polygyny in Malaysia

1. In addition to the references cited, information in this chapter is based on fieldwork carried out by the author in Kuala Lumpur in 1997–9, as well as a PhD thesis at the University of Cambridge, UK.

Chapter 5 Christian Polygamy in the USA

1. Many of the current events and statistics referred to in this section are sourced from BBC.co.uk.

Chapter 9 Polygamy in Contemporary Societies

1. Apart from references cited, sources include: Asianweek.com; BBC.co.uk; CBN. com; CNN.com; crosscurrents.org; islamfortoday.com; pbs.org; reason.com; washtimes.com; Africa chat groups.
2. K. Annan, *New York Times*, 29 December 2002; M. Buerk, BBC News, 20 February 2003; E. Rosenthal, *New York Times*, 21 November 2006.
3. C. Bond, CNN, 5 April 1998; H. French, *New York Times*, 5 April 1996; W. Ross, BBC News, 29 March 2005.
4. Source: rastafarispeaks.com.

References

Adams, B. and Mburugu, E. (1994), 'Kikuyu Bridewealth and Polygyny Today', *Journal of Comparative Family Studies*, 25(2): 159–66.

Agadjanian, V. and Ezeh, A.C. (2000), 'Polygyny, Gender Relations, and Reproduction in Ghana', *Journal of Comparative Family Studies*, 31(4): 427–41.

Al-Krenawi, A., Graham, J.R. and Izzeldin, A. (2001), 'The Psychosocial Impact of Polygamous Marriages on Palestinian Women', *Women and Health*, 34(1): 1–16.

Altman, I. and Ginat, J. (1996), *Polygamous Families in Contemporary Society*, Cambridge: Cambridge University Press.

Anderson, C.M. (2000), 'The Persistence of Polygyny as an Adaptive Response to Poverty and Oppression in Apartheid South Africa', *Cross-Cultural Resources*, 34(2): 99–112.

Anderson, N. (1937), 'The Mormon Family', *American Sociological Review*, 2(5): 601–8.

Argyll, Duke of (1881), 'The Unity of Nature. VII', *Science*, 2(44): 194–9.

Asante-Darko, N. and van der Geest, S. (1983), 'Male Chauvinism: Men and Women in Ghanaian Highlife Songs', in C. Oppong (ed.), *Female and Male in West Africa*, London: Allen & Unwin, pp. 244–55.

Bachofen, J. (1861), *Das Mutterrecht*, Frankfurt am Main: Suhrkamp Verlag, 1975.

Balikci, A. (1970), *The Netsilik Eskimo*, Garden City, NY: Natural History Press.

Banks, D.J. (1983), *Malay Kinship*, Philadelphia: ISHI.

Bascom, W. and Herskovits, M. (1959), 'The Problem of Stability and Change in African Culture', in W. Bascom and M. Herskovits (eds), *Continuity and Change in African Cultures*, Chicago: University of Chicago Press, pp. 1–14.

Bennion, J. (1998), *Women of Principle: Female Networking in Contemporary Mormon Polygyny*, Oxford: Oxford University Press.

Berreman, G. (1962), 'Pahari Polyandry: A Comparison', *American Anthropologist*, 64(1): 60–75.

Berreman, G. (1972), *Hindus of the Himalayas*, Berkeley: University of California Press.

Berreman, G. (1975), 'Himalayan Polyandry and the Domestic Cycle', *American Ethnologist*, 2: 127–38.

Berreman, G. (1978), 'Ecology, Demography and Domestic Strategies in the Western Himalayas', *Journal of Anthropological Research*, 34: 326–68.

Betzig, L. (1986), *Despotism and Differential Reproduction: A Darwinian View of History*, New York: Aldine Publishing Company.

Betzig, L. (1995), 'Medieval Monogamy', *Journal of Family History*, 20(2): 181–216.

Bhatt, G.S. and S.D. Jain (1987), 'Woman's Role in a Polyandrous Cis-Himalayan Society: An Overview', in Raha (ed.), *Polyandry in India*, Delhi: Gian Publishing House, pp. 405–21.

Birket-Smith, K. (1948), *Kulturens Veje*, København: Jespersen og Pios Forlag.

Bledsoe, C. (1980), *Women and Marriage in Kpelle Society*, Stanford, CA: Stanford University Press.

Bledsoe, C. (1990), 'The Politics of Children: Fosterage and the Social Management of Fertility among the Mende of Sierra Leone', in W.P. Handwerker (ed.), *Births and Power*, Boulder, CO: Westview Press, pp. 81–100.

Bledsoe, C. (1995), 'Marginal Members: Children of previous Unions in Mende Households in Sierra Leone', in S. Greenhalgh (ed.), *Situating Fertility*, Cambridge: Cambridge University Press, pp. 130–53.

Bledsoe, C. and Gage, A. (1994), 'The Effects of Education and Social Stratification on Marriage and the Transition to Parenthood in Freetown, Sierra Leone', in C. Bledsoe and G. Pison (eds), *Nuptiality in Sub-Saharan Africa. Contemporary Anthropological and Demographic Perspectives*, Oxford: Clarendon Press, pp. 148–64.

Bledsoe, C. and Pison, G. (1994), 'Introduction', in C. Bledsoe and G. Pison (eds), *Nuptiality in Sub-Saharan Africa. Contemporary Anthropological and Demographic Perspectives*, Oxford: Clarendon Press, pp. 1–22.

Bleek, W. (1987), 'Family and Family Planning in Southern Ghana', in C. Oppong (ed.), *Sex Roles, Population and Development in West Africa*, London: James Currey, pp. 138–53.

Blum, C. (1998), 'A Populationist Controversy in Eighteenth-Century France: Polygamy', *Population*, 53(1–2): 93–112.

Boserup, E. (1970), *Woman's Role in Economic Development*, London: George Allen & Unwin.

Bretschneider, P. (1995), *Polygyny: A Cross-Cultural Study*, Doctoral Thesis at Uppsala University, Uppsala Studies in Cultural Anthropology 20.

Buijs, G. (2002), 'Female Chiefs and Their Wives: Tradition and Modernity in Venda, South Africa', in W. Haviland, R. Gordon and L. Vivanco (eds), *Talking About People* (3rd edition), Boston: McGraw Hill, pp. 121–4.

Bunge, F. (1984), *Malaysia – A Country Study*, Washington DC: United States Government.

Burnham, P. (1987), 'Changing Themes in the Analysis of African Marriage', in D. Parkin and D. Nyamwaya (eds), *Transformations of African Marriage*, Manchester: Manchester University Press, pp. 37–54.

Cairncross, J. (1974), *After Polygamy was Made a Sin: The Social History of Christian Polygamy*, London: Routledge & Kegan Paul.

Carsten, J. (1997), *The Heat of the Hearth. The Process of Kinship in a Malay Fishing Community*, Oxford: Clarendon Press.

Cederoth, S. and Hassan, S. (1997), *Managing Marital Disputes in Malaysia*, Richmond: Curzon Press.

Chandra, R. (1981), 'Sex Role Arrangement to Achieve Economic Security in North Himalayas', in C. von Fürer-Haimendorf (ed.), *Asian Highland Societies in Anthropological Perspective*, New Delhi: Sterling Publishers, pp. 203–13.

Chapman, A. (1986), *Man Sharing: Dilemma of Choice, A Radical New Way of Relating to the Men in Your Life*, New York: William Morrow and Co.

Charles, M. (1987), 'Precedents for Mormon Women from Scriptures', in M. Beecher and L. Anderson (eds), *Sisters in Spirit. Mormon Women in Historical and Cultural Perspective*, Chicago: University of Illinois Press, 37–63.

Chisholm, J.S. and Burbank, V.K. (1991), 'Monogamy and Polygyny in Southeast Arnhemland – Male Coercion and Female Choice', *Ethnology and Sociobiology*, 12(4): 291–313.

Christiansen, J. (1963), 'Contemporary Mormons' Attitudes Towards Polygynous Practices', *Marriage and Family Living*, 25(2): 167–70.

Clignet, R. (1970), *Many Wives, Many Powers. Authority and Power in Polygynous Families*, Evanston, IL: Northwestern University Press.

Clignet, R. (1987), 'On dit que la Polygamie est Morte: Vive la Polygamie!', in D. Parkin and D. Nyamwaya (eds), *Transformations of African Marriage*, Manchester: Manchester University Press, pp. 199–209.

Clignet, R. and Sween, J. (1981), 'For a Revisionist Theory of Human Polygyny', *Signs*, 6: 445–68.

Collier, J. and Rosaldo, M. (1981), 'Politics and Gender in Simple Societies', in S. Ortner and H. Whitehead (eds), *Sexual Meanings. The Cultural Construction of Gender and Sexuality*, Cambridge: Cambridge University Press, pp. 275–329.

Colson, E. (1958), *Marriage and the Family among the Plateau Tonga of Northern Rhodesia*, Manchester: Manchester University Press.

Comaroff, J. (1980), 'Bridewealth and the Control of Ambiguity in a Tswana Chiefdom', in J. Comaroff (ed.), *The Meaning of Marriage Payments*, London: Academic Press, pp. 161–96.

Connell, R.W. (1987), *Gender and Power*, Oxford: Polity Press.

Crosby, K.H. (1937), 'Polygamy in Mende Country', *Africa*, 10(3): 249–64.

Cucchiari, S. (1981), 'The Gender Revolution and the Transition from Bisexual Horde to Patrilocal Band: The Origins of Gender Hierarchy', in S. Ortner and H. Whitehead (eds), *Sexual Meanings. The Cultural Construction of Gender and Sexuality*, Cambridge: Cambridge University Press, pp. 31–79.

Damas, D. (1975), 'Demographic Aspects of Central Eskimo Marriage Practices', *American Ethnologist*, 2(3): 409–18.

Dannin, R. (2002), *Black Pilgrimage to Islam*, Oxford: Oxford University Press.

Delaney, T. (2001), 'The Secret Story of Polygamy', Book Review, *Library Journal*, 126(19): 88–9.

Derr, J. (1987), 'Strength in Our Union: The Making of Mormon Sisterhood', in M. Beecher and L. Anderson (eds), *Sisters in Spirit. Mormon Women in Historical and Cultural Perspective*, Chicago: University of Illinois Press, pp. 153–207.

Dinan, C. (1983), 'Sugar Daddies and Gold-Diggers: the White-Collar Single Women in Accra', in C. Oppong (ed.), *Female and Male in West Africa*, London: Allen & Unwin, pp. 344–66.

Djamour, J. (1965), *Malay Kinship and Marriage in Singapore*, London: Athlone Press.

Dorjahn, V. (1959), 'The Factor of Polygyny in African Demography', in W. Bascom and M. Herskovits (eds), *Continuity and Change in African Cultures*, Chicago: University of Chicago Press, pp. 87–112.

Effah, K.B. (1999), 'A Reformulation of the Polygyny-Fertility Hypothesis', *Journal of Comparative Family Studies*, 30(3): 381–408.

Egbuna, O. (1964), *Wind versus Polygamy*, London: Faber & Faber.

Erlank, N. (2003), 'Gendering Commonality: African Men and the 1883 Commission on Native Law and Custom', *Journal of Southern African Studies*, 29(4): 937–53.

Evans-Pritchard, E.E. (1951), *Kinship and Marriage among the Nuer*, Oxford: Clarendon Press.

Ezeh, A.C. (1997), 'Polygyny and Reproductive Behavior in Sub-Saharan Africa: A Contextual Analysis', *Demography*, 34(3): 355–68.

Fainzang, S. and Journet, O. (1988), *La Femme de Mon Mari. Etude Ethnologique du Mariage Polygamique en Afrique et en France*, Paris: L'Harmattan.

Firth, R. (1943), *Housekeeping among Malay Peasants*, University of London: Athlone Press, 1966.

Fischer, H. (1952), 'Polyandry', *International Archives of Ethnography*, 46: 106–15.

Fortes, M. (1950), 'Kinship and Marriage among the Ashanti', in A.R. Radcliffe-Brown and C.D. Forde (eds), *African Systems of Kinship and Marriage*, London: Oxford University Press, pp. 252–84.

Fortes, M. (1962), *Marriage in Tribal Societies*, Cambridge: Cambridge University Press.

Fortes, M. and Evans-Pritchard, E.E. (eds) 1940, *African Political Systems*, Oxford: Oxford University Press, 1970.

Freeman, M. (1971), 'A Social and Ecologic Analysis of Systematic Female Infanticide among the Netsilik Eskimo', *American Anthropologist*, New Series, 73(5): 1011–18.

Gallichan, W. (1914), *Women under Polygamy*, London: Holden and Hardingham, 1974.

Garber, C. (1935), 'Marriage and Sex Customs of the Western Eskimos', *The Scientific Monthly*, 41(3): 215–27.

Garber, C. (1947), 'Eskimo Infanticide', *The Scientific Monthly*, 64(2): 98–102.

Garenne, M. and van de Walle, E. (1989), 'Polygyny and Fertility among the Sereer of Senegal', *Population Studies*, 43: 267–83.

Geertz, H. (1961), *The Javanese Family*, Glencoe: Free Press.

Goody, J. (1973a), 'Polygyny, Economy and the Role of Women', in J. Goody (ed.), *The Character of Kinship*, Cambridge: Cambridge University Press, pp. 175–90.

Goody, J. (1973b), 'Bridewealth and Dowry in Africa and Eurasia', in J. Goody and S. Tambiah, *Bridewealth and Dowry*, Cambridge: Cambridge University Press, pp. 1–58.

Goody, J. (1976), *Production and Reproduction*, Cambridge: Cambridge University Press.

Gordon, S. (1996), 'The Liberty of Self-Degradation: Polygamy, Woman Suffrage, and Consent in Nineteenth-Century America', *The Journal of American History*, 83(3): 815–47.

Goswami, B.B. (1987), 'Bow and Arrow Ceremony of the Toda – An Interpretation', in Raha (ed.), *Polyandry in India*, Delhi: Gian Publishing House, pp. 394–404.

Gough, K.E. (1959), 'The Nayars and the Definition of Marriage', *Journal of the Royal Anthropological Institute*, 89: 23–34.

Gough, K.E. (1961), 'Nayar: Central Kerala; Nayar: North Kerala', in D. Schneider and K.E. Gough (eds), *Matrilineal Kinship*, Berkeley: University of California Press, pp. 298–401.

Gough, K.E. (1965), 'A Note on Nayar Marriage', *Man*, 65: 8–11.

Guennec-Coppens, F. Le (1987), 'L'Instabilite conjugale et ses Consequences dans la Societe Swahili de Lamu (Kenya)', in D. Parkin and D. Nyamwaya (eds), *Transformations of African Marriage*, Manchester: Manchester University Press, pp. 233–46.

Gullick, J.M. (1987), *Malay Society in the Late Nineteenth Century: The Beginnings of Change*, Singapore: Oxford University Press.

Guyer, J. (1994), 'Lineal Identities and Lateral Networks: The Logics of Polyandrous Motherhood', in C. Bledsoe and G. Pison (eds), *Nuptiality in Sub-Saharan Africa. Contemporary Anthropological and Demographic Perspectives*, Oxford: Clarendon Press, pp. 231–52.

Gwako, E. (1998), 'Polygyny among the Logoli of Western Kenya', *Anthropos*, 93(4–6): 331–48.

Handwerker, W.P. (1982), 'Family, Fertility, and Economics', *Current Anthropology*, 18 (2): 259–87.

Harris, M. (1983), *Cultural Anthropology*, New York: Harper and Row Publishers.

Hartung, J. (1982), 'Polygyny and Inheritance of Wealth', *Current Anthropology*, 23(1): 1–12.

Haviland, W. (1983), *Cultural Anthropology* (4th edition), New York: Holt, Rhinehart and Winston.

Hern, W.M. (1992), 'Polygyny and Fertility among the Shipibo of the Peruvian Amazon', *Population Studies*, 46(1): 53–64.

Hetherington, P. (2001), 'Generational Changes in Marriage Patterns in the Central Province of Kenya, (1930–1990)', *Journal of Asian and African Studies*, 36(2): 157–80.

Hobsbawm, E. and Ranger, T. (eds) (1983), *The Invention of Tradition*, Cambridge: Cambridge University Press.

Hoebel, E.A. (1947), 'Eskimo Infanticide and Polyandry', *Scientific Monthly*, 64(6): 535.

Hughes, A.L. (1982), 'Confidence of Paternity and Wife Sharing in Polygynous and Polyandrous Systems', *Ethnology and Sociobiology*, 3: 125–9.

Hullet, J.E. (1943), 'The Social Role of the Mormon Polygamous Male', *American Sociological Review*, 8(3): 279–87.

Inhorn, M. (1996), *Infertility and Patriarchy*, Philadelphia: University of Pennsylvania Press.

Jankowiak, W. and Diderich, M. (2000), 'Sibling Solidarity in a Polygamous Community in the USA: Unpacking Inclusive Fitness', *Evolution of Human Behavior*, 21(2): 125–39.

Jenness, D. (1917), 'The Copper Eskimos', *The Geographical Review*, 4(2): 81–91.

Jenness, D. (1922), *The Life of the Copper Eskimos*, Ottawa: King's Printer.

Johnson, N.E. and Zhang, K.T. (1991), 'Matriarchy, Polyandry and Fertility amongst the Mosuos in China', *Journal of Biosocial Science*, 23(4): 499–505.

Jones, G.W. (1994), *Marriage and Divorce in Islamic South-East Asia*, Kuala Lumpur: Oxford University Press.

Karanja, W. (1987), '"Outside Wives" and "Inside Wives" in Nigeria: A Study of Changing Perceptions of Marriage', in D. Parkin and D. Nyamwaya (eds), *Transformations of African Marriage*, Manchester: Manchester University Press, pp. 247–61.

Karanja, W. (1994), 'The Phenomenon of "Outside Wives": Some Reflections on its Possible Influence on Fertility', in C. Bledsoe and G. Pison (eds), *Nuptiality in Sub-Saharan Africa. Contemporary Anthropological and Demographic Perspectives*, Oxford: Clarendon Press, pp. 194–214.

Karim, W. (1991), 'The Status of Muslim Marriages, Polygyny and Divorce in Peninsular Malaysia', in W. Karim (ed.), *Sociological and Legal Implications of the Implementation of Islamic Family Law in Malaysia*, Universiti Sains Malaysia, pp. 51–83.

Karim, W. (1992), *Women and Culture. Between Malay Adat and Islam*, Boulder, CO: Westview Press.

Kilbride, P. (1994), *Plural Marriage for our Times. A Reinvented Option?* London: Bergin and Garvey.

Kilbride, P. and Kilbride, J. (1990), *Changing Family Life in East Africa*, London: Pennsylvania State University Press.

Klomegah, R. (1997), 'Socio-Economic Characteristics of Ghanaian Women in Polygynous Marriages', *Journal of Comparative Family Studies*, 28(1): 73–88.

Kosack, G. (1999), 'Überlegungen zur Mehrfrauenehe am Beispiel der Mafa in Nordkamerun', *Anthropos*, 94(4–6): 554–63.

Krige, E.J. and Krige, J.D. (1943), *The Realm of A Rain-Queen*, London: Oxford University Press.

Krulfeld, R. (1986), 'Sasak Attitudes Towards Polygyny and the Changing Position of Women in Sasak Peasant Villages', in L. Dube, E. Leacock and S. Ardener (eds), *Visibility and Power*, Delhi: Oxford University Press, pp. 194–208.

Kuchiba, M., Tsubouchi, Y. and Maeda, N. (1979), *Three Malay Villages: A Sociology of Paddy Growers in West Malaysia*, Honolulu: The University Press of Hawaii.

Kumlien, L. (1880), 'Ethnology. Fragmentary Notes on the Eskimo of Cumberland Sound', *Science*, 1(8): 85–8.

Kuper, A. (1975), 'Preferential Marriage and Polygyny among the Tswana', in M. Fortes and S. Patterson (eds), *Studies in African Social Anthropology*, London: Academic Press, pp. 121–34.

Kuper, A. (1982), *Wives for Cattle*, London: Routledge & Kegan Paul.

Kuria, G. (1987), 'The African or Customary Marriage in Kenyan Law', in D. Parkin and D. Nyamwaya (eds), *Transformations of African Marriage*, Manchester: Manchester University Press, pp. 283–306.

Kurland, J.A. and Gaulin, S.J.C. (1984), 'Polygyny versus Polyandry – Why the Bias', *American Journal of Physical Anthropology*, 63(2): 180.

Lamphere, L. (1974), 'Strategies, Cooperation, and Conflict Among Women in Domestic Groups', in M.Z. Rosaldo and L. Lamphere (eds), *Woman, Culture and Society*, Stanford, CA: Stanford University Press, pp. 97–112.

Lang, G. and Smart, J. (2002), 'Migration and the "Second Wife", in South China: Toward Cross-Border Polygyny', *International Migration Review*, 36(2): 546–69.

Leach, E. (1955), 'Polyandry, Inheritance and the Definition of Marriage', *Man*, 55: 182–6.

Leete, R. (1996), *Malaysia's Demographic Transition*, Kuala Lumpur: Oxford University Press.

Lesthaeghe, R. (1989), 'Introduction', in Lesthaeghe (ed.): *Reproduction and Social Organization in Sub-Saharan Africa*, Berkeley: University of California Press, pp. 1–12.

Lesthaeghe, R., Kaufmann, G. and Meekers, D. (1989), 'Nuptiality Regimes in Sub-Saharan Africa', in R. Lesthaeghe (ed.), *Reproduction and Social Organization in Sub-Saharan Africa*, Berkeley: University of California Press, pp. 238–337.

Lévi-Strauss, C. (1969), *The Elementary Structures of Kinship*, Boston: Beacon Press.

Levine, N. (1980), 'Nyinba Polyandry and the Allocation of Paternity', *Journal of Comparative Family Studies*, 11(3): 283–98.

Levine, N. (1987a), 'Fathers and Sons – Kinship Value and Validation in Tibetan Polyandry', *Man*, 22(2): 267–86.

Levine, N. (1987b), 'Differential Childcare in three Tibetan communities: Beyond Son Preferences', *Population and Development Review*, 13(2): 281–304.

Levine, N. (1988), *The Dynamics of Polyandry. Kinship, Domesticity and Population on the Tibetan Border*, Chicago: University of Chicago Press.

Levine, N. and Sangree, W. (eds) (1980a), 'Women with many Husbands: Polyandrous Alliance and Marital Flexibility in Africa and Asia', Special Issue, *Journal of Comparative Family Studies*, 11(3).

Levine, N. and Sangree, W. (1980b), 'Conclusion: Asian and African Systems of Polyandry', *Journal of Comparative Family Studies*, 11(3): 385–410.

Lie, M. and Lund, R. (1994), *Renegotiating Local Values. Working Women and Foreign Industry in Malaysia*, London: Curzon Press.

Lienhardt, G. (1964), *Social Anthropology*, Oxford: Oxford University Press.

Little, M.A. (1951), *The Mende of Sierra Leone*, London: Routledge & Kegan Paul.

Locoh, T. (1994), 'Social Change and Marriage Arrangements: New Types of Union in Lome, Togo', in C. Bledsoe and G. Pison (eds), *Nuptiality in Sub-Saharan Africa. Contemporary Anthropological and Demographic Perspectives*, Oxford: Clarendon Press, pp. 215–30.

Lystad, R. (1959), 'Marriage and Kinship among the Ashanti and the Agni', in W. Bascom and M. Herskovits (eds), *Continuity and Change in African Cultures*, Chicago: University of Chicago Press, pp. 187–204.

MacCormack, C. (ed.) (1982), *Ethnography of Fertility and Birth* (2nd edition), Prospect Heights, IL: Waveland Press.

Madhavan, S. (2002), 'Best of Friends and Worst of Enemies: Competition and Collaboration in Polygyny', *Ethnology*, 41(1): 69–84.

Maillu, D. (1988), *Our Kind of Polygamy*, Nairobi: Heinemann Kenya.

Mair, L. (1953), 'African Marriage and Social Change', in A. Phillips (ed.), *Survey of African Marriage and Family Life*, London: Oxford University Press, pp. 1–171.

Mair, L. (1971), *Marriage*, Harmondsworth: Penguin Books.

Majumdar, D.N. (1962), *Himalayan Polyandry*, London: Asia Publishing House.

Mandelbaum, D. (1938), 'Polyandry in Kota Society', *American Anthropologist*, 40(4): 574–83.

Mann, K. (1985), *Marrying Well: Marriage, Status and Social Change among the Educated Elite in Colonial Lagos*, Cambridge: Cambridge University Press.

Mann, K. (1994), 'The Historical Roots and Cultural Logic of Outside Marriage in Colonial Lagos', in C. Bledsoe and G. Pison (eds), *Nuptiality in Sub-Saharan Africa. Contemporary Anthropological and Demographic Perspectives*, Oxford: Clarendon Press, pp. 167–93.

McDonald, P.F. (1985), 'Social Organization and Nuptiality in Developing Societies', in J. Cleland and J. Hobcraft (eds), *Reproductive Change in Developing Countries*, Oxford: Oxford University Press, pp. 87–114.

McLennan, J.F. (1865), *Primitive Marriage*, Chicago: University of Chicago Press, 1970.

McLennan, J.F. (1876), *Studies in Ancient History*, London: Quaritch.

Meek, C.K. (1925), *The Northern Tribes of Nigeria*. Vol. 1. London: Oxford University Press.

Meekers, D. and Franklin, N. (1995), 'Women's Perceptions of Polygyny Among the Kaguru of Tanzania', *Ethnology*, 34(4): 315–29.

Meier, B. (1999), 'Doglientiri: An Institutionalised Relationship Between Women among the Bulsa of Northern Ghana', *Africa*, 69(1): 87–107.

Meillassoux, C. (1981), *Maidens, Meal and Money: Capitalism and the Domestic Community*. Cambridge: Cambridge University Press.

Mernissi, F. (1987), *Beyond the Veil. Male–Female Dynamics in Modern Muslim Society*, Revised Edition. Bloomington: Indiana University Press.

Merrill, M. (1975), *Polygamist's Wife*, Salt Lake City: Olympus Publishing Company.

Moodey, R. (1978), 'Kinship and Culture in the Himalayan Region', in J. Fisher (ed.), *Himalayan Anthropology. The Indo-Tibetan Interface*, The Hague: Mouton Publishers, pp. 27–36.

Moore, H. (1988), *Feminism and Anthropology*, Oxford: Polity Press.

Morgan, L.H. (1877), *Ancient Society Or Researches in the Lines of Human Progress from Savagery, Through Barbarism to Civilization*, E.B. Leacock (ed.), Gloucester, MA: Peter Smith, 1974.

Mulder, M. (1989), 'Marital Status and Reproductive Performance in Kipsigis Women: Re-Evaluating the Polygyny-Fertility Hypothesis', *Population Studies*, 43: 285–304.

Murdock, G.P. (1949), *Social Structure*, New York: Macmillan.

Murdock, G.P. (1967), *Ethnographic Atlas*, Pittsburgh: University of Pittsburgh Press.

Nandi, S.B. (1987), 'Status of Women in Polyandrous Society', in M.K. Raha (ed.), *Polyandry in India*, Delhi: Gian Publishing House, pp. 422–34.

Nicolaisen, I. (1983), 'Introduction', in B. Utas (ed.), *Women in Islamic Societies*, London: Curzon Press, pp. 1–11.

Nimkoff, M.F. (1955), 'Isn't One Wife Enough?', *Marriage and Family Living*, 17(4): 374–5.

Notermans, C. (2002), 'True Christianity without Dialogue – Women and the Polygyny Debate in Cameroon', *Anthropos*, 97(2): 341–53.

Obbo, C. (1987), 'The Old and the New in East African Elite Marriages', in D. Parkin and D. Nyamwaya (eds), *Transformations of African Marriage*, Manchester: Manchester University Press, pp. 263–81.

Obi, C. (1970), *Marriage among the Igbo of Nigeria*, Unpublished Doctoral Thesis, Rome: Pontifical Urban University.

Oboler, R. (1980), 'Is the Female Husband a Man? Woman/Woman Marriage among the Nandi of Kenya', *Ethnology*, 19(1): 69–88.

Oppong, C. (1974), *Marriage among a Matrilineal Elite. A Family Study of Ghanaian Senior Civil Servants*, Cambridge: Cambridge University Press.

Oppong, C. (ed.) (1983), *Female and Male in West Africa*, London: Allen & Unwin.

Oppong, C. (1987), 'Responsible Fatherhood and Birth Planning', in C. Oppong (ed.), *Sex Roles, Population and Development in West Africa*, London: James Currey, pp. 164–78.

Ortner, S. and Whitehead, H. (eds) (1981), *Sexual Meanings. The Cultural Construction of Gender and Sexuality*, Cambridge: Cambridge University Press.

Pakrasi, K. (1987), 'A Note on Differential Sex-Ratios and Polyandrous People in India', in M.K. Raha (ed.), *Polyandry in India*, Delhi: Gian Publishing House, pp. 377–93.

Park, W. (1937), 'Paviotso Polyandry', *American Anthropologist*, New Series, 39(2): 366–8.

Parkin, D. and Nyamwaya, D. (1987), 'Introduction: Transformations of African Marriage: Change and Choice', in D. Parkin and D. Nyamwaya (eds), *Transformations of African Marriage*, Manchester: Manchester University Press, pp. 1–36.

Parmar, Y.S. (1975), *Polyandry in the Himalayas*, Delhi: Vikas Publishing House.

Pebley, A. and Mbugua, W. (1989), 'Polygyny and Fertility in Sub-Saharan Africa', in R. Lesthaeghe (ed.), *Reproduction and Social Organization in Sub-Saharan Africa*, Berkeley: University of California Press, pp. 338–64.

Peletz, M.G. (1996), *Reason and Passion. Representations of Gender in a Malay Society*, Berkeley: California University Press.

Peter, Prince of Denmark and Greece (1963), *A Study of Polyandry*, The Hague: Mouton and Co.

Phillips, A. (1953), 'Marriage Laws in Africa', in Phillips (ed.), *Survey of African Marriage and Family Life*, London: Oxford University Press, pp. 173–327.

Piot, C. (1999), *Remotely Global: Village Modernity in West Africa*, Chicago: Chicago University Press.

Pitshandenge, I.N. a (1994), 'Les Legislations sur le Marriage en Afrique au Sud du Sahara', in C. Bledsoe and G. Pison (eds), *Nuptiality in Sub-Saharan Africa. Contemporary Anthropological and Demographic Perspectives*, Oxford: Clarendon Press, pp. 117–29.

Price, N. (1996), 'The Changing Value of Children among the Kikuyu of Central Province, Kenya', *Africa*, 66(3): 411–36.

Radcliffe-Brown, A.R. (1950), 'Introduction', in A.R. Radcliffe-Brown and C.D. Forde (eds), *African Systems of Kinship and Marriage*, London: Oxford University Press, pp. 1–85.

Radcliffe-Brown, A.R. and Forde, C.D. (eds) (1950), *African Systems of Kinship and Marriage*, London: Oxford University Press.

Raha, M.K. (1987), 'Introduction', in M.K. Raha (ed.), *Polyandry in India*, Delhi: Gian Publishing House, pp. 1–22.

Raynes, M. (1987), Mormon Marriages in an American Context, in M. Beecher and L. Anderson (eds), *Sisters in Spirit. Mormon Women in Historical and Cultural Perspective*, Chicago: University of Illinois Press, pp. 227–48.

Renjini, D. (1996), 'Matrilineal System of Nayars of Kerala', *Man India*, 76(2): 173–80.

Reyburn, W.D. (1959), 'Polygamy, Economy and Christianity in the Eastern Cameroon', *Practical Anthropology*, 6: 1–19.

Reyher, R.H. (1948), *Zulu Woman*, New York: Columbia University Press.

Reyher, R.H. (1953), *The Fon and his Hundred Wives*, London: Gollancz.

Richards, A. (1940), 'The Political System of the Bemba Tribe – Northeastern Rhodesia', in M. Fortes and E.E. Evans-Pritchard (eds), *African Political Systems*, Oxford: Oxford University Press, 1970, pp. 83–120.

Rockwood, J. (1987), 'The Redemption of Eve', in M. Beecher and L. Anderson (eds), *Sisters in Spirit. Mormon Women in Historical and Cultural Perspective*, Chicago: University of Illinois Press, pp. 3–36.

Rouse, C.M. (2004), *Engaged Surrender: African American Women and Islam*, Berkeley: University of California Press.

Sahlins, M. (1999), 'What is Anthropological Enlightenment? Some Lessons of the Twentieth Century', *Annual Review of Anthropology*, 28: i–xxiii.

Saksena, R. (1962), *Social Economy of a Polyandrous People*, London: Asia Publishing House.

Samal P.K., Chauhan, M. and Fernando, R. (1996), 'The Functioning and Eco-Cultural Significance of Marriage Types among the Jaunsaries in Central Himalaya', *Man India*, 76(3): 199–214.

Samal, P.K., Farber, C., Farooquee, N.A. and Rawat, D.S. (1996), 'Polyandry in a Central Himalayan Community: An Eco-Cultural Analysis', *Man India*, 76(1): 51–65.

Sargent, C. and Cordell. D. (2003), 'Polygamy, Disrupted Reproduction, and the State: Malian Migrants in Paris, France', *Social Science Medicine*, 56(9): 1961–72.

Schapera, I. (1940), 'The Political Organization of the Ngwato of Bechuanaland Protectorate', in M. Fortes and E.E. Evans-Pritchard (eds), *African Political Systems*, Oxford: Oxford University Press, 1970, pp. 56–82.

Schuiling, G.A. (2003), 'The Benefit and the Doubt: Why Monogamy?', *Journal of Psychosomatic Obstetrics and Gynecology*, 24(1): 55–61.

Schneider, H. (1959), 'Pakot Resistance to Change', in W. Bascom and M. Herskovits (eds), *Continuity and Change in African Cultures*, Chicago: University of Chicago Press, pp. 144–67.

Seymour-Smith, C. (1986), *Macmillan Dictionary of Anthropology*, London: Macmillan.

Sharma, U. (1980), *Women, Work and Property in North-West India*, London: Tavistock.

Shipps, J. (1987), 'Foreword', in M. Beecher and L. Anderson (eds), *Sisters in Spirit. Mormon Women in Historical and Cultural Perspective*, Chicago: University of Illinois Press, pp. vii–xi.

Smith, J.E. and Kunz, P.R. (1976), 'Polygyny and Fertility in Nineteenth Century America', *Population Studies*, 30(3): 465–80.

Smith, M. (1953), *Baba of Karo. A Woman of the Muslim Hausa*, New Haven, CT: Yale University Press, 1981.

Smith, M.G. (1953), 'Secondary Marriage in Northern Nigeria', *Africa*, 23: 298–323.

Smith, M.G. (1980), 'After Secondary Marriage, What?', *Ethnology*, 19: 265–77.

Solway, J. (1990), 'Affines and Spouses, Friends and Lovers: The Passing of Polygyny in Botswana', *Journal of Anthropological Research*, 46: 41–66.

Speizer, I. (1995), 'Men's Desire for Additional Wives and Children', *Social Biology*, 42(3–4): 199–213.

Spencer, P. (1998), *The Pastoral Continuum. The Marginalization of Tradition in East Africa*, Oxford: Clarendon Press.

Stack, C. (1975), *All of Our Kin. Strategies for Survival in a Black Community*, New York: Harper and Row.

Stephens, M.E. (1988), 'Half a Wife is Better than None – A Practical Approach to Non-Adelphic Polyandry', *Current Anthropology*, 29(2): 354–6.

Steward, J. (1936), 'Shoshoni Polyandry', *American Anthropologist*, New Series, 38(4): 561–4.

Stivens, M. (1996), *Matriliny and Modernity. Sexual Politics and Social Change in Rural Malaysia*, St Leonards, Australia: Allen & Unwin.

Stone, L. (2006), *Kinship and Gender: An Introduction* (3rd edition), Boulder, CO: Westview Press.

Strange, H. (1981), *Rural Malay Women in Tradition and Transition*, New York: Praeger Publishers.

Sueyoshi, S. and Ohtsuka, R. (2003), 'Effects of Polygyny and Consanguinity on High Fertility in the Rural Arab Population in South Jordan', *Journal of Biosocial Science*, 35(4): 513–26.

Trevithick, A. (1997), 'On a Panhuman Preference for Monandry: Is Polyandry an Exception?', *Journal of Comparative Family Studies*, 28(3): 154–81.

Tyagi, D. (1997), 'Looking at Polyandry – A Dying or Dead Social Institution in India', *Man India*, 77(4): 329–43.

van Wagoner, R. (1989), *Mormon Polygamy. A History* (2nd edition), Salt Lake City: Signature Books.

van Wing, J. (1947), 'La polygamie au Congo Belge', *Africa*, 17: 93–102.

Vellenga, D. (1983), 'Who is a Wife? Legal Expressions of Heterosexual Conflicts in Ghana', in C. Oppong (ed.), *Female and Male in West Africa*, London: Allen & Unwin, pp. 144–55.

Ware, H. (1983), 'Female and Male Life Cycles', in C. Oppong (ed.), *Female and Male in West Africa*, London: Allen & Unwin, pp. 6–31.

Weber, M. (1948), *Essays in Sociology*, London: Routledge & Kegan Paul.

Welch, C. and Glick, P. (1981), 'The Incidence of Polygamy in Contemporary Africa: A Research Note', *Journal of Marriage and the Family*, 43(1): 191–3.

Westermarck, E. (1891), *The History of Human Marriage*, London: Macmillan and Co., 1925.

White, D. (1988), 'Rethinking Polygyny. Co-Wives, Codes, and Cultural Systems', *Current Anthropology*, 29(4): 529–72.

Whyte, S. (1980), 'Wives and Co-Wives in Marachi, Kenya', *Folk*, 21–22: 134–46.

Wittrup, I. (1990), 'Me and My Husband´s Wife: An Analysis of Polygyny Among Mandinka in the Gambia', *Folk*, 32: 117–41.

Wolfe, A. (1959), 'The Dynamics of the Ngombe Segmentary System', in W. Bascom and M. Herskovits (eds): *Continuity and Change in African Cultures*, Chicago: University of Chicago Press, pp. 168–86.

Yalman, N. (1967), *Under the Bo Tree: Studies in Caste, Kinship, and Marriage in the Interior of Ceylon*, Berkeley: University of California Press.

Yanca, C. and Low, B.S. (2004), 'Female Allies and Female Power – A Cross-Cultural Analysis', *Evolution and Human Behavior*, 25(1): 9–23.

Ethnographic Index

Africa

Benin
    Dahomey, 64–5
Cameroon, 32, 36–9, 137
    Bamenda (province), 178
Congo (DR), 145, 146
    Suku, 28
Cote d'Ivoire (Ivory Coast), 27, 177
Gambia
    Mandinka, 27, 53–4, 61, 125–6
Ghana, 8, 131, 161–4
    Bulsa, 129, 130, 152
Kenya, 154–6, 177, 179
    Kikuyu, 156
    Marachi, 127
    Samburu, 52
Mali, 36, 130
Morocco, 167, 177
Nigeria, 19, 54–5, 158
    Hausa, 127
    Igbo, 155
    Lagos (former capital), 159–60
    Nupe, 149
Senegal, 60–1, 153
Sierra Leone
    Mende, 4, 54, 129, 132, 133
South Africa, 145–6
    Bantu, 48
    Lovedu, 9–10, 132
    Tshidi, 26
    Zulu, 4, 11
Sudan
    Nuer, 10, 26, 116, 132
Swaziland, 176
Togo, 147
Tunisia, 167

Uganda, 177
    Ganda, 28
Zambia
    Bemba, 48
    Tonga, 11, 61, 150

America

Brazil
    Amazonian Indians, 9
    Kaingang, 13
Canada, 168–9, 171
    Inuit (Eskimo), 4, 5, 26, 42, 47, 51, 141
        Copper and Netsilik Inuit, 43–7
    Mormons, 91, 94
Mexico
    Mormons, 91, 94, 172
Peru
    Inca, 53
    Shipibo, 62
United States of America (USA), 3, 7, 27, 34, 165–74
    African Americans, 12, 136,180
        Muslims, 165–6, 180–1
        Rastafarians, 180
    Alternative Communities
        Keriste Commune, 13
        Oneida Community, 13
    Mormons, 3, 7, 9, 27, 34, 38, 89–107, 147, 151, 165–6, 179–81
        Apostolic United Brethren (AUB), 94, 104
        Church of Jesus Christ of Latter Day Saints (LDS), 89–107
        Fundamentalist Church of Jesus Christ of Latter Day Saints (FLDS), 94, 174

Subject Index